English/Spanish Edition

The New Oxford Picture Dictionary

E. C. Parnwell

Translated by Sergio Gaitán

Illustrations by:
Ray Burns
Bob Giuliani
Laura Hartman
Pamela Johnson
Melodye Rosales
Raymond Skibinski
Joel Snyder

Oxford University Press

P9-CDF-375

Oxford University Press

198 Madison Avenue
New York, NY 10016 USA

Great Clarendon Street
Oxford OX2 6DP

Oxford New York
Athens Auckland Bangkok Bogotá Buenos Aires Cape Town Chennai
Dar es Salaam Delhi Florence Hong Kong Istanbul Karachi Kolkata
Kuala Lumpur Madrid Melbourne Mexico City Mumbai Nairobi
Paris São Paulo Shanghai Singapore Taipei Tokyo Toronto Warsaw

and associated companies in
Berlin Ibadan

OXFORD is a trademark of Oxford University Press

Library of Congress Cataloging-in-Publication Data

Parnwell, E. C.
    The new Oxford picture dictionary.

    Rev. ed. of: Oxford picture dictionary of American
English. English/Spanish ed. 1978.
    Includes index.
    Summary: Teaches English as a second language to
Spanish speakers through the use of pictures dealing with
everyday topics such as the body, post office, law, travel,
and family.
    1. Picture dictionaries, English.   2. English language—
United States—Dictionaries.   3. Americanisms—
Dictionaries.   4. English Language—Textbooks for foreign
speakers—Spanish.   [1. English language—Textbooks for
foreign speakers—Spanish] I. Parnwell, E. C. Oxford
picture dictionary of American English. II. Burns,
Raymond, 1924–   , ill. III. Title. PE2835.5.P28 1989 423'.1
88–345432
    ISBN 0-19-434355-3

Copyright © 1989 by Oxford University Press

No unauthorized photocopying.

All rights reserved. No part of this publication may be
reproduced, stored in a retrieval system, or transmitted, in
any form or by any means, electronic, mechanical,
photocopying, recording, or otherwise, without the prior
written permission of Oxford University Press.

This book is sold subject to the condition that it shall not,
by way of trade or otherwise, be lent, resold, hired out, or
otherwise circulated without the publisher's prior consent
in any form of binding or cover other than that in which it
is published and without a similar condition including
this condition being imposed on the subsequent
purchaser.

Developmental Editor: Margot Gramer
Associate Editor: Mary Lynne Nielsen
Art Director: Lynn Luchetti
Production Coordinator: Claire Nicholl

*The publisher would like to thank the following agents for their
cooperation:*

Carol Bancroft and Friends, representing Bob Giuliani,
Laura Hartman, and Melodye Rosales.

Publishers Graphics Inc., representing Ray Burns,
Pamela Johnson, and Joel Snyder.

Cover illustration by Laura Hartman.

Printing (last digit): 30 29 28 27 26

Printed in China

The New Oxford Picture Dictionary contextually illustrates over 2,400 words. The book is a unique language learning tool for students of English. It provides students with a glance at American lifestyle, as well as a compendium of useful vocabulary.

The *Dictionary* is organized thematically, beginning with topics that are most useful for the "survival" needs of students in an English-speaking country. However, pages may be used at random, depending on the students' particular needs. The book need not be taught in order.

The New Oxford Picture Dictionary contextualizes vocabulary whenever possible. Verbs have been included on separate pages, but within a topic area where they are most likely to occur. However, this does not imply that these verbs only appear within these contexts.

Articles are shown only with irregular nouns. Regional variations of the primary translation are listed following a slash (/). A complete index with pronunciation guide in English is in the Appendix.

For further ideas on using *The New Oxford Picture Dictionary*, see the *Listening and Speaking Activity Book*, the *Teacher's Guide*, and the two workbooks: *Beginner's* and *Intermediate* levels. Also available in the program are a complete set of *Cassettes*, offering a reading of all the words in the *Dictionary; Vocabulary Playing Cards*, featuring 40 words and the corresponding prictures on 80 cards, with ideas for many games; sets of *Wall Charts*, available in one complete package, or in three smaller packages; and *Overhead Transparencies*, featuring color transparencies of all the *Dictionary* pages (all of these items are available in English only). The *NOPD CD-ROM* offers the *Dictionary* in an interactive multimedia format and includes exercises and activities.

The New Oxford Picture Dictionary (El Nuevo Diccionario Ilustrado Oxford) presenta más de 2,400 palabras dentro de sus contextos. Este libro es un instrumento único en el aprendizaje de lenguas para estudiantes de inglés o de español. Además de ser un compendio de vocabulario práctico, el diccionario proporciona al alumno la oportunidad de conocer parte del estilo de vida americano.

Los temas en que está organizado el libro, comienzan con los más prácticos para alumnos principiantes en un país de habla inglesa. Sin embargo, los temas pueden utilizarse sin seguir el orden en que se presentan, y de acuerdo a las necesidades del usuario. Como libro de texto, tampoco es necesario seguir un orden.

Hasta donde ha sido posible, el *New Oxford Picture Dictionary* presenta el vocabulario dentro de un contexto. Los verbos se presentan juntos, en páginas separadas, después de ciertos temas y dentro de los contextos donde generalmente se utilizan. Estos verbos también se presentan en otros contextos.

El uso de los artículos ha sido limitado a algunos sustantivos irregulares. Cualquier variante regional de la primera traducción está en lista despúes de una línea diagonal (/). En el Apéndice aparece una guía para la pronunciación del inglés.

Para obtener más ideas sobre el uso del *New Oxford Picture Dictionary*, consulte la Guía del Maestro, *Teacher's Guide*, y los dos cuadernos de trabajo, (workbooks): *Beginner's and Intermediate*, Principiantes y el nivel Intermedio. Además se cuenta con un equipo de audiocintas que contienen la pronunciación de todas las palabras incluídas en el diccionario; un juego de vocabulario en tarjetas con 40 diferentes palabras con el respectivo dibujo impreso en otras 80 tarjetas separadas; y grandes láminas de las ilustraciones del libro, todo esto disponible en un sólo paquete o en tres paquetes más pequeños. Todos estos materiales se ofrecen únicamente en inglés.

iv Contents

Contenido

People and Relationships   *Gente y parentesco*   Page 2
The Family   *La familia*   3
The Human Body   *El cuerpo humano*   4–5
Vegetables   *Legumbres/Verduras/Vegetales*   6–7
Fruits   *Frutas*   8–9
Meat, Poultry, and Seafood   *Carnes, aves, y mariscos*   10–11
Containers, Quantities, and Money   *Envases, cantidades, y dinero*   12–13
The Supermarket   *El supermercado*   14–15
Family Restaurant and Cocktail Lounge   *Restorán familiar y bar*   16
Restaurant Verbs   *Verbos relacionados con el restorán*   17
Common Prepared Foods   *Alimentos preparados comunes*   18
Outdoor Clothes   *Ropa de exteriores*   19
Everyday Clothes   *Ropa del día*   20–21
Underwear and Sleepwear   *Ropa interior y de dormir*   22
Jewelry and Cosmetics   *Joyería y cosméticos*   23
Describing Clothes   *Descripción de ropa*   24
Describing the Weather   *Descripción del clima*   25
Seasonal Verbs   *Verbos relacionados con las estaciones del año*   *26*
Houses   *Casas*   27
The Living Room   *La sala*   28
The Dining Room   *El comedor*   29
The Kitchen   *La cocina*   30
Kitchen Verbs   *Verbos relacionados con la cocina*   31
The Bedroom   *La recámara*   32
The Baby's Room   *El cuarto del bebé*   33
The Bathroom   *El baño*   34
The Utility Room   *El cuarto de servicios*   35
A Workshop   *Un taller de trabajo*   36–37
Housework and Repair Verbs   *Verbos relacionados con el trabajo del hogar*   38
Medical and Dental Care   *Cuidado médico y dental*   39
Ailments and Injuries   *Enfermedades y heridas*   40
Treatments and Remedies   *Tratamientos y remedios*   41
Firefighting and Rescue   *Combate del fuego y rescate*   42
Crime and Punishment   *Crimen y castigo*   43
The City   *La ciudad*   44–45
The U.S. Postal System   *El sistema postal de los Estados Unidos*   46
The Public Library   *La biblioteca pública*   47
The Armed Forces   *Las fuerzas armadas*   48
Trucks   *Camiones*   49
Cars   *Coches/Carros*   50–51
Bikes   *Bicicletas*   52
Highway Travel   *Viaje por carretera*   53
Public Transportation   *El transporte público*   54–55
Air Travel   *Viaje aéreo*   56
Aircraft   *Aviones*   57
In Port   *El puerto*   58
Pleasure Boating   *Paseo por agua*   59
Plants and Trees   *Plantas y árboles*   60–61
Simple Animals   *Animales simples*   62
Insects   *Insectos*   63
Birds   *Pájaros/Aves*   64
Fish and Reptiles   *Peces y reptiles*   65
Mammals I   *Mamíferos I*   66–67
Mammals II   *Mamíferos II*   68–69
Map of the World   *Mapa del mundo*   70–71
The United States of America   *Los Estados Unidos*   72–73
The Universe   *El universo*   74
The Space Program   *El programa espacial*   75

A Classroom   *Un salón de clase*   *Page*   76
School Verbs   *Verbos relacionados con la escuela*   77
A Science Lab   *Un laboratorio de ciencias*   78
Math   *Matemáticas*   79
Energy   *La energía*   80
Farming and Ranching   *La granja y el rancho*   81
Construction   *Construcción*   82
An Office   *Una oficina*   83
Occupations I: Main Street USA   *Ocupaciones I: La calle principal en*   84
    los Estados Unidos
Occupations II   *Ocupaciones II*   85
Occupations III   *Ocupaciones III*   86
Neighborhood Parks   *Parques del vecindario*   87
Outdoor Activities   *Actividades al aire libre*   88–89
At the Beach   *En la playa*   90–91
Team Sports   *Deportes en equipo*   92
Ballfields   *Campos de juego*   93
Individual Sports   *Deportes individuales*   94
Fields and Courses   *Campos y canchas de juego*   95
Sports Verbs   *Verbos relacionados con el deporte*   96–97
Musical Instruments   *Instrumentos musicales*   98
Music, Dance, and Theater   *Música, baile/danza, y teatro*   99
Electronics and Photography   *Electrónica y fotografía*   100
Handicrafts   *Trabajos manuales*   101
Prepositions of Description   *Preposiciones de descripción*   102
Prepositions of Motion   *Preposiciones de movimiento*   103
Appendix   *Apéndice*   104
Index   *Indice*   105

mujer	**1.** woman		niños	**7.** children
hombre	**2.** man		niño/muchacho	**8.** boy
esposo	**3.** husband		niña/muchacha	**9.** girl
esposa	**4.** wife		abuelos	**10.** grandparents
bebé	**5.** baby		nieta	**11.** granddaughter
padres	**6.** parents		nieto	**12.** grandson

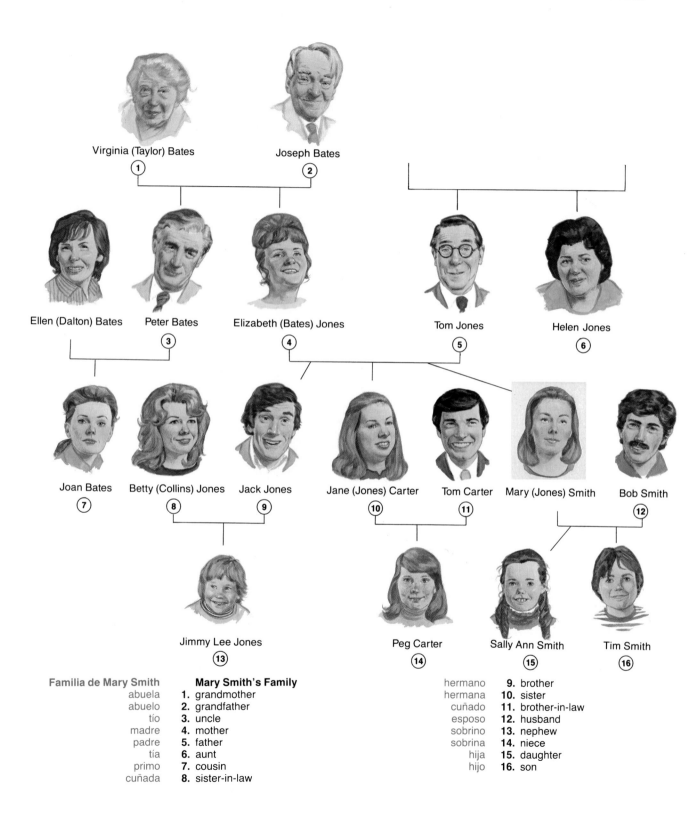

Virginia (Taylor) Bates ①

Joseph Bates ②

Ellen (Dalton) Bates   Peter Bates ③

Elizabeth (Bates) Jones ④

Tom Jones ⑤

Helen Jones ⑥

Joan Bates ⑦

Betty (Collins) Jones ⑧

Jack Jones ⑨

Jane (Jones) Carter ⑩

Tom Carter ⑪

Mary (Jones) Smith

Bob Smith ⑫

Jimmy Lee Jones ⑬

Peg Carter ⑭

Sally Ann Smith ⑮

Tim Smith ⑯

Familia de Mary Smith	Mary Smith's Family		
abuela	**1.** grandmother	hermano	**9.** brother
abuelo	**2.** grandfather	hermana	**10.** sister
tío	**3.** uncle	cuñado	**11.** brother-in-law
madre	**4.** mother	esposo	**12.** husband
padre	**5.** father	sobrino	**13.** nephew
tía	**6.** aunt	sobrina	**14.** niece
primo	**7.** cousin	hija	**15.** daughter
cuñada	**8.** sister-in-law	hijo	**16.** son

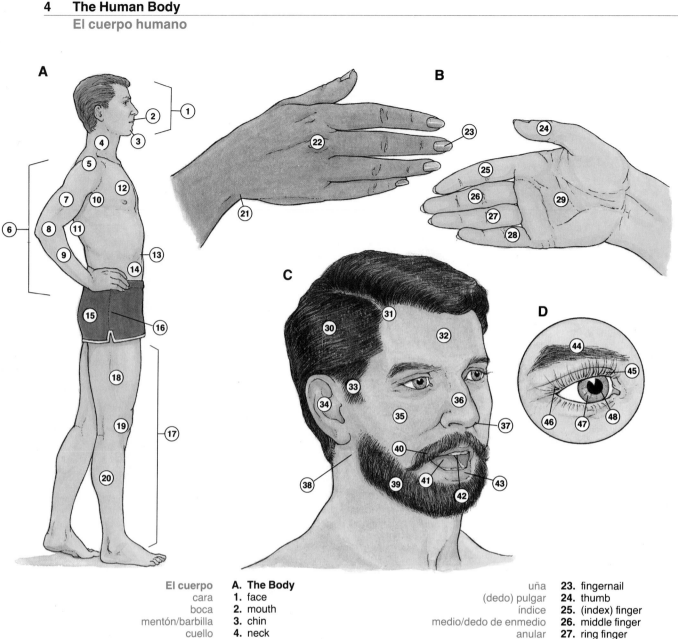

El cuerpo	**A. The Body**
cara	**1.** face
boca	**2.** mouth
mentón/barbilla	**3.** chin
cuello	**4.** neck
hombro	**5.** shoulder
brazo	**6.** arm
parte superior del brazo	**7.** upper arm
codo	**8.** elbow
antebrazo	**9.** forearm
axila/sobaco	**10.** armpit
espalda	**11.** back
pecho	**12.** chest
cintura	**13.** waist
abdomen	**14.** abdomen
nalgas	**15.** buttocks
cadera	**16.** hip
pierna	**17.** leg
muslo	**18.** thigh
rodilla	**19.** knee
pantorrilla	**20.** calf

La mano	**B. The Hand**
muñeca	**21.** wrist
nudillo	**22.** knuckle

uña	**23.** fingernail
(dedo) pulgar	**24.** thumb
índice	**25.** (index) finger
medio/dedo de enmedio	**26.** middle finger
anular	**27.** ring finger
meñique	**28.** little finger
palma	**29.** palm

La cabeza	**C. The Head**
cabello/pelo	**30.** hair
raya/partidura	**31.** part
frente	**32.** forehead
patilla	**33.** sideburn
oreja/oído	**34.** ear
mejilla/cachete	**35.** cheek
nariz	**36.** nose
orificio nasal	**37.** nostril
quijada/mandíbula	**38.** jaw
barba	**39.** beard
bigote	**40.** mustache
lengua	**41.** tongue
diente	**42.** tooth
labio	**43.** lip

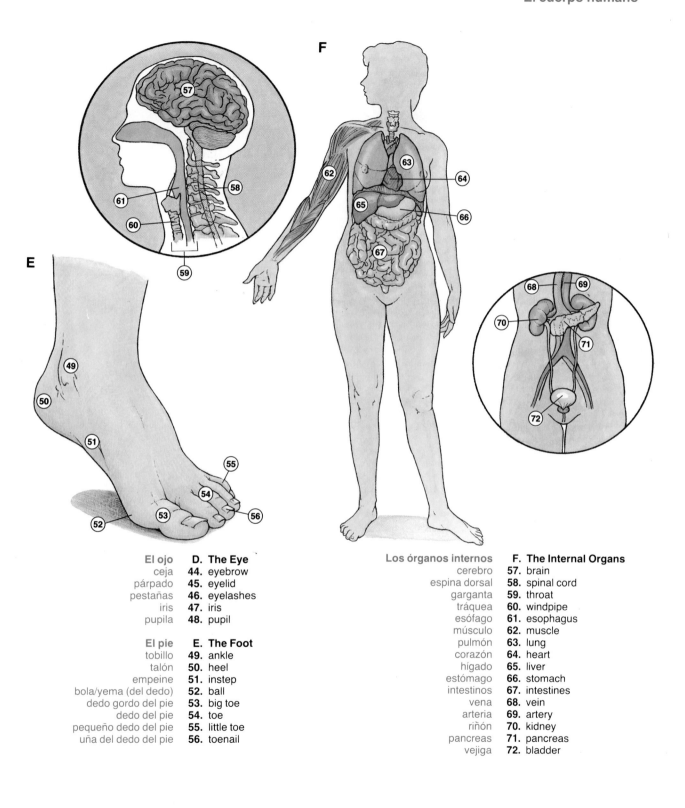

El ojo	D. The Eye
ceja	**44.** eyebrow
párpado	**45.** eyelid
pestañas	**46.** eyelashes
iris	**47.** iris
pupila	**48.** pupil

El pie	E. The Foot
tobillo	**49.** ankle
talón	**50.** heel
empeine	**51.** instep
bola/yema (del dedo)	**52.** ball
dedo gordo del pie	**53.** big toe
dedo del pie	**54.** toe
pequeño dedo del pie	**55.** little toe
uña del dedo del pie	**56.** toenail

Los órganos internos	F. The Internal Organs
cerebro	**57.** brain
espina dorsal	**58.** spinal cord
garganta	**59.** throat
tráquea	**60.** windpipe
esófago	**61.** esophagus
músculo	**62.** muscle
pulmón	**63.** lung
corazón	**64.** heart
hígado	**65.** liver
estómago	**66.** stomach
intestinos	**67.** intestines
vena	**68.** vein
arteria	**69.** artery
riñón	**70.** kidney
páncreas	**71.** pancreas
vejiga	**72.** bladder

Verduras/Legumbres/Vegetales

(cabeza de) coliflor	**1.** (head of) cauliflower	alcachofa	**11.** artichoke
brocoli	**2.** broccoli	mazorca de maíz	**12.** (ear of) corn
col/repollo	**3.** cabbage	elote	**a.** cob
coles pequeñas	**4.** brussels sprouts	habichuela(s)/coloradas	**13.** kidney bean(s)
berro	**5.** watercress	frijol(es) negro(s)	**14.** black bean(s)
lechuga	**6.** lettuce	ejote(s)/habichuelas tiernas	**15.** string bean(s)
lechuga	**7.** escarole	haba(s)	**16.** lima bean(s)
espinaca	**8.** spinach	chícharo(s)/petit pois	**17.** pea(s)
yerba(s)/hierba(s)	**9.** herb(s)	vaina	**a.** pod
apio	**10.** celery	espárragos	**18.** asparagus

Verduras/Legumbres/Vegetales

(ji) tomate(s)	**19.** tomato(es)		calabacita	**27.** zucchini
pepino(s)	**20.** cucumber(s)		calabaza pequeña	**28.** acorn squash
berenjena	**21.** eggplant		rábano(s)	**29.** radish(es)
pimiento(s)	**22.** pepper(s)		hongo(s)/seta(s)	**30.** mushroom(s)
papa(s)	**23.** potato(es)		cebolla(s)	**31.** onion(s)
ñame	**24.** yam		zanahoria(s)	**32.** carrot(s)
ajo	**25.** garlic		betabel(es)/remolacha	**33.** beet(s)
diente de ajo	**a.** clove		nabo	**34.** turnip
calabaza	**26.** pumpkin			

(un racimo de) uvas	**1.** (a bunch of) grapes	limón	**9.** lemon
manzana	**2.** apple	limón verde/lima	**10.** lime
tallo	**a.** stem		
corazón/centro	**b.** core	**Bayas/Frutas pequeñas**	**Berries**
coco	**3.** coconut	grosellas	**11.** gooseberries
piña	**4.** pineapple	moras/zarzamoras	**12.** blackberries
mango	**5.** mango	arándano agrios	**13.** cranberries
papaya	**6.** papaya	arándano azules	**14.** blueberries
		fresa	**15.** strawberry
Frutas cítricas	**Citrus Fruits**	frambuesas	**16.** raspberries
toronja	**7.** grapefruit		
naranja/china	**8.** orange	nectarín	**17.** nectarine
gajo	**a.** section	pera	**18.** pear
cáscara	**b.** rind		
semilla/pepita	**c.** seed		

cerezas	**19.** cherries
plátanos/guineo	**20.** (a bunch of) bananas
cáscara	**a.** peel
Frutas secas	**Dried Fruits**
higo	**21.** fig
ciruela pasa	**22.** prune
dátil	**23.** date
pasa(s)	**24.** raisin(s)
chabacano/albaricoque	**25.** apricot
sandía/melón	**26.** watermelon

Nueces	**Nuts**
anacardo(s)/marañón(es)	**27.** cashew(s)
cacahuate(s)/maní	**28.** peanut(s)
nuez (nueces) de nogal	**29.** walnut(s)
avellana(s)	**30.** hazelnut(s)
almendra(s)	**31.** almond(s)
castaña(s)	**32.** chestnut(s)
aguacate/palta	**33.** avocado
ciruela	**34.** plum
melón (verde)	**35.** honeydew melon
melón	**36.** cantaloupe
durazno/melocotón	**37.** peach
hueso/semilla	**a.** pit
cáscara	**b.** skin

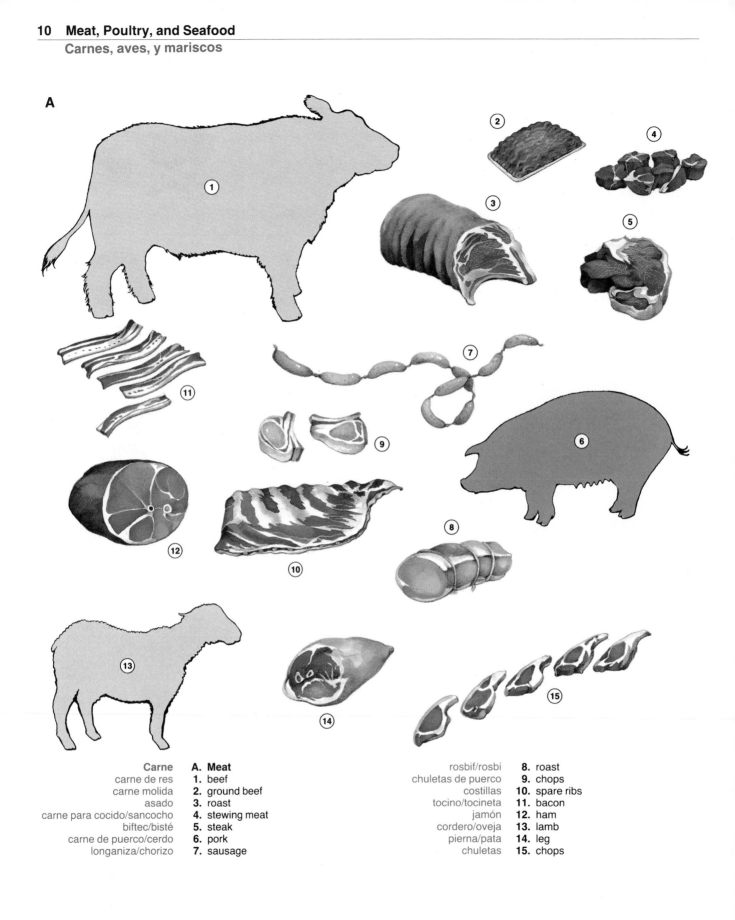

Carne	**A. Meat**		rosbif/rosbí	**8.** roast
carne de res	**1.** beef		chuletas de puerco	**9.** chops
carne molida	**2.** ground beef		costillas	**10.** spare ribs
asado	**3.** roast		tocino/tocineta	**11.** bacon
carne para cocido/sancocho	**4.** stewing meat		jamón	**12.** ham
biftec/bisté	**5.** steak		cordero/oveja	**13.** lamb
carne de puerco/cerdo	**6.** pork		pierna/pata	**14.** leg
longaniza/chorizo	**7.** sausage		chuletas	**15.** chops

B

C

D

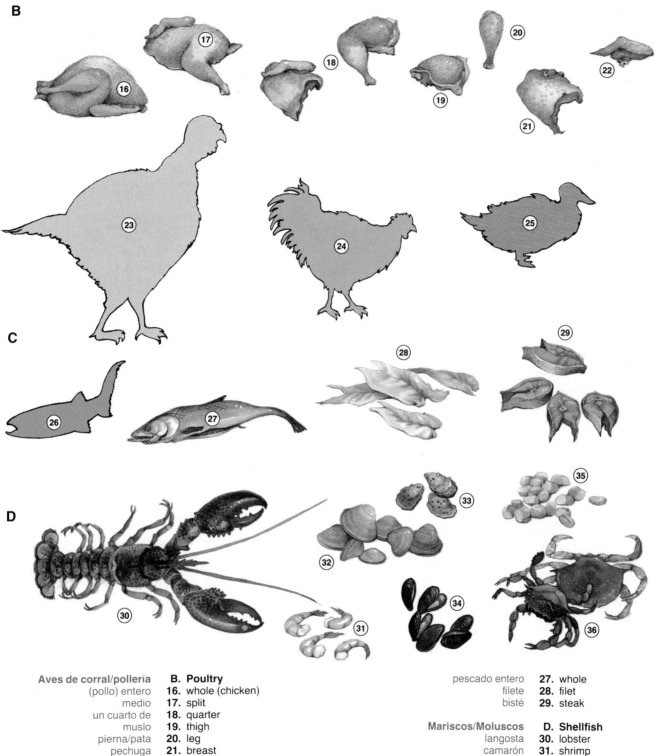

Aves de corral/pollería	**B. Poultry**
(pollo) entero	**16.** whole (chicken)
medio	**17.** split
un cuarto de	**18.** quarter
muslo	**19.** thigh
pierna/pata	**20.** leg
pechuga	**21.** breast
ala	**22.** wing
pavo	**23.** turkey
pollo	**24.** chicken
pato	**25.** duck

Alimentos de mar/Mariscos	**C. Seafood**
pescado	**26.** fish

pescado entero	**27.** whole
filete	**28.** filet
bisté	**29.** steak

Mariscos/Moluscos	**D. Shellfish**
langosta	**30.** lobster
camarón	**31.** shrimp
almeja(s)	**32.** clam(s)
ostión(es)/ostras	**33.** oyster(s)
mejillón(es)	**34.** mussel(s)
molusco(s) bivalvo(s)/escalopes	**35.** scallop(s)
jaiba(s)/juey(es)	**36.** crab(s)

cartón	**1.** carton
envase	**2.** container
botella	**3.** bottle
paquete	**4.** package
barrita	**5.** stick
batea	**6.** tub

barra de pan/hogaza de pan/ libra de pan	**7.** loaf
bolsa	**8.** bag
frasco/pote	**9.** jar
lata	**10.** can
rollo	**11.** roll

caja	**12.** box	tazón/plato hondo	**23.** bowl
paquete de seis	**13.** six-pack	lata rociadora	**24.** spray can
pompa	**14.** pump		
tubo	**15.** tube	**Dinero**	**Money**
paquete/cajetilla	**16.** pack	billete(s)	**25.** dollar bills
carterita/librito	**17.** book	monedas	**26.** coins
pastilla/barra	**18.** bar	centavo/chavito prieto	**27.** penny
taza	**19.** cup	moneda de cinco/vellón	**28.** nickel
vaso	**20.** glass	moneda de diez/sencillo	**29.** dime
rebanada	**21.** slice	moneda de veinticinco/peseta	**30.** quarter
pieza/pedazo	**22.** piece		

mostrador de fiambre y quesos	**1.** deli counter	canasta de compras	**8.** shopping basket
alimentos congelados	**2.** frozen foods	frutas y legumbres	**9.** produce
congelador	**3.** freezer	pasillo	**10.** aisle
productos lácteos	**4.** dairy products	repostería	**11.** baked goods
leche	**5.** milk	pan	**12.** bread
estante/tablilla	**6.** shelf	productos enlatados	**13.** canned goods
escala/pesa	**7.** scale	bebidas	**14.** beverages

FISH MEAT POULTRY

EXPRESS LANE 10 ITEMS OR LESS

artículos del hogar	**15.** household items	caja	**21.** cash register
depósito/arcón/canasta	**16.** bin	cajera/cajero	**22.** cashier
comprador/cliente	**17.** customer	banda	**23.** conveyor belt
confitería/bocadillos	**18.** snacks	abarrotes/compra	**24.** groceries
porta compras/carrito de compras	**19.** shopping cart	bolsa/funda	**25.** bag
		mostrador de chequeo	**26.** checkout counter
recibo	**20.** receipt	cheque	**27.** check

Restorán familiar	A. Family Restaurant	Bar/Cantina	B. Cocktail Lounge
cocinero	1. cook	sacacorcho/titabuzón	17. corkscrew
mesera	2. waitress	corcho	18. cork
limpiamesas/ayudante de camarero	3. busboy	vino	19. wine
		cerveza de barril	20. tap
salsa de tomate/catsup	4. ketchup	cantinero	21. bartender
mesero	5. waiter	(botella de) licor	22. liquor (bottle)
delantal	6. apron	cerveza	23. beer
menú	7. menu	barra/bar	24. bar
silla para niño/sillita	8. high chair	asiento	25. bar stool
caseta/casilla	9. booth	pipa	26. pipe
popote/pitillo/sorbeto	10. straw	porta vaso	27. coaster
refresco	11. soft drink	(carterita de) cerillos/fósforos	28. (book of) matches
sinfonola/vellonera	12. jukebox	cenicero	29. ashtray
(paquetito de) azúcar/(sobrecito de) azúcar	13. sugar (packet)	encendedor	30. lighter
		cigarro/cigarrillo	31. cigarette
cuenta	14. check	mesera (de bebidas)	32. cocktail waitress
té	15. tea	charola/bandeja	33. tray
sandwich	16. sandwich		

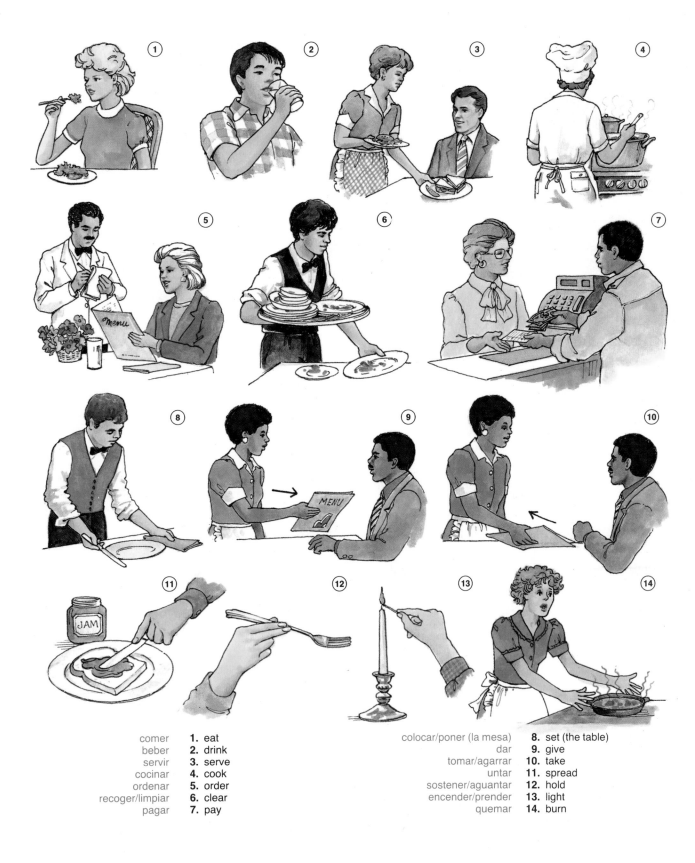

comer	**1.** eat	colocar/poner (la mesa)	**8.** set (the table)
beber	**2.** drink	dar	**9.** give
servir	**3.** serve	tomar/agarrar	**10.** take
cocinar	**4.** cook	untar	**11.** spread
ordenar	**5.** order	sostener/aguantar	**12.** hold
recoger/limpiar	**6.** clear	encender/prender	**13.** light
pagar	**7.** pay	quemar	**14.** burn

Alimentos preparados comunes

mostaza	**1.**	mustard
hot dog/perro caliente	**2.**	hot dog
frijoles cocidos/habichuelas cocidas	**3.**	baked beans
papas fritas/papitas	**4.**	potato chips
panqueques/pancakes	**5.**	pancakes
almíbar	**6.**	syrup
panecillo	**7.**	bun
pepinillo	**8.**	pickle
hamburguesa	**9.**	hamburger
espagueti	**10.**	spaghetti
albóndigas	**11.**	meatballs
aderezo	**12.**	salad dressing
ensalada	**13.**	tossed salad
asado/sancocho	**14.**	beef stew
chuletas de puerco	**15.**	pork chops
verduras mixtas/vegetales mixtos	**16.**	mixed vegetables
puré de papas/papas majadas	**17.**	mashed potatoes
mantequilla	**18.**	butter
panecillo	**19.**	roll
papa al horno	**20.**	baked potato
bisté	**21.**	steak
galleta	**22.**	cookie
sundae	**23.**	sundae
taco	**24.**	taco
rollo relleno de carne con verduras	**25.**	egg roll
pastelillo de fresa	**26.**	strawberry shortcake
bisquet/panecillo	**27.**	biscuit
papas fritas	**28.**	french fries
pollo frito	**29.**	fried chicken
pizza	**30.**	pizza
jalea	**31.**	jelly
huevo (estrellado)	**32.**	(sunnyside-up) egg
tocino/tocineta	**33.**	bacon
pan tostado/tostada	**34.**	toast
café	**35.**	coffee
barquillo de nieve/helado/barquilla	**36.**	ice cream cone

guantes	**1.** gloves	suéter (cuello de tortuga)	**13.** (turtleneck) sweater
gorra	**2.** cap	medias de invierno	**14.** tights
camisa de franela	**3.** flannel shirt	patines de hielo	**15.** ice skates
mochila	**4.** backpack	gorro de esquiar	**16.** ski cap
rompeviento	**5.** windbreaker	chaqueta/chamarra	**17.** jacket
pantalón de mezclilla/mahón	**6.** (blue) jeans	sombrero	**18.** hat
suéter (cerrado)	**7.** (crewneck) sweater	bufanda	**19.** scarf
abrigo de invierno/chamarra de invierno	**8.** parka	sobreabrigo	**20.** overcoat
botas de excursionismo	**9.** hiking boots	botas	**21.** boots
orejeras	**10.** earmuffs	boina	**22.** beret
guante entero/mitón	**11.** mittens	suéter (cuello V)	**23.** (V-neck) sweater
chaleco de plumas de ganso	**12.** down vest	abrigo/sobretodo	**24.** coat
		botas de lluvia	**25.** rain boots

solapa	**1.** lapel		pantaloncillo/shorts	**14.** shorts
saco "sport"	**2.** blazer		manga larga	**15.** long sleeve
botón	**3.** button		cinturón/correa	**16.** belt
pantalón	**4.** slacks		hebilla	**17.** buckle
tacón	**5.** heel		bolsa de compras	**18.** shopping bag
suela	**6.** sole		sandalia	**19.** sandal
agujeta/cordón/gavetes	**7.** shoelace		cuello	**20.** collar
sudadera	**8.** sweatshirt		manga corta	**21.** short sleeve
cartera/billetera	**9.** wallet		vestido	**22.** dress
pantalón de sudadera/pants	**10.** sweatpants		bolso/cartera	**23.** purse
tenis	**11.** sneakers		paraguas/sombrilla	**24.** umbrella
banda/cinta	**12.** sweatband		zapatos de tacón (alto)	**25.** (high) heels
camiseta sin mangas	**13.** tank top			

suéter abierto	**26.** cardigan	impermeable/capa de agua	**38.** raincoat
pantalón (de pana)	**27.** (corduroy) pants	chaleco	**39.** vest
sombrero duro/casco	**28.** hard hat	traje de tres piezas	**40.** three-piece suit
camiseta manga corta	**29.** T-shirt	bolsa/bolsillo	**41.** pocket
overol/mameluco	**30.** overalls	mocasín	**42.** loafer
lonchera	**31.** lunch box	cachucha/gorra	**43.** cap
botas	**32.** (construction) boots	lentes/anteojos/gafas	**44.** glasses
saco de vestir	**33.** jacket	uniforme	**45.** uniform
blusa	**34.** blouse	camisa	**46.** shirt
bolso	**35.** (shoulder) bag	corbata	**47.** tie
falda	**36.** skirt	periódico	**48.** newspaper
portafolio/maletín	**37.** briefcase	zapato	**49.** shoe

camiseta	**1.** undershirt
calzoncillo boxer	**2.** boxer shorts
calzón/calzoncillo	**3.** underpants
suspensorio	**4.** athletic supporter
pantimedia	**5.** pantyhose
medias	**6.** stockings
calzón largo	**7.** long johns
medio fondo/enagua	**8.** half slip
camisola/bustillo	**9.** camisole
fondo entero/refajo	**10.** full slip
pantaleta (bikini)	**11.** (bikini) panties

pantaleta	**12.** briefs
sostén/porta bustos	**13.** bra(ssiere)
liguero	**14.** garter belt
faja	**15.** girdle
calcetines largos	**16.** knee socks
calcetines/medias	**17.** socks
pantuflas/chancletas	**18.** slippers
pijamas	**19.** pajamas
bata (de baño)	**20.** bathrobe
camisón/bata de noche	**21.** nightgown

Joyería/Prendas	A. Jewelry		frente/gancho	18. post
aretes/pantallas	1. earrings		trasero/atrás	19. back
anillo(s)/sortija(s)	2. ring(s)			
anillo de compromiso/sortija de compromiso	3. engagement ring		**Artículos de tocador y maquillaje**	**B. Toiletries and Makeup**
anillo de boda/ sortija de boda	4. wedding ring		rastrillo	20. razor
cadena	5. chain		loción para después de afeitar	21. after-shave lotion
collar	6. necklace		crema de afeitar	22. shaving cream
(collar de) cuentas	7. (strand of) beads		navajas para afeitar	23. razor blades
prendedor	8. pin		lima	24. emery board
pulsera/brazalete	9. bracelet		esmalte para uñas	25. nail polish
reloj de pulsera	10. watch		lápiz para cejas	26. eyebrow pencil
extensible/correa de reloj	11. watchband		perfume	27. perfume
mancuernas/yuntas	12. cuff links		máscara	28. mascara
prendedor/alfiler de corbata	13. tie pin		lápiz labial	29. lipstick
broche de corbata	14. tie clip		sombra para ojos	30. eye shadow
arete de presión/pantalla de pinchar	15. clip-on earring		cortauñas	31. nail clippers
arete de broche/pantalla de gancho	16. pierced earring		rubor/colorete	32. blush
broche	17. clasp		delineador	33. eyeliner

corta	**1.** short	bajo	**12.** low
larga	**2.** long	nueva	**13.** new
apretado	**3.** tight	vieja	**14.** old
flojo/suelto/holgado	**4.** loose	abierto	**15.** open
sucio	**5.** dirty	cerrado	**16.** closed
limpio	**6.** clean	rayado/de líneas (rayitas)	**17.** striped
chico/pequeño	**7.** small	a cuadros/de cuadritos	**18.** checked
grande	**8.** big	punteado/de bolitas	**19.** polka dot
claro	**9.** light	sólido/entero (color)	**20.** solid
obscuro	**10.** dark	estampado	**21.** print
alto	**11.** high	diseño a cuadros/madras	**22.** plaid

lluvioso	**1.** rainy	fresco	**9.** cool
nublado	**2.** cloudy	frío	**10.** cold
con nieve/nevado	**3.** snowy	helando/helado	**11.** freezing
soleado	**4.** sunny	con neblina	**12.** foggy
termómetro	**5.** thermometer	con viento	**13.** windy
temperatura	**6.** temperature	seco	**14.** dry
caliente	**7.** hot	mojado	**15.** wet
caluroso	**8.** warm	helado/congelado (y resbaloso)	**16.** icy

Primavera	Spring	Verano	Summer	Otoño	Fall	Invierno	Winter
pintar	**1.** paint	regar	**5.** water	llenar	**9.** fill	traspalar/palear	**13.** shovel
limpiar	**2.** clean	cortar el césped/cortar la grama	**6.** mow	rastrillar	**10.** rake	enarenar	**14.** sand
excavar	**3.** dig	recoger	**7.** pick	cortar	**11.** chop	raspar	**15.** scrape
plantar	**4.** plant	recortar/podar	**8.** trim	empujar	**12.** push	cargar	**16.** carry

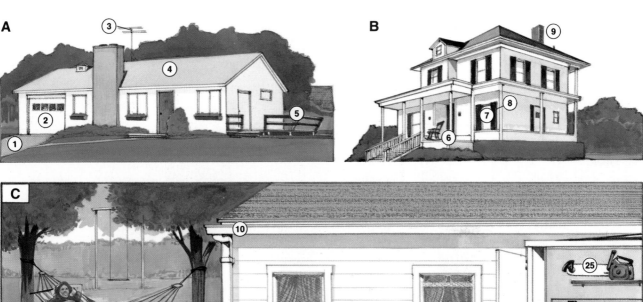

Casa de rancho	**A. Ranch House**
entrada de carro	**1.** driveway
garaje/marquesina	**2.** garage
antena de televisión	**3.** TV antenna
techo	**4.** roof
asoleadera	**5.** deck
Casa estilo colonial	**B. Colonial-style House**
porche/balcón	**6.** porch
ventana	**7.** window
contraventana	**8.** shutter
chimenea	**9.** chimney
El patio interior	**C. The Backyard**
gotera/desagüe	**10.** gutter
hamaca	**11.** hammock
cortadora de césped (grama)	**12.** lawn mower
rociador/regadera	**13.** sprinkler
manguera	**14.** garden hose
césped/pasto/grama	**15.** grass

regadera de mano	**16.** watering can
patio	**17.** patio
desagüe de lluvia	**18.** drainpipe
mosquitero	**19.** screen
guante	**20.** mitt
espátula	**21.** spatula
parrilla	**22.** grill
carbón	**23.** charcoal briquettes
soleadero	**24.** lounge chair
sierra eléctrica	**25.** power saw
guantes de trabajo	**26.** work gloves
cuchara (de albañil)/pala de jardín	**27.** trowel
tejadillo de herramientas	**28.** toolshed
tijeras de césped	**29.** hedge clippers
rastrillo	**30.** rake
pala	**31.** shovel
carretilla	**32.** wheelbarrow

ventilador de techo	**1.** ceiling fan		reclinador	**16.** recliner
techo	**2.** ceiling		control remoto	**17.** remote control
pared	**3.** wall		televisor	**18.** television
marco/cuadro	**4.** frame		mueble de pared	**19.** wall unit
pintura	**5.** painting		estéreo	**20.** stereo system
jarrón	**6.** vase		bocina	**21.** speaker
repisa	**7.** mantel		librero	**22.** bookcase
chimenea	**8.** fireplace		cortinas	**23.** drapes
fuego	**9.** fire		cojín	**24.** cushion
leña	**10.** log		sofá	**25.** sofa
pasamano	**11.** banister		mesita central	**26.** coffee table
escalera	**12.** staircase		pantalla de lámpara	**27.** lampshade
escalón	**13.** step		lámpara	**28.** lamp
escritorio	**14.** desk		mesita	**29.** end table
alfombrado (de pared a pared)	**15.** wall-to-wall carpeting			

vajilla/loza	**1.** china	mantel	**16.** tablecloth
armario/alacena de loza/chinero	**2.** china closet	silla	**17.** chair
candil	**3.** chandelier	cafetera	**18.** coffeepot
jarra	**4.** pitcher	tetera	**19.** teapot
copa de vino	**5.** wine glass	taza	**20.** cup
vaso	**6.** water glass	platito/platillo	**21.** saucer
mesa	**7.** table	juego de cubiertos	**22.** silverware
cuchara	**8.** spoon	azucarera	**23.** sugar bowl
pimentero	**9.** pepper shaker	cremera	**24.** creamer
salero	**10.** salt shaker	ensaladera	**25.** salad bowl
platito para mantequilla y pan	**11.** bread and butter plate	flama/llama	**26.** flame
tenedor	**12.** fork	vela	**27.** candle
plato	**13.** plate	candelero	**28.** candlestick
servilleta	**14.** napkin	aparador/mostrador	**29.** buffet
cuchillo	**15.** knife		

lavaplatos/máquina de lavar platos	**1.** dishwasher	secador/paño de platos	**18.** dish towel
escurridor	**2.** dish drainer	refrigerador/nevera	**19.** refrigerator
vaporera	**3.** steamer	congelador	**20.** freezer
abrelatas	**4.** can opener	charola para cubitos de hielo/	**21.** ice tray
sartén	**5.** frying pan	cubeta de hielo	
destapador	**6.** bottle opener	gabinete	**22.** cabinet
coladera/colador	**7.** colander	horno microondas	**23.** microwave oven
cacerola/olla	**8.** saucepan	molde	**24.** mixing bowl
tapa	**9.** lid	rodillo/rolo	**25.** rolling pin
jabón líquido para trastes/jabón de fregar	**10.** dishwashing liquid	picador/tabla para cortar	**26.** cutting board
		mostrador	**27.** counter
cojincillo de restregar/brillo	**11.** scouring pad	tetera	**28.** teakettle
licuadora	**12.** blender	quemador/hornilla	**29.** burner
olla/caldero	**13.** pot	estufa	**30.** stove
cacerola	**14.** casserole dish	cafetera	**31.** coffeemaker
latería	**15.** canister	horno	**32.** oven
tostador	**16.** toaster	asador	**33.** broiler
cazuela/bandeja de asar	**17.** roasting pan	sostén de ollas/agarradera	**34.** pot holder

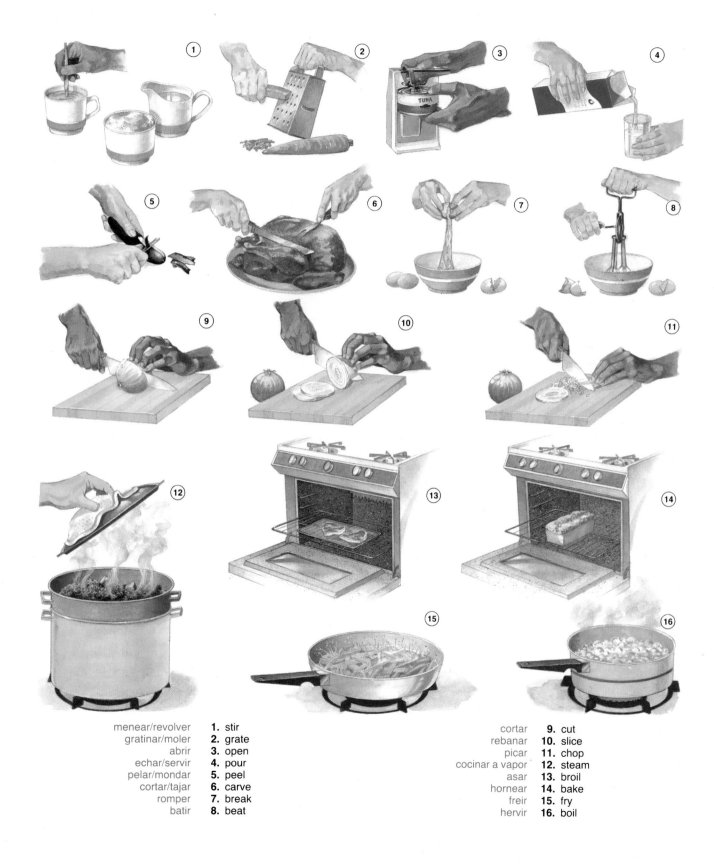

menear/revolver	**1.** stir
gratinar/moler	**2.** grate
abrir	**3.** open
echar/servir	**4.** pour
pelar/mondar	**5.** peel
cortar/tajar	**6.** carve
romper	**7.** break
batir	**8.** beat

cortar	**9.** cut
rebanar	**10.** slice
picar	**11.** chop
cocinar a vapor	**12.** steam
asar	**13.** broil
hornear	**14.** bake
freír	**15.** fry
hervir	**16.** boil

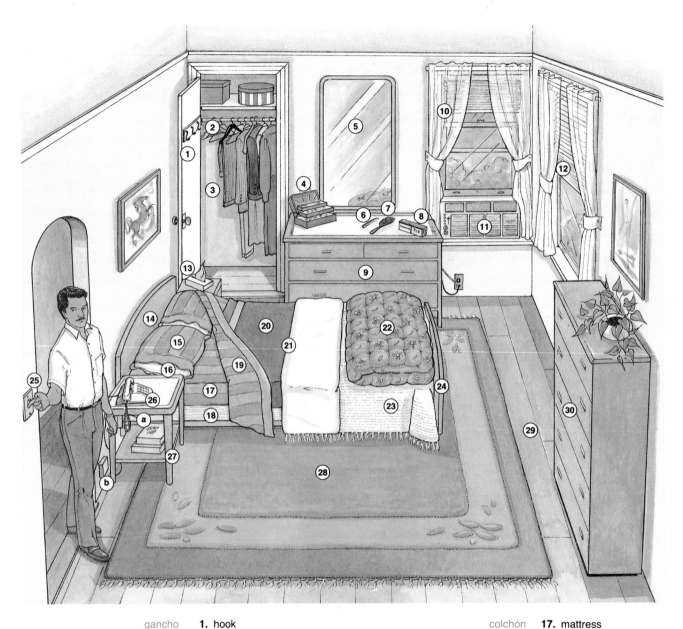

gancho	**1.** hook	colchón	**17.** mattress
gancho para ropa	**2.** hanger	colchón de muelles	**18.** box spring
closet	**3.** closet	sábana	**19.** (flat) sheet
joyero	**4.** jewelry box	cobija	**20.** blanket
espejo	**5.** mirror	cama	**21.** bed
peine/peinilla	**6.** comb	cobertor acolchado	**22.** comforter
cepillo de pelo	**7.** hairbrush	colcha/sobrecama	**23.** bedspread
despertador	**8.** alarm clock	pie de la cama	**24.** footboard
buró/gavetero/ropero	**9.** bureau	interruptor de luz/apagador	**25.** light switch
cortina	**10.** curtain	teléfono	**26.** phone
aire acondicionado	**11.** air conditioner	cordón	**a.** cord
persianas	**12.** blinds	conexión/enchufe	**b.** jack
pañuelos faciales	**13.** tissues	nochero/mesita de noche	**27.** night table
cabecera	**14.** headboard	alfombra/tapete	**28.** rug
funda	**15.** pillowcase	piso	**29.** floor
almohada	**16.** pillow	cómoda/gavetero	**30.** chest of drawers

cortinilla	**1.** shade		biberón	**17.** bottle
móvil	**2.** mobile		tetilla/pezón/mamadera	**18.** nipple
oso de peluche	**3.** teddy bear		trajecito	**19.** stretchie
cuna	**4.** crib		babero	**20.** bib
colchón protector/orillero	**5.** bumper		sonaja/maraquita	**21.** rattle
loción para bebé	**6.** baby lotion		chupón	**22.** pacifier
talco para bebé	**7.** baby powder		andadera/andador	**23.** walker
toallitas para bebé	**8.** baby wipes		columpio	**24.** swing
mesita (portátil)	**9.** changing table		casa de muñecas	**25.** doll house
cotonete/algodoncito/palitos de algodón	**10.** cotton swab		cuna mecedora	**26.** cradle
			animal de peluche	**27.** stuffed animal
seguro/imperdibles	**11.** safety pin		muñeca	**28.** doll
pañal desechable	**12.** disposable diaper		juguetero/baúl de juguetes	**29.** toy chest
pañal	**13.** cloth diaper		corral de juego	**30.** playpen
carrito de bebé	**14.** stroller		rompecabezas	**31.** puzzle
detector de humo	**15.** smoke detector		bloques	**32.** block
(silla) mecedora	**16.** rocking chair		basinica/escupidera	**33.** potty

cortinero/palo de cortina	**1.** curtain rod	llave del agua caliente	**17.** hot water faucet
aros para cortina	**2.** curtain rings	llave del agua fría	**18.** cold water faucet
gorro de baño	**3.** shower cap	lavabo/lavamanos	**19.** sink
regadera/ducha	**4.** shower head	cepillo para uñas	**20.** nailbrush
cortina de baño	**5.** shower curtain	cepillo de dientes	**21.** toothbrush
jabonera	**6.** soap dish	toallita	**22.** washcloth
esponja	**7.** sponge	toalla de manos	**23.** hand towel
shampú/champú	**8.** shampoo	toalla de baño	**24.** bath towel
drenaje/desagüe	**9.** drain	toallero	**25.** towel rack
tapón	**10.** stopper	secador	**26.** hair dryer
tina/bañera	**11.** bathtub	azulejo/loseta	**27.** tile
tapete de baño/alfombra de baño	**12.** bath mat	canasto	**28.** hamper
basurero/zafacón	**13.** wastepaper basket	excusado/inodoro	**29.** toilet
botiquín	**14.** medicine chest	papel de baño/papel higiénico	**30.** toilet paper
jabón	**15.** soap	cepillo de baño	**31.** toilet brush
pasta de dientes	**16.** toothpaste	báscula/pesa	**32.** scale

escalera	**1.** stepladder	accesorios	**17.** attachments
plumero/sacudidor	**2.** feather duster	tubo	**18.** pipe
lámpara (de mano)	**3.** flashlight	tendedero	**19.** clothesline
trapos	**4.** rags	pinzas/pinches de ropa	**20.** clothespins
caja de fusibles/corta circuitos	**5.** circuit breaker	almidón en lata rociadora	**21.** spray starch
limpiador (de esponja)	**6.** (sponge) mop	foco/bombilla	**22.** lightbulb
escoba	**7.** broom	papel absorbente	**23.** paper towels
recogedor	**8.** dustpan	secadora	**24.** dryer
limpiador en polvo	**9.** cleanser	detergente	**25.** laundry detergent
líquido limpia ventanas	**10.** window cleaner	blanqueador	**26.** bleach
repuesto	**11.** (mop) refill	suavizante	**27.** fabric softener
plancha	**12.** iron	lavandería	**28.** laundry
mesa de planchar	**13.** ironing board	canasto de lavandería	**29.** laundry basket
bomba/destapa caños	**14.** plunger	lavadora	**30.** washing machine
cubeta/cubo	**15.** bucket	basurero/zafacón	**31.** garbage can
aspiradora	**16.** vacuum cleaner	ratonera	**32.** mousetrap

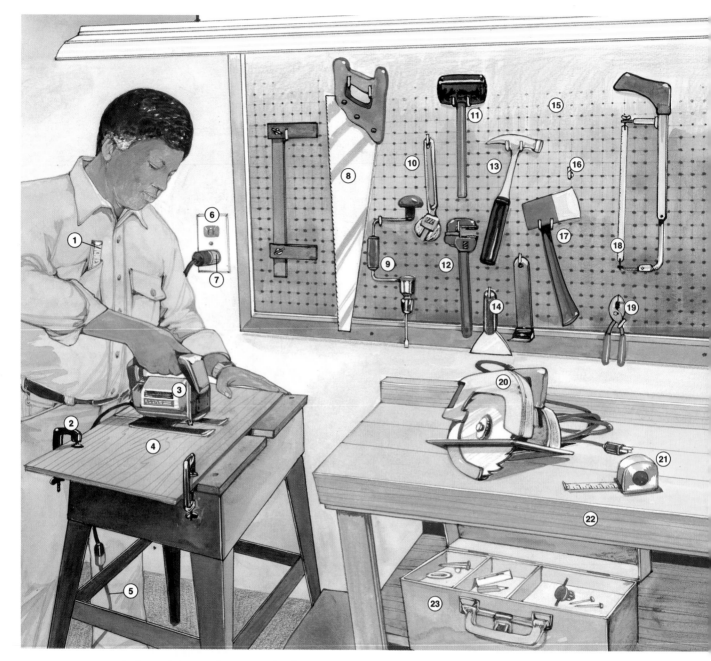

regla de carpintero	**1.** carpenter's rule	martillo	**13.** hammer
tornillo de banco	**2.** C-clamp	espátula/alijadora	**14.** scraper
sierra	**3.** jigsaw	tablero para colgar herramientas	**15.** pegboard
madera	**4.** wood		
extensión	**5.** extension cord	gancho	**16.** hook
contacto/enchufe	**6.** outlet	hacha	**17.** hatchet
clavija de tierra	**7.** grounding plug	serrucho	**18.** hacksaw
serrote/serrucho	**8.** saw	pinzas/alicate	**19.** pliers
taladro de mano	**9.** brace	sierra circular	**20.** circular saw
llave de tuercas/llave de perro	**10.** wrench	cinta de medir	**21.** tape measure
mazo	**11.** mallet	mesa de trabajo	**22.** workbench
llave inglesa	**12.** monkey wrench	caja de herramientas	**23.** toolbox

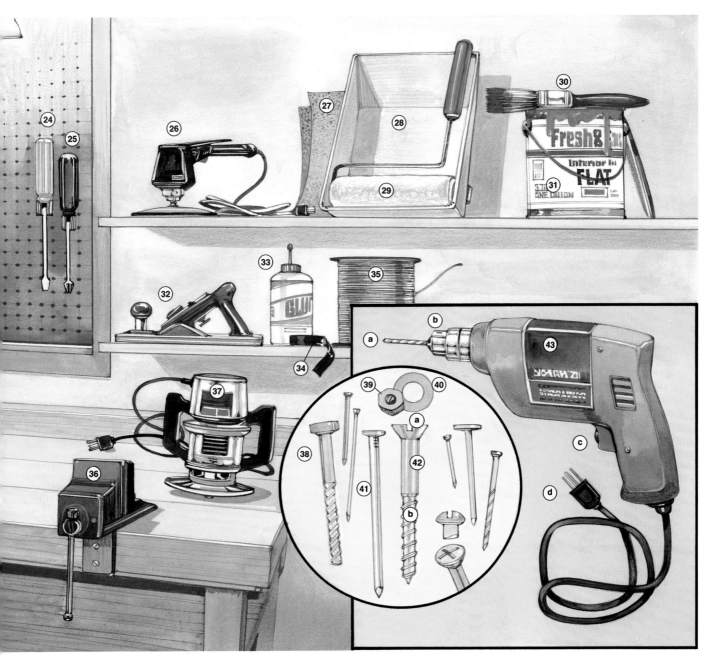

destornillador/desarmador	**24.** screwdriver	canalizador/ranurador	**37.** router
desarmador Phillips	**25.** Phillips screwdriver	perno/tornillo grande	**38.** bolt
pulidora	**26.** power sander	tuerca	**39.** nut
lija	**27.** sandpaper	rondalla/arandela	**40.** washer
cacerola/bandeja	**28.** pan	clavo	**41.** nail
rodillo	**29.** roller	tornillo	**42.** screw
brocha	**30.** paintbrush	cabeza	**a.** head
pintura	**31.** paint	rosca	**b.** thread
cepillo de madera	**32.** wood plane	taladro eléctrico	**43.** electric drill
pegamento	**33.** glue	taladro	**a.** bit
cinta de aislar	**34.** electrical tape	astil	**b.** shank
cable eléctrico	**35.** wire	interruptor	**c.** switch
tornillo de banco	**36.** vise	clavija	**d.** plug

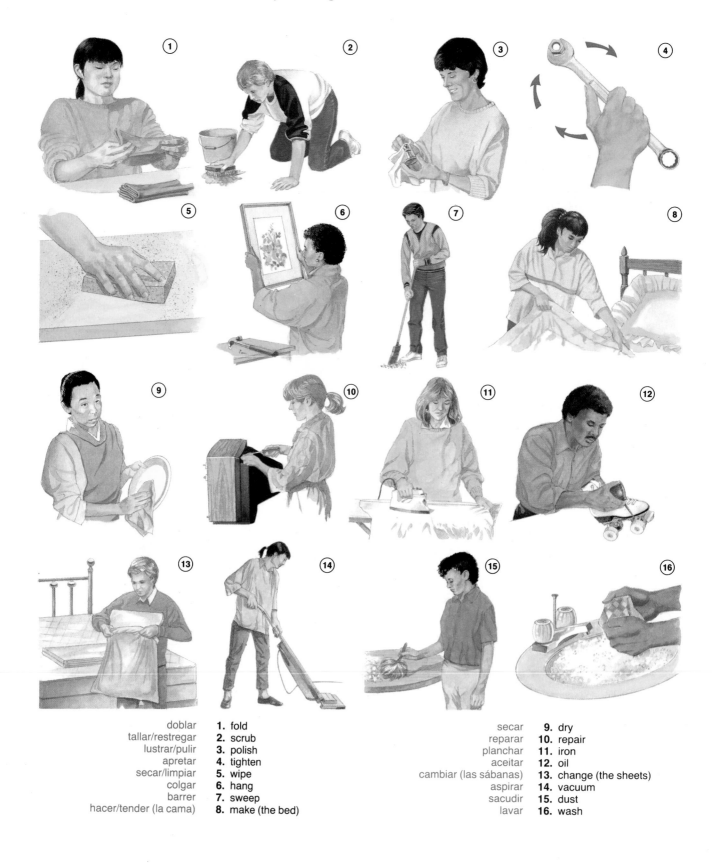

doblar	**1.** fold
tallar/restregar	**2.** scrub
lustrar/pulir	**3.** polish
apretar	**4.** tighten
secar/limpiar	**5.** wipe
colgar	**6.** hang
barrer	**7.** sweep
hacer/tender (la cama)	**8.** make (the bed)

secar	**9.** dry
reparar	**10.** repair
planchar	**11.** iron
aceitar	**12.** oil
cambiar (las sábanas)	**13.** change (the sheets)
aspirar	**14.** vacuum
sacudir	**15.** dust
lavar	**16.** wash

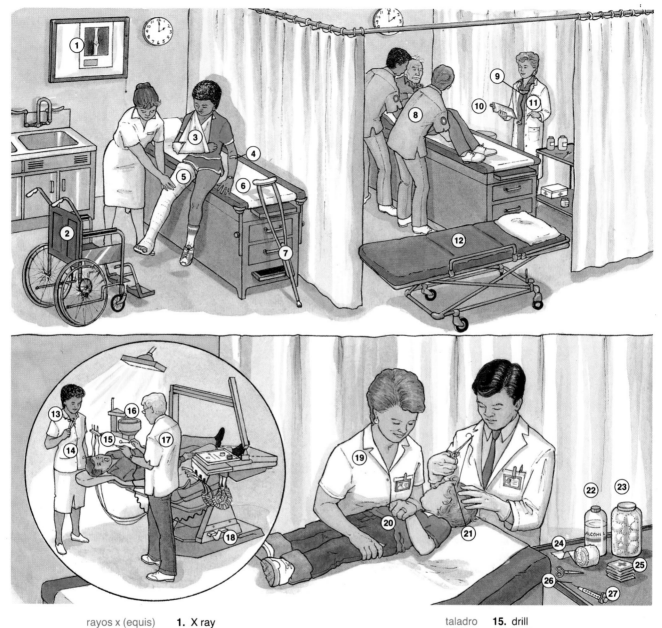

rayos x (equis)	**1.** X ray		taladro	**15.** drill
silla de ruedas	**2.** wheelchair		escupidero	**16.** basin
soporte	**3.** sling		dentista	**17.** dentist
curita	**4.** Band-Aid		pedal	**18.** pedal
enyesado	**5.** cast		enfermera	**19.** nurse
mesa de reconocimiento	**6.** examining table		paciente	**20.** patient
muleta	**7.** crutch		puntadas/puntos	**21.** stitches
ayudante	**8.** attendant		alcohol	**22.** alcohol
estetoscopio	**9.** stethoscope		algodón	**23.** cotton balls
cuadro médico	**10.** chart		vendas (de gaza)	**24.** (gauze) bandage
doctor	**11.** doctor		gaza	**25.** gauze pads
camilla	**12.** stretcher		aguja	**26.** needle
instrumentos	**13.** instruments		jeringa	**27.** syringe
higienista bucal	**14.** oral hygienist			

sarpullido	**1.** rash
fiebre	**2.** fever
piquete de insecto/picada	**3.** insect bite
resfríos/escalofríos	**4.** chills
ojo morado	**5.** black eye
dolor de cabeza	**6.** headache
dolor de estómago	**7.** stomachache
dolor de espalda	**8.** backache
dolor de muela	**9.** toothache
alta presión sanguínea/presión alta	**10.** high blood pressure
resfriado/resfrío	**11.** cold
dolor de garganta	**12.** sore throat
depresor de lengua/paleta	**a.** tongue depressor
torcedura	**13.** sprain
venda elástica	**a.** stretch bandage
infección	**14.** infection
fractura	**15.** broken bone
cortada	**16.** cut
golpe	**17.** bruise
quemadura	**18.** burn

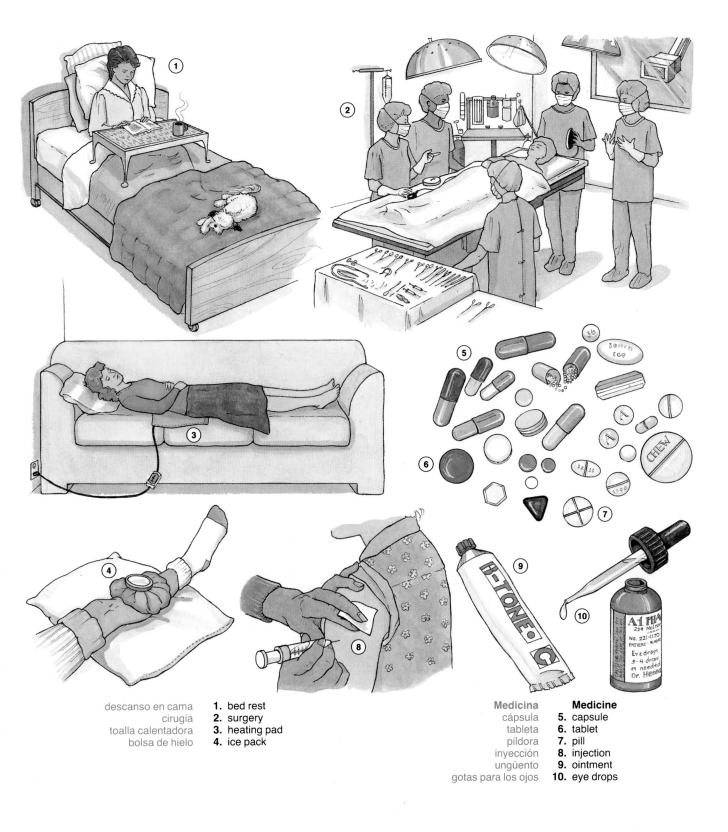

descanso en cama	**1.** bed rest	**Medicina**	**Medicine**
cirugía	**2.** surgery	cápsula	**5.** capsule
toalla calentadora	**3.** heating pad	tableta	**6.** tablet
bolsa de hielo	**4.** ice pack	píldora	**7.** pill
		inyección	**8.** injection
		ungüento	**9.** ointment
		gotas para los ojos	**10.** eye drops

escalera	**1.** ladder	bomba de agua para incendios	**9.** fire hydrant
carro tanque de bomberos/	**2.** fire engine	bombero	**10.** fire fighter
carro bombas		extinguidor	**11.** fire extinguisher
carro de bomberos	**3.** fire truck	casco	**12.** helmet
escape de incendio	**4.** fire escape	abrigo	**13.** coat
fuego/incendio	**5.** fire	hacha	**14.** ax
ambulancia	**6.** ambulance	humo	**15.** smoke
enfermero/paramédico	**7.** paramedic	agua	**16.** water
manguera	**8.** hose	lanza agua	**17.** nozzle

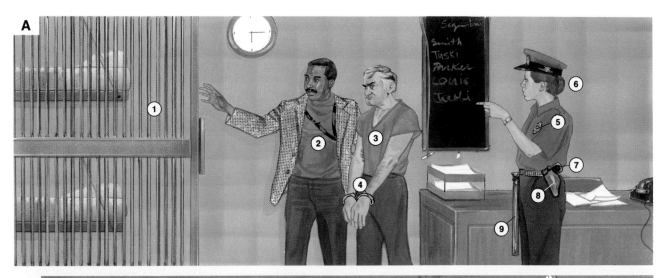

Estación de policía	**A. Police Station**
cárcel	**1.** jail
detective	**2.** detective
sospechoso	**3.** suspect
esposas	**4.** handcuffs
escudo/insignia/chapa	**5.** badge
(oficial de) policía	**6.** police officer
arma/pistola/revólver	**7.** gun
funda/baqueta	**8.** holster
macana	**9.** nightstick
Corte/Sala de Juicio	**B. Court**
juez	**10.** judge
bata	**11.** robes

martillo	**12.** gavel
testigo	**13.** witness
anotador	**14.** court reporter
transcripción	**15.** transcript
tribunal/banco	**16.** bench
fiscal acusador	**17.** prosecuting attorney
tribuna del testigo/silla del testigo	**18.** witness stand
oficial de la corte	**19.** court officer
tribunal del jurado	**20.** jury box
jurado	**21.** jury
abogado defensor	**22.** defense attorney
demandado/acusado	**23.** defendant
huellas digitales	**24.** fingerprints

edificio de oficinas	**1.** office building	policía de tránsito	**10.** traffic cop
recibidor	**2.** lobby	cruce	**11.** intersection
esquina	**3.** corner	peatón	**12.** pedestrian
vía peatonal	**4.** crosswalk	parada de autobús	**13.** bus stop
tienda de departamentos	**5.** department store	banca	**14.** bench
panadería/pastelería	**6.** bakery	basurero/zafacón	**15.** trash basket
teléfono público	**7.** public telephone	estación del metro/estación del subterráneo	**16.** subway station
letrero	**8.** street sign		
oficina de correo	**9.** post office		

elevador/ascensor	**17.** elevator	acera/banqueta	**25.** sidewalk
librería	**18.** bookstore	reborde/cuneta	**26.** curb
estacionamiento	**19.** parking garage	carro para bebé	**27.** baby carriage
parquímetro	**20.** parking meter	mercado de frutas y legumbres	**28.** fruit and vegetable market
semáforo	**21.** traffic light	poste de luz	**29.** streetlight
farmacia	**22.** drugstore	puesto de periódicos y revistas	**30.** newsstand
apartamentos	**23.** apartment house	calle	**31.** street
número del edificio	**24.** building number	alcantarilla	**32.** manhole

Entrega de correo	**A. Delivering Mail**		Oficina de correos	**B. The Post Office**
buzón	**1.** mailbox		ranura	**13.** mail slot
correo	**2.** mail		empleado postal	**14.** postal worker
cartero	**3.** letter carrier		ventanilla	**15.** window
bolsa de correo	**4.** mailbag			
camión de correo	**5.** mail truck		**Tipos de correo**	**C. Types of Mail**
buzón de los Estados Unidos	**6.** U.S. mailbox		sobre (aéreo)	**16.** (airmail) envelope
carta	**7.** letter		tarjeta postal	**17.** postcard
remitente	**8.** return address		orden monetaria/giro postal	**18.** money order
sello de correo	**9.** postmark		paquete	**19.** package
estampilla/timbre (de correo)	**10.** stamp		cordón/cuerda	**20.** string
dirección	**11.** address		etiqueta	**21.** label
código postal/área postal	**12.** zip code		cinta	**22.** tape
			(paquete) correo express	**23.** Express Mail (package)

empleado de biblioteca	**1.**	library clerk
mostrador de chequeo	**2.**	checkout desk
tarjeta de biblioteca	**3.**	library card
catálogo/tarjetero	**4.**	card catalog
cajón/gaveta	**5.**	drawer
tarjeta informativa	**6.**	call card
número de clasificación	**7.**	call number
autor	**8.**	author
título	**9.**	title
tema/materia	**10.**	subject
fila	**11.**	row
ficha de reclamo	**12.**	call slip
microfilm	**13.**	microfilm
amplificador de microfilm	**14.**	microfilm reader
sección de revistas/ publicaciones periódicas	**15.**	periodicals section
revista	**16.**	magazine
estante	**17.**	rack
fotocopiadora/sacacopias	**18.**	photocopy machine
globo/esfera	**19.**	globe
atlas	**20.**	atlas
sección de referencia	**21.**	reference section
información	**22.**	information desk
bibliotecaria	**23.**	(reference) librarian
diccionario	**24.**	dictionary
enciclopedia	**25.**	encyclopedia
repisa/tablilla	**26.**	shelf

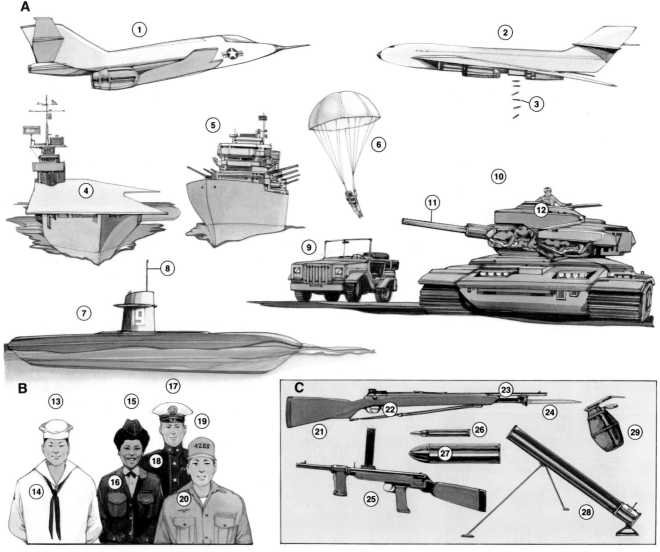

Vehículos y equipo	A. Vehicles and Equipment	Armada/Ejército	15. Army
avión de caza	1. fighter plane	soldado	16. soldier
bombardero	2. bomber	Marina	17. Marines
bomba	3. bomb	marino	18. marine
portaviones	4. aircraft carrier	Fuerza Aérea	19. Air Force
barco de guerra	5. battleship	aviador	20. airman
paracaídas	6. parachute		
submarino	7. submarine	Armas y munición	C. Weapons and Ammunition
periscopio	8. periscope	rifle	21. rifle
jeep	9. jeep	gatillo	22. trigger
tanque	10. tank	cañón	23. barrel
cañón	11. cannon	bayoneta	24. bayonet
torre blindada de armas	12. gun turret	ametralladora	25. machine gun
		bala	26. bullet
Personal	**B. Personnel**	casquillo	27. shell
Naval/Marina	13. Navy	mortero	28. mortar
marinero	14. sailor	granada (de mano)	29. hand grenade

barredora/limpia calles	1. street cleaner		persona de entrega	10. delivery person
grúa	2. tow truck		carro de mudanza	11. moving van
carro tanque	3. fuel truck		mudador	12. mover
camioneta	4. pickup truck		mezcladora de cemento/	13. cement truck
pala de nieve	5. snow plow		revolvedora de cemento	
camión de la basura	6. garbage truck		camión de volteo	14. dump truck
empleado de limpieza	7. sanitation worker		trailer	15. tractor trailer
camioneta de lonchar/cantina	8. lunch truck		chofer/camionero	16. truck driver
rodante			transportador/porta autos	17. transporter
camión	9. panel truck		acoplado	18. flatbed

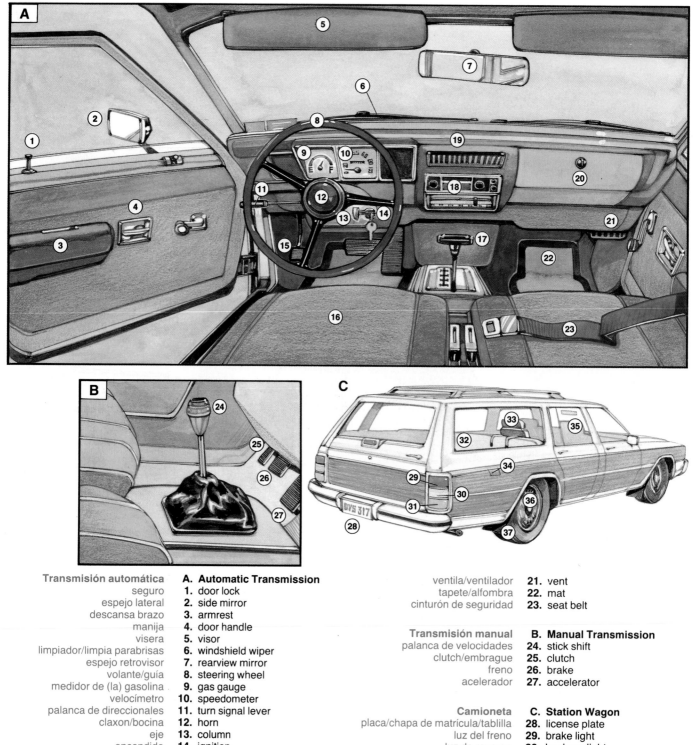

Transmisión automática	A. Automatic Transmission
seguro	1. door lock
espejo lateral	2. side mirror
descansa brazo	3. armrest
manija	4. door handle
visera	5. visor
limpiador/limpia parabrisas	6. windshield wiper
espejo retrovisor	7. rearview mirror
volante/guía	8. steering wheel
medidor de (la) gasolina	9. gas gauge
velocímetro	10. speedometer
palanca de direccionales	11. turn signal lever
claxon/bocina	12. horn
eje	13. column
encendido	14. ignition
freno de emergencia	15. emergency brake
asiento deportivo	16. bucket seat
cambio de velocidades/palanca de cambios	17. gearshift
radio	18. radio
tablero	19. dashboard
guantera/gaveta para guantes	20. glove compartment

ventila/ventilador	21. vent
tapete/alfombra	22. mat
cinturón de seguridad	23. seat belt

Transmisión manual	B. Manual Transmission
palanca de velocidades	24. stick shift
clutch/embrague	25. clutch
freno	26. brake
acelerador	27. accelerator

Camioneta	C. Station Wagon
placa/chapa de matrícula/tablilla	28. license plate
luz del freno	29. brake light
luz de reversa	30. back-up light
luz trasera	31. taillight
asiento trasero	32. backseat
asiento para niño	33. child's seat
tanque de gasolina	34. gas tank
respaldo	35. headrest
tapón/tapacubo/tapabocina	36. hubcap
llanta/goma	37. tire

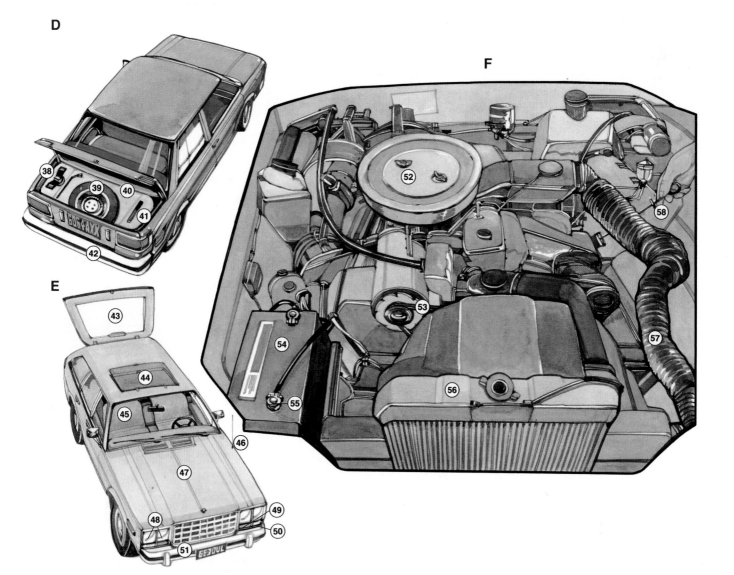

Sedán (dos puertas)	**D. (Two-door) Sedan**	luces delanteras	**48.** headlights
gato	**38.** jack	luces para estacionarse	**49.** parking lights
llanta de repuesto/refacción/repuesta	**39.** spare tire	luces direccionales	**50.** turn signal (lights)
cajuela/maletera/baúl	**40.** trunk	defensa delantera	**51.** front bumper
señal luminosa preventiva	**41.** flare		
defensa trasera	**42.** rear bumper	**Motor**	**F. Engine**
		filtro	**52.** air filter
Camioneta cuatro puertas	**E. Four-door Hatchback**	banda (del ventilador)	**53.** fan belt
compuerta trasera	**43.** hatchback	acumulador/batería	**54.** battery
quemacoco	**44.** sunroof	terminal	**55.** terminal
el parabrisas	**45.** windshield	radiador	**56.** radiator
antena	**46.** antenna	manguera	**57.** hose
toldo/capota	**47.** hood	varilla del aceite	**58.** dipstick

ruedas de entrenamiento	**1.** training wheels	cadena	**18.** chain
manubrios(de carreras)	**2.** (racing) handlebars	pedal	**19.** pedal
bicicleta de mujer	**3.** girl's frame	engrane	**20.** sprocket
rueda	**4.** wheel	pompa	**21.** pump
claxon/bocina	**5.** horn	palanca de velocidades	**22.** gear changer
triciclo	**6.** tricycle	cable	**23.** cable
casco	**7.** helmet	freno manual	**24.** hand brake
bicicleta para campo	**8.** dirt bike	reflector	**25.** reflector
soporte	**9.** kickstand	rayo	**26.** spoke
defensa	**10.** fender	válvula	**27.** valve
bicicleta de hombre	**11.** boy's frame	llanta/goma	**28.** tire
manubrios de viaje	**12.** touring handlebars	moto pequeña	**29.** motor scooter
seguro	**13.** lock	motocicleta	**30.** motorcycle
estante de bicicleta	**14.** bike stand	amortiguadores	**31.** shock absorbers
bicicleta	**15.** bicycle	motor	**32.** engine
asiento	**16.** seat	escape	**33.** exhaust pipe
freno	**17.** brake		

carretera interestatal	**1.** interstate highway	carro de pasajeros	**15.** passenger car
carril de salida	**2.** exit ramp	vehículo de remolque para	**16.** camper
paso a desnivel	**3.** overpass	acampar/carro casa	
cruce de trébol	**4.** cloverleaf	carro deportivo	**17.** sports car
carril izquierdo	**5.** left lane	división central/divisor	**18.** center divider
carril central	**6.** center lane	motocicleta	**19.** motorcycle
carril derecho	**7.** right lane	autobús	**20.** bus
letrero de límite de velocidad	**8.** speed limit sign	carril de entrada	**21.** entrance ramp
persona que viaja pidiendo	**9.** hitchhiker	borde/orilla de la carretera	**22.** shoulder
aventón/ponero		letrero de carretera	**23.** road sign
casa-remolque	**10.** trailer	letrero de salida	**24.** exit sign
área de servicios	**11.** service area	camión	**25.** truck
ayudante/asistente	**12.** attendant	camión de mudanza	**26.** van
bomba de aire/pompa de aire	**13.** air pump	caseta de cobro/peaje	**27.** tollbooth
bomba de gasolina/pompa de	**14.** gas pump		
gasolina			

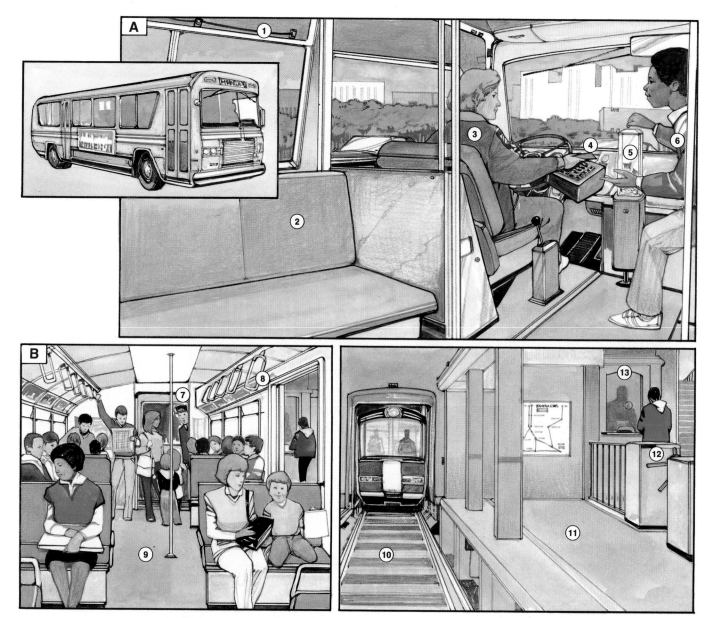

<table>
<tr><td colspan="2" align="right">**Autobús/Guagua**</td><td colspan="2">**A. Bus**</td></tr>
</table>

Autobús/Guagua	**A. Bus**
cordón	1. cord
asiento	2. seat
chofer/conductor	3. bus driver
boleto/billete de transbordo	4. transfer
alcancía de cuota/tarifa	5. fare box
pasajero	6. rider

Tren subterráneo/Metro	**B. Subway**
conductor	7. conductor
agarradera	8. strap
coche/carro de ferrocarril	9. car
vía/carril	10. track
plataforma	11. platform
torniquete de entrada/torno	12. turnstile
casilla/taquilla de fichas	13. token booth

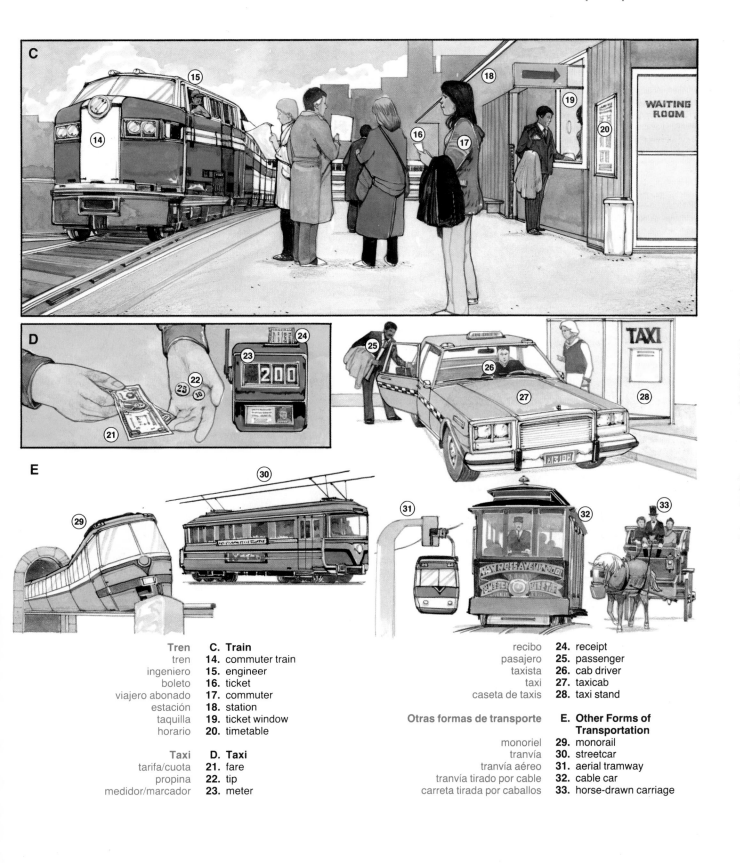

Tren	C. Train		recibo	24. receipt
tren	14. commuter train		pasajero	25. passenger
ingeniero	15. engineer		taxista	26. cab driver
boleto	16. ticket		taxi	27. taxicab
viajero abonado	17. commuter		caseta de taxis	28. taxi stand
estación	18. station			
taquilla	19. ticket window		Otras formas de transporte	E. Other Forms of Transportation
horario	20. timetable			
			monoriel	29. monorail
Taxi	D. Taxi		tranvía	30. streetcar
tarifa/cuota	21. fare		tranvía aéreo	31. aerial tramway
propina	22. tip		tranvía tirado por cable	32. cable car
medidor/marcador	23. meter		carreta tirada por caballos	33. horse-drawn carriage

Registro en el aeropuerto

Airport Check-In

porta ropa
bolso de mano
viajero
boleto/pasaje
mozo/maletero
carrito de equipaje
maleta
equipaje

1. garment bag
2. carry-on bag
3. traveler
4. ticket
5. porter
6. dolly
7. suitcase
8. baggage

Seguridad

Security

el guardia de seguridad
detector de metales
seleccionador de rayos
banda

9. security guard
10. metal detector
11. X-ray screener
12. conveyor belt

Abordaje

Boarding

cabina de mando
instrumentos
piloto
copiloto
ingeniero de vuelo
pase de abordar
cabina
el, la sobrecargo
compartimento de equipaje
mesita
pasillo

13. cockpit
14. instruments
15. pilot
16. copilot
17. flight engineer
18. boarding pass
19. cabin
20. flight attendant
21. luggage compartment
22. tray table
23. aisle

A

B

Clases de aviones	**A. Aircraft Types**	Despegue	**B. Takeoff**
globo	**1.** hot air balloon	turbina	**11.** jet engine
helicóptero	**2.** helicopter	el área de carga	**12.** cargo area
hélice	**a.** rotor	puerta de carga	**13.** cargo door
jet privado	**3.** private jet	fuselaje	**14.** fuselage
planeador	**4.** glider	tren de aterrizaje	**15.** landing gear
dirigible	**5.** blimp	la terminal	**16.** terminal building
deslizador	**6.** hang glider	el hangar	**17.** hangar
avión de motor	**7.** propeller plane	el jet	**18.** (jet) plane
trompa (del avión)/nariz	**8.** nose	pista	**19.** runway
ala	**9.** wing	torre de control	**20.** control tower
cola	**10.** tail		

bote de pesca	**1.** fishing boat
pescador	**2.** fisherman
muelle/malecón	**3.** pier
porta carga	**4.** forklift
proa	**5.** bow
grúa	**6.** crane
caja	**7.** container
bodega	**8.** hold
barco de carga	**9.** (container)ship
carga	**10.** cargo
popa	**11.** stern
barcaza/lanchón	**12.** barge
remolcador	**13.** tugboat
faro	**14.** lighthouse
barco tanque	**15.** tanker

boya	**16.** buoy
transbordador	**17.** ferry
chimenea	**18.** smokestack
bote salvavidas	**19.** lifeboat
portalón	**20.** gangway
ventanilla/portilla/clarabolla	**21.** porthole
cubierta	**22.** deck
molinete	**23.** windlass
el ancla	**24.** anchor
cuerda/lazo	**25.** line
bolardo	**26.** bollard
buque (transatlántico)	**27.** ocean liner
dique/desembarcadero	**28.** dock
estación de carga	**29.** terminal

chaleco salvavidas	**1.** life jacket	lancha de motor	**13.** motorboat
canoa	**2.** canoe	deslizador de vela	**14.** windsurfer
remo/paleta (de agua)	**3.** paddle	veleta	**15.** sailboard
bote de vela	**4.** sailboat	bote de paseo	**16.** cabin cruiser
timón	**5.** rudder	canoa de los esquimales	**17.** kayak
orza de deriva/quilla	**6.** centerboard	bote/lancha/botecito	**18.** dinghy
botalón/botavara	**7.** boom	anclaje/bolla	**19.** mooring
mástil	**8.** mast	flotador inflable	**20.** inflatable raft
vela	**9.** sail	escálamo/horquilla	**21.** oarlock
esquiador	**10.** water-skier	remo	**22.** oar
sirga/cuerda de remolque	**11.** towrope	bote de remo	**23.** rowboat
motor exterior	**12.** outboard motor		

Flores	Flowers		gardenia	**14.** gardenia
tulipán	**1.** tulip		flor de nochebuena/pascua	**15.** poinsettia
tallo	**a.** stem		violeta	**16.** violet
pensamiento	**2.** pansy		botón de oro	**17.** buttercup
azucena	**3.** lily		rosa	**18.** rose
crisantemo	**4.** (chrysanthe)mum		botón	**a.** bud
margarita	**5.** daisy		pétalo	**b.** petal
maravilla/clavelón	**6.** marigold		espina	**c.** thorn
petunia	**7.** petunia		girasol	**19.** sunflower
narciso	**8.** daffodil			
bulbo	**a.** bulb		**Yerbas y granos**	**Grasses and Grains**
azafrán croco	**9.** crocus		caña de azúcar	**20.** sugarcane
jacinto	**10.** hyacinth		arroz	**21.** rice
lirio	**11.** iris		trigo	**22.** wheat
orquídea	**12.** orchid		(granos de) avena	**23.** oats
pompón	**13.** zinnia		maíz	**24.** corn

Arboles	Trees	olmo	36. elm
secoya	**25.** redwood	hoja	**a.** leaf
palmera	**26.** palm	acebo/agrifolio	**37.** holly
eucalipto	**27.** eucalyptus	arce/meple	**38.** maple
cornejo	**28.** dogwood		
magnolia	**29.** magnolia	**Otras plantas**	**Other Plants**
álamo/chopo	**30.** poplar	plantas caseras	**39.** house plants
sauce	**31.** willow	cactus	**40.** cactus
abedul	**32.** birch	arbustos	**41.** bushes
roble	**33.** oak	enredadera	**42.** vine
ramita	**a.** twig		
bellota	**b.** acorn	**Plantas venenosas**	**Poisonous Plants**
pino	**34.** pine	roble venenoso	**43.** poison oak
aguja	**a.** needle	zumaque venenoso	**44.** poison sumac
cono	**b.** cone	hiedra venenosa	**45.** poison ivy
árbol	**35.** tree		
rama	**a.** branch		
tronco	**b.** trunk		
corcho	**c.** bark		
raíz	**d.** root		

caracol	**1.**	snail
concha	**a.**	shell
antena	**b.**	antenna
ostra	**2.**	oyster
almeja	**3.**	mussel
baboso/babosa	**4.**	slug
calamar	**5.**	squid
pulpo	**6.**	octopus
pez estrella	**7.**	starfish

camarón	**8.**	shrimp
cangrejo/juey	**9.**	crab
escalope/concha	**10.**	scallop
lombriz	**11.**	worm
medusa/aguaviva	**12.**	jellyfish
tentáculo	**a.**	tentacle
langosta	**13.**	lobster
pinza/boca	**a.**	claw

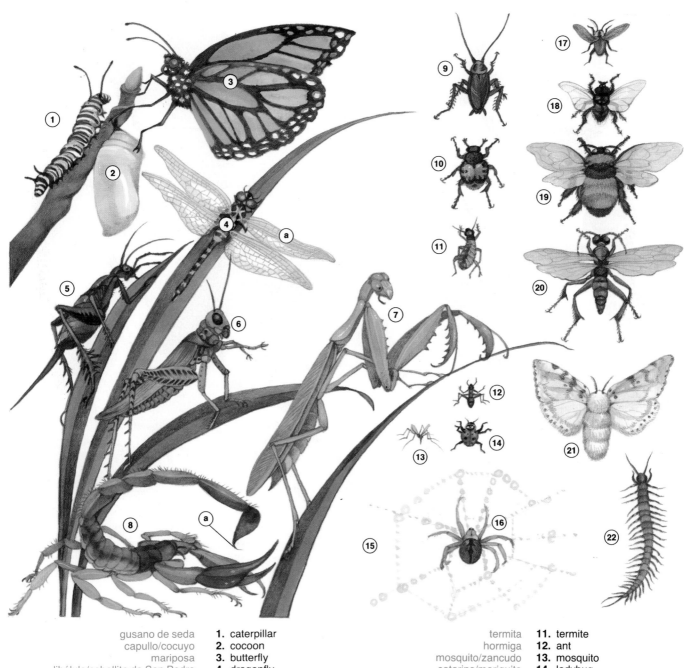

gusano de seda	**1.** caterpillar
capullo/cocuyo	**2.** cocoon
mariposa	**3.** butterfly
libélula/caballito de San Pedro	**4.** dragonfly
ala	**a.** wing
grillo	**5.** cricket
chapulín/saltamonte	**6.** grasshopper
mantis	**7.** mantis
alacrán	**8.** scorpion
aguijón	**a.** sting
cucaracha	**9.** cockroach
escarabajo	**10.** beetle

termita	**11.** termite
hormiga	**12.** ant
mosquito/zancudo	**13.** mosquito
catarina/mariquita	**14.** ladybug
telaraña	**15.** web
araña	**16.** spider
luciérnaga/cucubano	**17.** firefly
mosca	**18.** fly
abeja	**19.** bee
avispa	**20.** wasp
mariposa nocturna	**21.** moth
ciempiés	**22.** centipede

pichón/paloma	**1.** pigeon	perico/cotorra/loro	**16.** parrot
ala	**a.** wing	pájaro carpintero	**17.** woodpecker
colibrí	**2.** hummingbird	pavo real	**18.** peacock
cuervo	**3.** crow	el faisán	**19.** pheasant
pico	**a.** beak	pavo	**20.** turkey
gaviota	**4.** sea gull	gallo	**21.** rooster
águila	**5.** eagle	pollito	**22.** chick
búho/lechuza	**6.** owl	pollo	**23.** chicken
halcón/falcón	**7.** hawk	pelícano	**24.** pelican
pluma	**a.** feather	pico	**a.** bill
pájaro azul	**8.** blue jay	pato	**25.** duck
petirrojo/pechicolorado	**9.** robin	ganso	**26.** goose
gorrión	**10.** sparrow	pingüino	**27.** penguin
cardenal	**11.** cardinal	cisne	**28.** swan
el avestruz	**12.** ostrich	flamingo	**29.** flamingo
huevo	**13.** egg	cigüeña	**30.** stork
canario	**14.** canary	nido	**31.** nest
periquito	**15.** parakeet	correcaminos	**32.** roadrunner

A

B

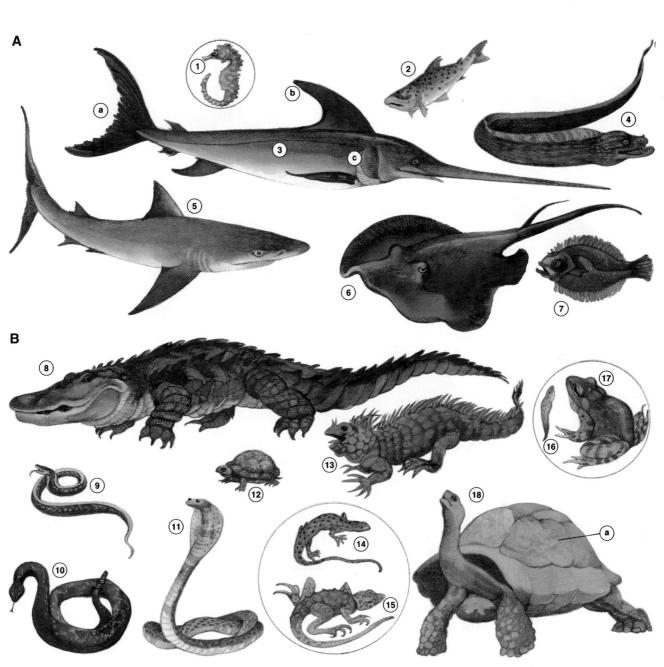

Peces	**A. Fish**		Anfibios y reptiles	**B. Amphibians and Reptiles**
caballo de mar	**1.** sea horse		cocodrilo	**8.** alligator
trucha	**2.** trout		culebra/víbora	**9.** (garter) snake
pez espada	**3.** swordfish		víbora de cascabel	**10.** rattlesnake
cola	**a.** tail		cobra	**11.** cobra
aleta	**b.** fin		tortuga	**12.** turtle
agalla	**c.** gill		iguana	**13.** iguana
anguila	**4.** eel		salamandra	**14.** salamander
tiburón	**5.** shark		lagartija	**15.** lizard
mantaraya	**6.** stingray		renacuajo/ajolote	**16.** tadpole
robalo/mojarra	**7.** flounder		rana	**17.** frog
			tortuga gigante	**18.** tortoise
			concha/carapacho	**a.** shell

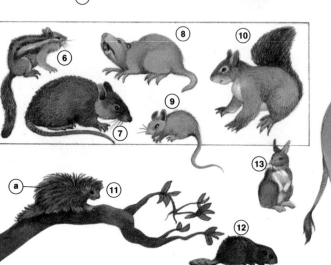

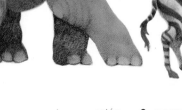

Mamíferos de bolsa, sin dientes, y voladores

(oso) koala
armadillo
canguro
cola
patas traseras
bolsa
patas frontales
murciélago
oso hormiguero

Pouched, Toothless, or Flying Mammals

1. koala
2. armadillo
3. kangaroo
   a. tail
   b. hind legs
   c. pouch
   d. forelegs
4. bat
5. anteater

Roedores

ardillita
rata
topo

Rodents

6. chipmunk
7. rat
8. gopher

ratón
ardilla
puerco espín
púa
castor
conejo

9. mouse
10. squirrel
11. porcupine
    a. quill
12. beaver
13. rabbit

Mamíferos de pezuña

hipopótamo
llama
rinoceronte
cuerno
elefante
trompa
colmillo
cebra

Hoofed Mammals

14. hippopotamus
15. llama
16. rhinoceros
    a. horn
17. elephant
    a. trunk
    b. tusk
18. zebra

bisonte	**19.** bison		girafa	**29.** giraffe
pony	**20.** pony		cerdo	**30.** hog
caballo	**21.** horse		becerro/ternero	**31.** calf
crin de caballo	**a.** mane		vaca	**32.** cow
potro	**22.** foal		camello	**33.** camel
burro	**23.** donkey		joroba	**a.** hump
borrego/oveja pequeña	**24.** lamb		toro	**34.** bull
cordero/oveja	**25.** sheep		alce	**35.** moose
venado	**26.** deer		cuerno/asta	**a.** antler
cervato/venadito	**27.** fawn		pezuña	**b.** hoof
chivo	**28.** goat			

		Mamíferos acuáticos	**Aquatic Mammals**
leopardo	**1.** leopard	ballena	**9.** whale
tigre	**2.** tiger	nutria	**10.** otter
garra	**a.** claw	morsa	**11.** walrus
león	**3.** lion	foca	**12.** seal
gato	**4.** cat	pata de foca	**a.** flipper
gatito	**5.** kitten	delfín	**13.** dolphin
zorro	**6.** fox		
mapache	**7.** raccoon		
zorrillo	**8.** skunk		

Primates	Primates
chango/mico	**14.** monkey
mono de Asia	**15.** gibbon
chimpancé	**16.** chimpanzee
gorila	**17.** gorilla
orangután	**18.** orangutan
mandril	**19.** baboon

Osos	Bears
oso panda	**20.** panda
oso negro	**21.** black bear
oso polar	**22.** polar bear
oso pardo	**23.** grizzly bear

Perros	Dogs
spaniel/perro de aguas	**24.** spaniel
terrier	**25.** terrier
perro cobrador	**26.** retriever
cachorro	**27.** puppy
pastor	**28.** shepherd
lobo	**29.** wolf
pata/garra	**a.** paw
hiena	**30.** hyena

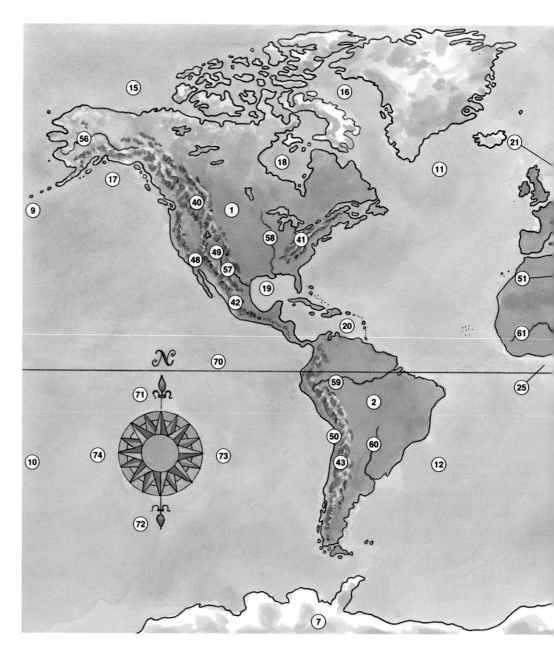

Continentes	Continents	Mares, golfos y bahías	Seas, Gulfs, and Bays		
Norteamérica	**1.** North America	Mar de Beaufort	**15.** Beaufort Sea	Mar Arábigo	**30.** Arabian Sea
Sudamérica	**2.** South America	Bahía Baffin	**16.** Baffin Bay	Mar de Kara	**31.** Kara Sea
Europa	**3.** Europe	Golfo de Alaska	**17.** Gulf of Alaska	Bahía de Bengala	**32.** Bay of Bengal
Africa	**4.** Africa	Bahía del Hudson	**18.** Hudson Bay	Mar de Laptev	**33.** Laptev Sea
Asia	**5.** Asia	Golfo de México	**19.** Gulf of Mexico	Mar de Bering	**34.** Bering Sea
Australia	**6.** Australia	Mar del Caribe/Mar Caribe	**20.** Caribbean Sea	Mar de Okhotsk	**35.** Sea of Okhotsk
Antártica	**7.** Antarctica	Mar del Norte	**21.** North Sea	Mar del Japón	**36.** Sea of Japan
		Mar Báltico	**22.** Baltic Sea	Mar Amarillo	**37.** Yellow Sea
Océanos	Oceans	Mar de Barents	**23.** Barents Sea	Mar del Este de China	**38.** East China Sea
Artico	**8.** Arctic	Mar Mediterráneo	**24.** Mediterranean Sea	Mar del Sur de China	**39.** South China Sea
Pacífico del norte	**9.** North Pacific	Golfo de Guinea	**25.** Gulf of Guinea		
Pacífico del sur	**10.** South Pacific	Mar Negro	**26.** Black Sea		
Atlántico del norte	**11.** North Atlantic	Mar Caspiano	**27.** Caspian Sea		
Atlántico del sur	**12.** South Atlantic	Golfo Pérsico	**28.** Persian Gulf		
Indico	**13.** Indian	Mar Rojo	**29.** Red Sea		
Antártico	**14.** Antarctic				

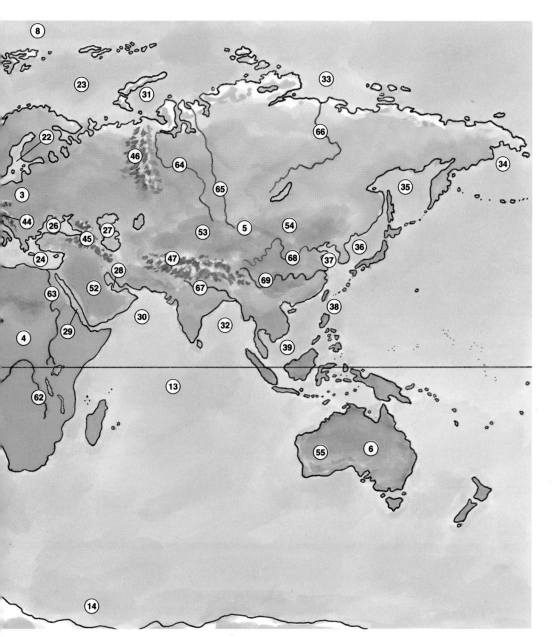

Cordilleras	**Mountain Ranges**
Montañas Rocallosas	**40.** Rocky Mountains
Montañas Apalaches/Montes Apalaches	**41.** Appalachian Mountains
Sierra Madre	**42.** Sierra Madre
Andes	**43.** Andes
Alpes	**44.** Alps
Montañas Cáucaso	**45.** Caucasus
Montes Urales	**46.** Urals
Himalayas	**47.** Himalayas

Desiertos	**Deserts**
Mojave	**48.** Mojave
Pintado	**49.** Painted
Atacama	**50.** Atacama
Sahara	**51.** Sahara

Rubalcali	**52.** Rub' al Khali
Takla Makan	**53.** Takla Makan
Gobi	**54.** Gobi
Arenoso	**55.** Great Sandy

Ríos	**Rivers**
Yukón	**56.** Yukon
Río Grande	**57.** Rio Grande
Misisipí	**58.** Mississippi
Amazonas	**59.** Amazon
Paraná	**60.** Paraná
Níger	**61.** Niger
Congo	**62.** Congo
Nilo	**63.** Nile
Ob	**64.** Ob

Yenisey	**65.** Yenisey
Lena	**66.** Lena
Ganges	**67.** Ganges
Huang	**68.** Huang
Yangtzé	**69.** Yangtze

ecuador	**70.** equator
norte	**71.** north
sur	**72.** south
este	**73.** east
oeste	**74.** west

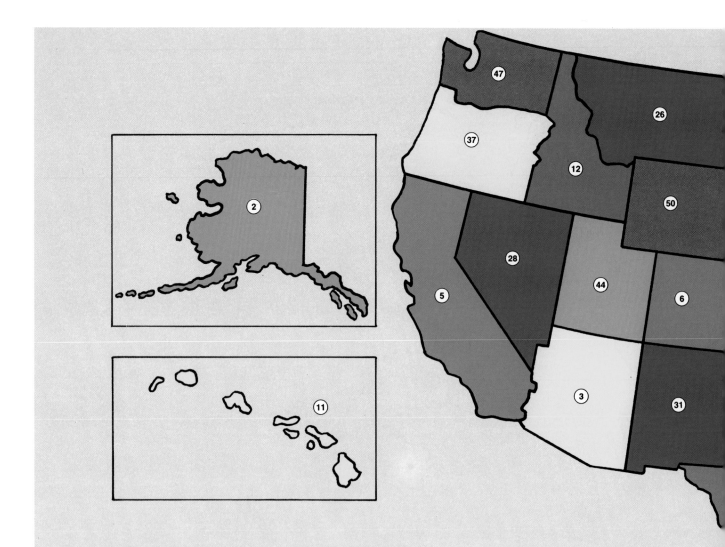

Alabama	**1.** Alabama		Illinois	**13.** Illinois
Alaska	**2.** Alaska		Indiana	**14.** Indiana
Arizona	**3.** Arizona		Iowa	**15.** Iowa
Arkansas	**4.** Arkansas		Kansas	**16.** Kansas
California	**5.** California		Kentucky	**17.** Kentucky
Colorado	**6.** Colorado		Louisiana	**18.** Louisiana
Connecticut	**7.** Connecticut		Maine	**19.** Maine
Delaware	**8.** Delaware		Maryland	**20.** Maryland
Florida	**9.** Florida		Massachusetts	**21.** Massachusetts
Georgia	**10.** Georgia		Michigan	**22.** Michigan
Hawaii	**11.** Hawaii		Minnesota	**23.** Minnesota
Idaho	**12.** Idaho		Misisipí	**24.** Mississippi

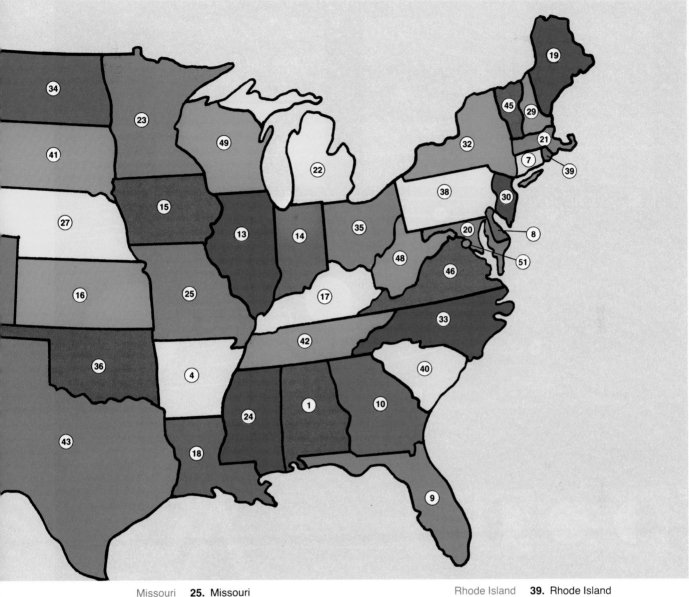

Missouri	**25.** Missouri		Rhode Island	**39.** Rhode Island
Montana	**26.** Montana		Carolina del sur	**40.** South Carolina
Nebraska	**27.** Nebraska		Dakota del sur	**41.** South Dakota
Nevada	**28.** Nevada		Tennessee	**42.** Tennessee
Nueva Hampshire	**29.** New Hampshire		Texas	**43.** Texas
Nueva Jersey	**30.** New Jersey		Utah	**44.** Utah
Nuevo México	**31.** New Mexico		Vermont	**45.** Vermont
Nueva York	**32.** New York		Virginia	**46.** Virginia
Carolina del norte	**33.** North Carolina		Washington	**47.** Washington
Dakota del norte	**34.** North Dakota		West Virginia	**48.** West Virginia
Ohio	**35.** Ohio		Wisconsin	**49.** Wisconsin
Oklahoma	**36.** Oklahoma		Wyoming	**50.** Wyoming
Oregon	**37.** Oregon			
Pennsylvania	**38.** Pennsylvania		Distrito de Columbia	**51.** District of Columbia

Espacio exterior | **A. Outer Space**
galaxia | **1.** galaxy
cometa | **2.** comet
constelación (Osa Mayor) | **3.** (Big Dipper) constellation
estrella | **4.** star
meteoro | **5.** meteor

El Sistema Solar | **B. The Solar System**
eclipse lunar | **6.** lunar eclipse
sol | **7.** Sun
tierra | **8.** Earth
luna | **9.** Moon
eclipse solar | **10.** solar eclipse

Los Planetas | *The Planets*
Mercurio | **11.** Mercury
Venus | **12.** Venus
Tierra | **13.** Earth

Marte | **14.** Mars
Júpiter | **15.** Jupiter
Saturno | **16.** Saturn
anillo | **a.** ring
Urano | **17.** Uranus
Neptuno | **18.** Neptune
Plutón | **19.** Pluto

asteroide | **20.** asteroid
órbita | **21.** orbit
telescopio | **22.** telescope

Fases de la luna | **C. Phases of the Moon**
primer cuarto | **23.** first quarter
luna llena | **24.** full moon
cuarto menguante | **25.** last quarter
luna nueva | **26.** new moon

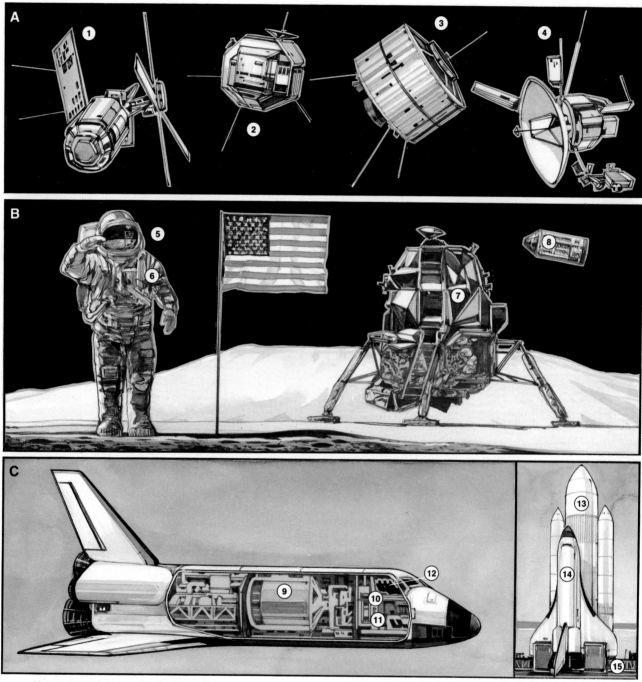

Naves espaciales	**A. Spacecraft**	El transbordador espacial	**C. The Space Shuttle**
estación espacial	**1.** space station	sección de carga	**9.** cargo bay
satélite de comunicación	**2.** communication satellite	cubierta de vuelo	**10.** flight deck
satélite climatológico	**3.** weather satellite	área habitacional	**11.** living quarters
explorador espacial	**4.** space probe	tripulación	**12.** crew
		cohete	**13.** rocket
Alunizaje	**B. Landing on the Moon**	transbordador espacial	**14.** space shuttle
astronauta	**5.** astronaut	plataforma de despegue	**15.** launchpad
traje espacial	**6.** space suit		
módulo lunar	**7.** lunar module		
módulo de comando	**8.** command module		

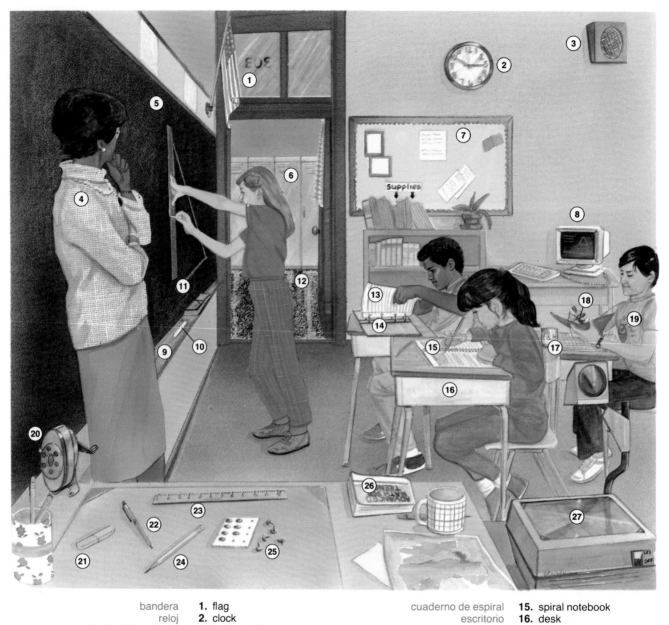

bandera	**1.** flag	cuaderno de espiral	**15.** spiral notebook
reloj	**2.** clock	escritorio	**16.** desk
bocina/altoparlante	**3.** loudspeaker	pegamento/pega	**17.** glue
maestra	**4.** teacher	brocha	**18.** brush
pizarrón/pizarra	**5.** chalkboard	el, la estudiante	**19.** student
armario/locker	**6.** locker	sacapuntas	**20.** pencil sharpener
tablero de anuncios/tablón de edictos	**7.** bulletin board	borrador/goma	**21.** pencil eraser
		pluma atómica/bolígrafo	**22.** ballpoint pen
computadora	**8.** computer	regla	**23.** ruler
repisa del gis/canal de tizas	**9.** chalk tray	lápiz	**24.** pencil
gis/tiza	**10.** chalk	tachuela	**25.** thumbtack
borrador	**11.** eraser	libro (de texto)	**26.** (text)book
pasillo	**12.** hall	retroproyector	**27.** overhead projector
(hojas sueltas de) papel	**13.** (loose-leaf) paper		
carpeta	**14.** ring binder		

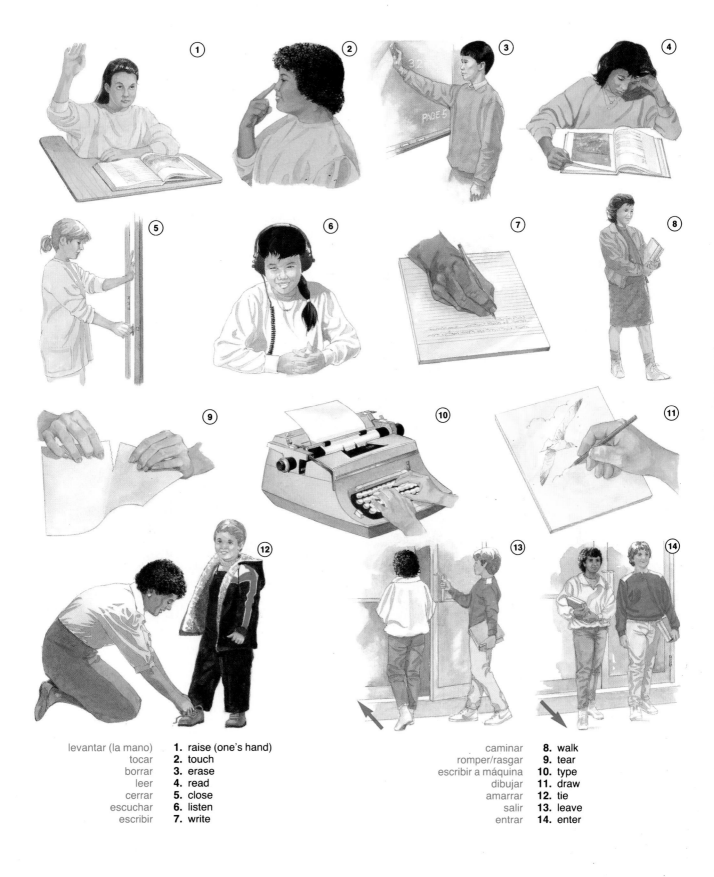

levantar (la mano)	**1.** raise (one's hand)	caminar	**8.** walk
tocar	**2.** touch	romper/rasgar	**9.** tear
borrar	**3.** erase	escribir a máquina	**10.** type
leer	**4.** read	dibujar	**11.** draw
cerrar	**5.** close	amarrar	**12.** tie
escuchar	**6.** listen	salir	**13.** leave
escribir	**7.** write	entrar	**14.** enter

Spanish	English	Spanish	English
prisma	**1.** prism	tubo de hule/goma	**18.** rubber tubing
frasco	**2.** flask	soporte del aro	**19.** ring stand
platito de muestras	**3.** petri dish	quemador	**20.** Bunsen burner
escala/pesa balanza	**4.** scale	flama	**21.** flame
pesas	**5.** weights	termómetro	**22.** thermometer
red metálica	**6.** wire mesh screen	tazón	**23.** beaker
tornillo	**7.** clamp	mesa de trabajo	**24.** bench
estante	**8.** rack	cilindro graduado	**25.** graduated cylinder
proveta	**9.** test tube	gotero	**26.** medicine dropper
tapón	**10.** stopper	imán	**27.** magnet
papel de gráficas/gráfico	**11.** graph paper	tenazas/pinzas	**28.** forceps
lentes de seguridad	**12.** safety glasses	pinzas	**29.** tongs
medidor de tiempo	**13.** timer	microscopio	**30.** microscope
popote/tubo de vidrio	**14.** pipette	muestra en transparencia	**31.** slide
lupa	**15.** magnifying glass	pincitas/tenacillas	**32.** tweezers
papel filtro	**16.** filter paper	estuche de disección	**33.** dissection kit
embudo	**17.** funnel	banco	**34.** stool

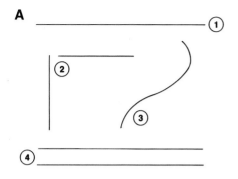

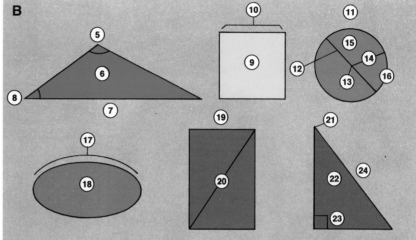

A

B

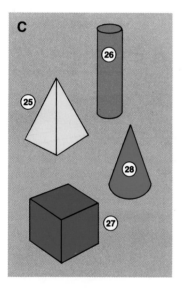

C

D

E

Líneas	A. Lines
línea recta	1. straight line
líneas perpendiculares	2. perpendicular lines
curva	3. curve
líneas paralelas	4. parallel lines

Figuras geométricas	B. Geometrical Figures
ángulo obtuso	5. obtuse angle
triángulo	6. triangle
base	7. base
ángulo agudo	8. acute angle
cuadrado	9. square
lado	10. side
círculo	11. circle
diámetro	12. diameter
centro	13. center
radio	14. radius
sección	15. section
arco	16. arc
circunferencia	17. circumference
óvalo	18. oval
rectángulo	19. rectangle
diagonal	20. diagonal

ápice/cumbre	21. apex
triángulo recto	22. right triangle
ángulo recto	23. right angle
hipotenusa	24. hypotenuse

Figuras sólidas	C. Solid Figures
pirámide	25. pyramid
cilindro	26. cylinder
cubo	27. cube
cono	28. cone

Fracciones	D. Fractions
entero	29. whole
un medio	30. a half (1/2)
un cuarto	31. a quarter (1/4)
un tercio	32. a third (1/3)

Medidas	E. Measurement
profundidad	33. depth
altura	34. height
ancho	35. width
largo	36. length

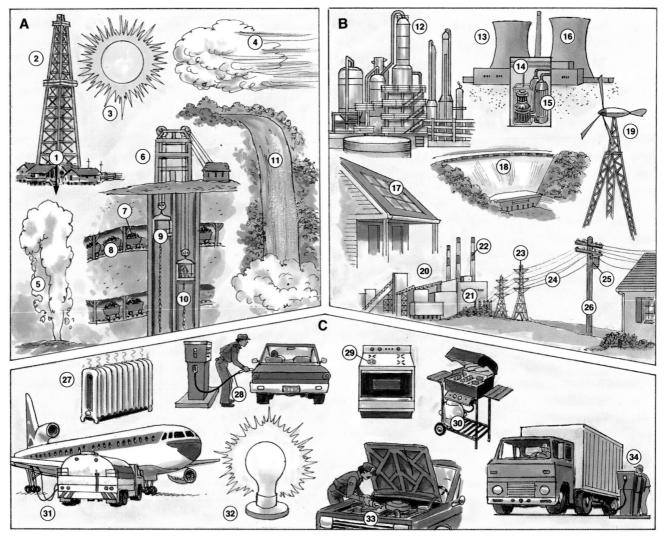

Fuentes de fuerza/energía	A. Sources of Power
pozo petrolero	1. oil well
armazón	2. derrick
sol	3. sun
viento	4. wind
geyser	5. geyser
mina de carbón	6. coal mine
carbón	7. coal
vagón transportador	8. shuttle car
elevador	9. elevator
(pozo) tiro de elevador	10. shaft
cascada/caída de agua	11. waterfall

Producción de energía	B. Generation of Power
refinería	12. refinery
reactor nuclear	13. nuclear reactor
núcleo	14. core
varillas de uranio	15. uranium rods
torre enfriadora	16. cooling tower
colector solar	17. solar collector

presa	18. dam
molino de viento	19. windmill
casa de fuerza/casa de energía	20. power station
generador eléctrico	21. electrical generator
chimenea	22. smokestack
torres transmisoras	23. transmission towers
líneas de corriente/energía	24. power lines
transformador	25. transformer
poste de servicio	26. utility pole

Usos y productos	C. Uses and Products
calefacción	27. heat
gasolina	28. gas(oline)
gas natural	29. natural gas
gas propano	30. propane gas
combustible para jet	31. jet fuel
electricidad	32. electricity
aceite de motor	33. motor oil
combustible diesel	34. diesel fuel

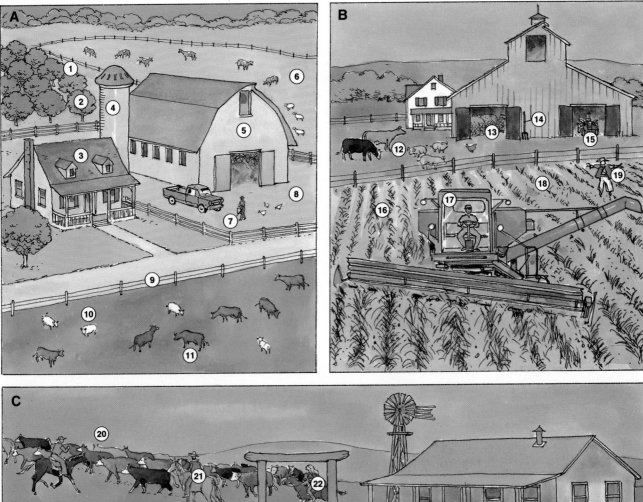

Granja lechera	**A. Dairy Farm**
huerta	**1.** orchard
árbol frutal	**2.** fruit tree
casa de granja	**3.** farmhouse
silo	**4.** silo
granero	**5.** barn
pastura/pastisal	**6.** pasture
granjero	**7.** farmer
corral	**8.** barnyard
cerca	**9.** fence
borregos/ovejas	**10.** sheep
vaca lechera	**11.** dairy cow
Granja de trigo	**B. Wheat Farm**
ganado	**12.** livestock
(bulto de) paja/(mazo de) paja	**13.** (bale of) hay

trinche	**14.** pitchfork
tractor	**15.** tractor
trigal	**16.** (wheat) field
segadora trilladora	**17.** combine
surco/fila	**18.** row
espantapájaros	**19.** scarecrow
Rancho	**C. Ranch**
(manada de) ganado	**20.** (herd of) cattle
vaquero	**21.** cowboy
vaquera	**22.** cowgirl
caballos	**23.** horses
corral	**24.** corral
bebedero	**25.** trough

Local de construcción	**A. Construction Site**		pala	**15.** shovel
vigas	**1.** rafters		tabla	**16.** board
tejas	**2.** shingle		operario que repara la línea	**17.** linesman
nivel	**3.** level		grúa con plataforma movible	**18.** cherry picker
sombrero duro/casco	**4.** hard hat			
constructor	**5.** builder		**Trabajo en carretera**	**B. Road Work**
planos	**6.** blueprints		cono preventivo	**19.** cone
andamiaje	**7.** scaffolding		banderín	**20.** flag
escalera	**8.** ladder		barricada	**21.** barricade
escalón	**9.** rung		martillo perforador	**22.** jackhammer
cemento	**10.** cement		carretilla	**23.** wheelbarrow
cimiento	**11.** foundation		muro central/divisorio	**24.** center divider
ladrillos	**12.** bricks		mezcladora de cemento	**25.** cement mixer
pico	**13.** pickax		pala mecánica	**26.** backhoe
trabajador de construcción	**14.** construction worker		excavadora	**27.** bulldozer

operadora de conmutador	**1.** switchboard operator
auriculares/audífonos	**2.** headset
conmutador	**3.** switchboard
impresora	**4.** printer
cubículo	**5.** cubicle
mecanógrafa	**6.** typist
procesador de palabras	**7.** word processor
listado	**8.** printout
calendario	**9.** calendar
máquina de escribir	**10.** typewriter
secretaria	**11.** secretary
documentación recibida	**12.** in-box
escritorio	**13.** desk
rolodex	**14.** rolodex
teléfono	**15.** telephone
computadora	**16.** computer

silla de mecanógrafa	**17.** typing chair
gerente	**18.** manager
calculadora	**19.** calculator
librero	**20.** bookcase
archivero	**21.** file cabinet
archivo	**22.** file folder
archivista	**23.** file clerk
fotocopiadora	**24.** photocopier
block para mensajes	**25.** message pad
block (de papel)	**26.** (legal) pad
engrapadora/grapadora	**27.** stapler
sujeta papel	**28.** paper clips
desengrapador/uña	**29.** staple remover
sacapuntas	**30.** pencil sharpener
sobre	**31.** envelope

farmacéutica/farmaceuta	**1.** pharmacist	panadero	**8.** baker
mecánico	**2.** mechanic	el, la oculista/óptico	**9.** optician
peluquero	**3.** barber	el, la estilista	**10.** hairdresser
agente de viajes	**4.** travel agent	el florista	**11.** florist
técnica en reparación	**5.** repairperson	joyera	**12.** jeweller
costurera/sastre	**6.** tailor	carnicero	**13.** butcher
verdulera	**7.** greengrocer		

Reparación y mantenimiento	A. Repair and Maintenance
plomera	1. plumber
carpintero	2. carpenter
jardinero	3. gardener
cerrajero	4. locksmith
agente de bienes raíces	5. real estate agent
el, la electricista	6. electrician
pintora	7. painter

Servicios domésticos	B. Household Services
ama de llaves	8. housekeeper
empleado de limpieza	9. janitor
mensajero	10. delivery boy
portero	11. doorman

Trabajo en fábrica	C. Factory Work
operario	12. shop worker
el, la capataz	13. foreman

Medios de comunicación y las artes	**A. Media and Arts**
pronosticador del tiempo	**1.** weather forecaster
locutor de noticiero	**2.** newscaster
el, la artista	**3.** artist
fotógrafo	**4.** photographer
el, la modelo	**5.** model
diseñador de moda	**6.** fashion designer
escritor	**7.** writer
arquitecto	**8.** architect
disc jockey	**9.** disc jockey (DJ)
camarógrafo	**10.** cameraperson
reportero	**11.** reporter
vendedor(a)	**12.** salesperson

Transacciones bancarias	**B. Banking**
oficial	**13.** officer
guardia de seguridad	**14.** security guard
cajero	**15.** teller

Empleados de negocios	**C. Business Workers**
programador (de computadora)	**16.** computer programmer
el, la recepcionista	**17.** receptionist
contador	**18.** accountant
mensajero/mandadero	**19.** messenger

zoológico	**1.** zoo	basurero/zafacón	**11.** trash can
teatro al aire libre	**2.** band shell	resbaladilla/chorrera	**12.** slide
vendedor	**3.** vendor	cajón de arena	**13.** sandbox
carrito manual	**4.** hand truck	rociador/chorrito	**14.** sprinkler
caballitos	**5.** merry-go-round	área de juego/parque	**15.** playground
caballista	**6.** horseback rider	columpios	**16.** swings
camino de harradura	**7.** bridle path	juegos infantiles	**17.** jungle gym
estanque (de patos)	**8.** (duck) pond	subibaja	**18.** seesaw
pista para correr	**9.** jogging path	bebedero/fuente	**19.** water fountain
banca	**10.** bench		

meseta	**1.** plateau
excursionistas	**2.** hikers
cañón	**3.** canyon
colina	**4.** hill
el, la guarda parques/guarda bosques	**5.** park ranger

Pesca	**Fishing**
arroyuelo	**6.** stream
caña de pesca	**7.** fishing rod
cordón de pesca	**8.** fishing line
red de pesca	**9.** fishing net
botas/pantalones impermeables para pescar	**10.** waders
rocas	**11.** rocks

Area de picnic	**Picnic Area**
parrilla	**12.** grill
canasta de día de campo	**13.** picnic basket
termo	**14.** thermos
mesa de día de campo	**15.** picnic table

Viajando en balsa	**Rafting**	Acampando	**Camping**
balsa	16. raft	casa de campaña	24. tent
rápidos de río	17. rapids	estufa de campamento	25. camp stove
cascada	18. waterfall	bolsa para dormir	26. sleeping bag
		equipo (de alpinismo)	27. gear
Alpinismo	**Mountain Climbing**	mochila con armazón	28. frame backpack
montaña	19. mountain	linterna/lámpara	29. lantern
pico	20. peak	estaca	30. stake
barranca	21. cliff	fogata	31. campfire
guarniciones/aparejo	22. harness	bosques	32. woods
cuerda/soga	23. rope		

En la playa

camino entarimado/entablado	**1.** boardwalk
puesto de refrescos	**2.** refreshment stand
motel	**3.** motel
ciclista	**4.** biker
silbato	**5.** whistle
el, la salvavidas (persona)	**6.** lifeguard
binoculares/gemelos	**7.** binoculars
silla del salvavidas	**8.** lifeguard chair
salvavidas (objeto)	**9.** life preserver
bote salvavidas	**10.** lifeboat
pelota de playa	**11.** beach ball

dunas de arena	**12.** sand dunes
frisbee/platillo	**13.** Frisbee ™
lentes para el sol/gafas de sol	**14.** sunglasses
toalla de playa	**15.** beach towel
cubeta/cubito/balde	**16.** pail
pala	**17.** shovel
traje de baño	**18.** bathing suit
el, la bañista	**19.** sunbather
silla de playa	**20.** beach chair
parasol/sombrilla de playa	**21.** beach umbrella

cometa/papalote/chiringa	**22.** kite	castillo de arena	**32.** sandcastle
corredores	**23.** runners	shorts de baño	**33.** bathing trunks
ola	**24.** wave	respirador	**34.** snorkel
planeador de mar/tabla	**25.** surfboard	visor/careta	**35.** mask
colchón de aire	**26.** air mattress	aletas/chapaletas	**36.** flippers
planeador pequeño de agua	**27.** kickboard	tanque de oxígeno	**37.** scuba tank
nadador	**28.** swimmer	traje de buceo	**38.** wet suit
llanta inflable/tubo	**29.** tube	loción para el sol	**39.** suntan lotion
agua	**30.** water	concha/caracol	**40.** shell
arena	**31.** sand	hielera/nevera	**41.** cooler

Béisbol	**Baseball**
árbitro	**1.** umpire
cácher/receptor	**2.** catcher
máscara del cácher	**3.** catcher's mask
guante del cácher	**4.** catcher's mitt
bate	**5.** bat
casco del bateador	**6.** batting helmet
bateador	**7.** batter

Pequeña Liga de béisbol	**Little League Baseball**
pequeño jugador de liga	**8.** Little Leaguer
uniforme	**9.** uniform

Softball	**Softball**
pelota de softball	**10.** softball
gorra	**11.** cap
guante	**12.** glove

Fútbol	**Football**
fútbol	**13.** football
casco	**14.** helmet

Lacrosse	**Lacrosse**
careta	**15.** face guard
raqueta de lacrosse	**16.** lacrosse stick

Hockey sobre hielo	**Ice Hockey**
disco de (hule duro) hockey	**17.** puck
palo de hockey	**18.** hockey stick

Baloncesto	**Basketball**
tablero	**19.** backboard
canasta	**20.** basket
balón	**21.** basketball

Vólibol	**Volleyball**
vólibol	**22.** volleyball
red	**23.** net

Fútbol	**Soccer**
portero	**24.** goalie
gol	**25.** goal
balón	**26.** soccer ball

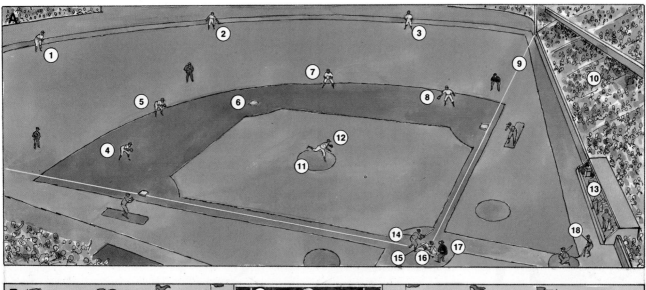

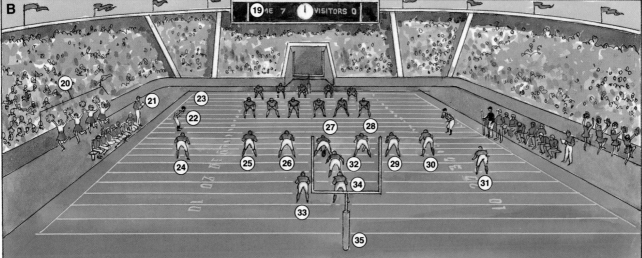

Diamante de béisbol	**A. Baseball Diamond**	Campo de fútbol	**B. Football Field**
campista izquierdo	**1.** left fielder	tablero (de puntuación/puntaje)	**19.** scoreboard
campista central	**2.** center fielder	porristas	**20.** cheerleaders
campista derecho	**3.** right fielder	entrenador	**21.** coach
tercera base	**4.** third baseman	árbitro	**22.** referee
campo/campista delantero	**5.** shortstop	zona de gol	**23.** end zone
base	**6.** base	ala/extremo	**24.** split end
segunda base	**7.** second baseman	atajador izquierdo	**25.** left tackle
primera base	**8.** first baseman	defensa izquierdo	**26.** left guard
línea de fuera	**9.** foul line	centro	**27.** center
tribunas	**10.** stands	defensa derecho	**28.** right guard
montículo	**11.** pitcher's mound	atajador derecho	**29.** right tackle
lanzador	**12.** pitcher	ala extrema	**30.** tight end
banco	**13.** dugout	flanqueador	**31.** flanker
bateador	**14.** batter	mariscal de campo	**32.** quarterback
base	**15.** home plate	medio trasero	**33.** halfback
cácher/receptor	**16.** catcher	trasero	**34.** fullback
árbitro	**17.** umpire	poste del gol	**35.** goalpost
muchacho de los bates	**18.** batboy		

Tenis	**Tennis**
bola de tenis	**1.** tennis ball
raqueta	**2.** racket

Boliche/Bolos	**Bowling**
canal	**3.** gutter
carril	**4.** lane
pino/bolo	**5.** pin
bola de boliche	**6.** bowling ball

Golf	**Golf**
bola de golf	**7.** golf ball
hoyo	**8.** hole
palo	**9.** putter
golfista	**10.** golfer

Frontón de mano	**Handball**
guante	**11.** glove
bola de frontón	**12.** handball
cancha	**13.** court

Boxeo	**Boxing**
casco protector	**14.** head protector
guante	**15.** glove
árbitro	**16.** referee
cuadrilátero	**17.** ring

Ping-pong	**Ping-Pong**
raqueta/paleta	**18.** paddle
bola de ping-pong	**19.** ping-pong ball

Carreras de caballo	**Horse Racing**
silla de montar	**20.** saddle
jockey/jinete (profesional)	**21.** jockey
riendas	**22.** reins

Gimnasia	**Gymnastics**
el, la gimnasta	**23.** gymnast
barra de balance	**24.** balance beam

Patinaje en hielo	**Ice Skating**
pista	**25.** rink
patín	**26.** skate
hoja/navaja	**27.** blade

Frontón con raqueta	**Racquetball**
lentes de protección	**28.** safety goggles
raqueta	**29.** racquet
bola de frontón con raqueta	**30.** racquetball

Atletismo	**Track and Field**
corredor	**31.** runner
pista	**32.** track

Esquiando a campo traviesa	**Cross-Country Skiing**
esquíes	**33.** skis
palo largo	**34.** pole
esquiador	**35.** skier

Cancha de tenis	**A. Tennis Court**
sección del saque	**1.** service court
red	**2.** net
línea del saque	**3.** service line
línea de fuera	**4.** baseline

Campo de golf	**B. Golf Course**
palos de golf	**5.** clubs
escabroso	**6.** rough
bolsa de golf	**7.** golf bag
carrito de golf	**8.** golf cart
bandera/banderín	**9.** flag
área verde	**10.** green
trampa de arena	**11.** sand trap
área verde y plana	**12.** fairway
portabola	**13.** tee

Bajada/cuesta abajo de esquiar	**C. Ski Slope**
palo largo	**14.** pole
bota de esquiar	**15.** ski boot
ribete	**16.** binding
esquí	**17.** ski
ascensor de esquíes	**18.** ski lift

Pista de carreras	**D. Race Track**
trecho	**19.** stretch
puerta de salida	**20.** starting gate
meta	**21.** finish line

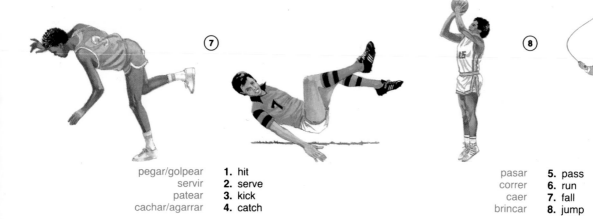

pegar/golpear	**1.** hit	pasar	**5.** pass
servir	**2.** serve	correr	**6.** run
patear	**3.** kick	caer	**7.** fall
cachar/agarrar	**4.** catch	brincar	**8.** jump

Verbos relacionados con el deporte

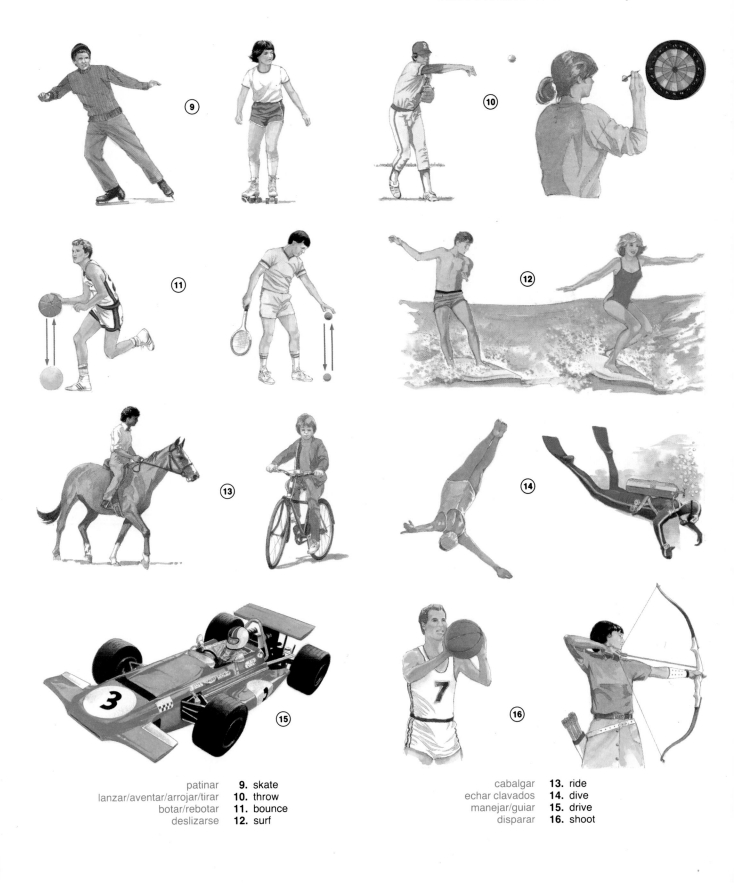

patinar	**9.** skate	cabalgar	**13.** ride
lanzar/aventar/arrojar/tirar	**10.** throw	echar clavados	**14.** dive
botar/rebotar	**11.** bounce	manejar/guiar	**15.** drive
deslizarse	**12.** surf	disparar	**16.** shoot

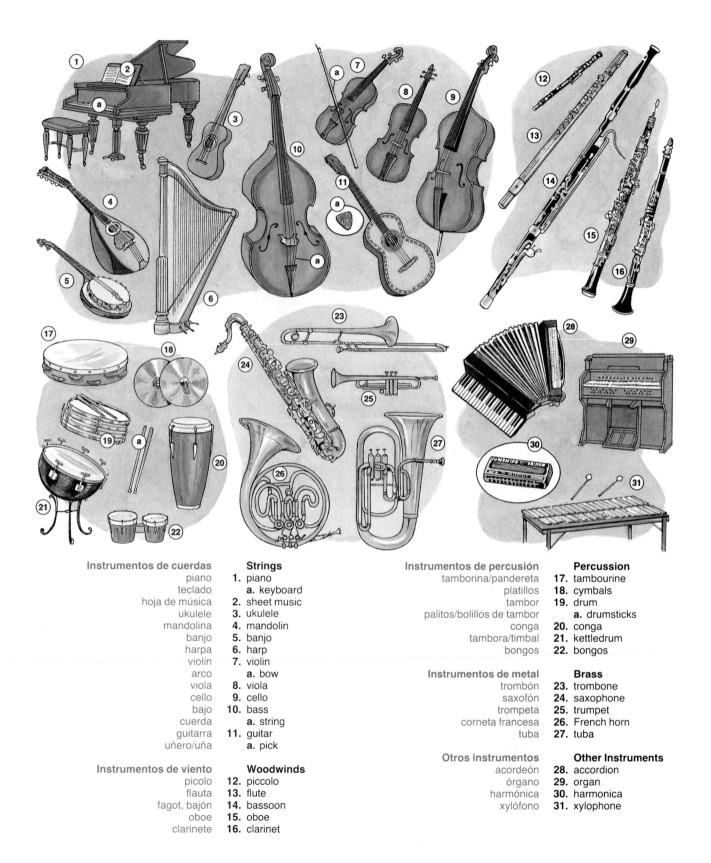

Instrumentos de cuerdas	Strings		Instrumentos de percusión	Percussion
piano	**1.** piano		tamborina/pandereta	**17.** tambourine
teclado	**a.** keyboard		platillos	**18.** cymbals
hoja de música	**2.** sheet music		tambor	**19.** drum
ukulele	**3.** ukulele		palitos/bolillos de tambor	**a.** drumsticks
mandolina	**4.** mandolin		conga	**20.** conga
banjo	**5.** banjo		tambora/timbal	**21.** kettledrum
harpa	**6.** harp		bongos	**22.** bongos
violín	**7.** violin			
arco	**a.** bow		**Instrumentos de metal**	**Brass**
viola	**8.** viola		trombón	**23.** trombone
cello	**9.** cello		saxofón	**24.** saxophone
bajo	**10.** bass		trompeta	**25.** trumpet
cuerda	**a.** string		corneta francesa	**26.** French horn
guitarra	**11.** guitar		tuba	**27.** tuba
uñero/uña	**a.** pick			
			Otros instrumentos	**Other Instruments**
Instrumentos de viento	**Woodwinds**		acordeón	**28.** accordion
picolo	**12.** piccolo		órgano	**29.** organ
flauta	**13.** flute		harmónica	**30.** harmonica
fagot, bajón	**14.** bassoon		xilófono	**31.** xylophone
oboe	**15.** oboe			
clarinete	**16.** clarinet			

El ballet	**A. The Ballet**
cortina	**1.** curtain
decoración	**2.** scenery
la bailarina/el bailarín	**3.** dancer
reflector	**4.** spotlight
foro/escenario	**5.** stage
orquesta	**6.** orchestra
podio	**7.** podium
conductor	**8.** conductor
batuta	**9.** baton
músico	**10.** musician
palco	**11.** box seat
luneta	**12.** orchestra seating
entresuelo/mezanine	**13.** mezzanine
balcón	**14.** balcony
auditorio	**15.** audience
acomodador	**16.** usher
programas	**17.** programs

Comedia musical	**B. Musical Comedy**
coro	**18.** chorus
actor	**19.** actor
actriz	**20.** actress

Grupo (musical) de Rock	**C. Rock Group**
sintetizador	**21.** synthesizer
arreglista	**22.** keyboard player
bajo	**23.** bass guitarist
cantante	**24.** singer
guitarrista principal	**25.** lead guitarist
guitarra eléctrica	**26.** electric guitar
tamborilero/baterista	**27.** drummer

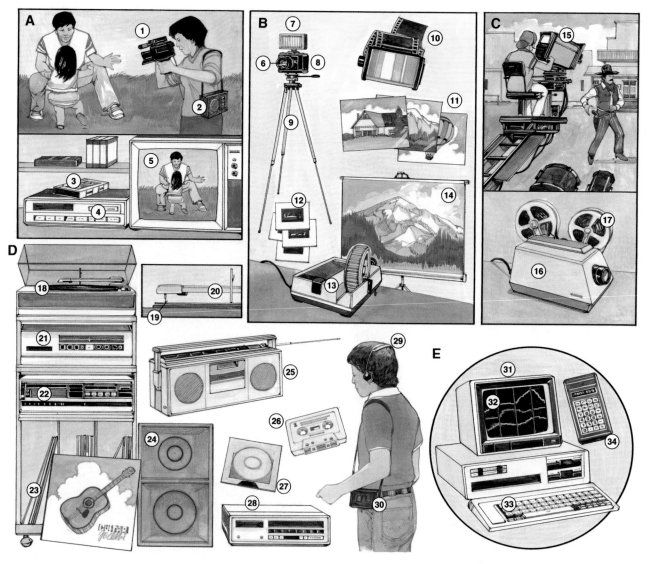

Video	**A. Video**	**Audio**	**D. Audio**
cámara de video	**1.** video camera	tocadiscos/tornamesa	**18.** turntable
mini-cámara	**2.** Minicam ™	aguja de cartucho	**19.** cartridge needle
videocassette (cinta)	**3.** videocassette (tape)	brazo	**20.** arm
videograbadora	**4.** VCR (videocassette recorder)	sintonizador/receptor	**21.** receiver
		grabadora	**22.** cassette deck
televisor/televisión	**5.** television	discos	**23.** records
		bocina/altoparlante	**24.** speaker
Fotografía	**B. Photography**	toca cassettes/cintas	**25.** stereo cassette player
lente	**6.** lens	cassette/cinta	**26.** cassette
flash/destello	**7.** flash	disco compacto	**27.** compact disc (CD)
cámara	**8.** camera	tocadiscos compacto	**28.** compact disc player
tripié/trípode	**9.** tripod	audífonos	**29.** headphones
(rollo de) película	**10.** (roll of) film	walkman	**30.** Sony Walkman
fotos/impresiones	**11.** prints		
transparencias	**12.** slides	**Computadoras**	**E. Computers**
proyector de transparencias	**13.** slide projector	mini-computadora	**31.** personal computer (PC)
pantalla	**14.** screen	monitor	**32.** monitor
		teclado	**33.** keyboard
Película	**C. Film**	calculadora	**34.** calculator
cámara de cine	**15.** movie camera		
proyector	**16.** projector		
(rollo de) película	**17.** (reel of) film		

A

B

Costura		A. Sewing	
máquina de coser		**1.**	sewing machine
(carrete de) hilo		**2.**	(spool of) thread
alfiletero		**3.**	pincushion
tela/material/género		**4.**	material
tijeras de piquitos		**5.**	pinking shears
pieza del patrón		**6.**	pattern piece
patrón/modelo		**7.**	pattern
ojal		**8.**	buttonhole
botón		**9.**	button
costura		**10.**	seam
dobladillo/ruedo		**11.**	hem
bastilla		**12.**	hem binding
broche de presión		**13.**	snap
presillas		**14.**	hook and eye
cinta métrica		**15.**	tape measure
cierre		**16.**	zipper
(par de) tijeras		**17.**	(pair of) scissors

aguja		**18.**	needle
puntada		**19.**	stitch
alfiler		**20.**	pin
dedal		**21.**	thimble

Otras actividades de costura		B. Other Needlecrafts	
tejido		**22.**	knitting
lana		**23.**	wool
madeja		**24.**	skein
aguja de tejer		**25.**	knitting needle
depunto/caneva		**26.**	needlepoint
bordado		**27.**	embroidery
labor de gancho		**28.**	crochet
aguja de gancho		**29.**	crochet hook
tejido/tejedora		**30.**	weaving
estambre		**31.**	yarn
acolchado (sustantivo)		**32.**	quilting

en (la ventana)	**1.** at (the window)
sobre/por encima de (el gato negro)	**2.** above (the black cat)
abajo (del gato blanco)	**3.** below (the white cat)
entre (los cojines)	**4.** between (the pillows)
sobre (la alfombra)	**5.** on (the rug)
frente a (la chimenea)	**6.** in front of (the fireplace)
dentro de (el cajón)	**7.** in (the drawer)
debajo de (el escritorio)	**8.** under (the desk)
detrás de (la silla)	**9.** behind (the chair)
sobre (la mesa)	**10.** on top of (the table)
junto a (la TV)	**11.** next to (the TV)

a través de (el faro)	**1.** through (the lighthouse)	fuera de (el agua)	**7.** out of (the water)
alrededor de (el faro)	**2.** around (the lighthouse)	sobre (el puente)	**8.** over (the bridge)
hacia abajo de (la colina)	**3.** down (the hill)	a/hacia (la cancha de golf)	**9.** to (the course)
hacia (el hoyo)	**4.** toward (the hole)	de/desde (la cancha de golf)	**10.** from (the course)
lejos de (el hoyo)	**5.** away from (the hole)	a/hacia arriba de (la colina)	**11.** up (the hill)
al otro lado de (el agua)	**6.** across (the water)	hacia dentro de (el hoyo)	**12.** into (the hole)

Días de la semana	Days of the Week		Números		Numbers
domingo	Sunday		cero	0	zero
lunes	Monday		uno	1	one
martes	Tuesday		dos	2	two
miércoles	Wednesday		tres	3	three
jueves	Thursday		cuatro	4	four
viernes	Friday		cinco	5	five
sábado	Saturday		seis	6	six
			siete	7	seven
Meses del año	**Months of the Year**		ocho	8	eight
enero	January		nueve	9	nine
febrero	February		diez	10	ten
marzo	March		once	11	eleven
abril	April		doce	12	twelve
mayo	May		trece	13	thirteen
junio	June		catorce	14	fourteen
julio	July		quince	15	fifteen
agosto	August		dieciséis	16	sixteen
septiembre	September		diecisiete	17	seventeen
octubre	October		dieciocho	18	eighteen
noviembre	November		diecinueve	19	nineteen
diciembre	December		veinte	20	twenty
			veintiuno	21	twenty-one
			treinta	30	thirty
			cuarenta	40	forty
			cincuenta	50	fifty
			sesenta	60	sixty
			setenta	70	seventy
			ochenta	80	eighty
			noventa	90	ninety
			cien/un ciento	100	a/one hundred
			quinientos	500	five hundred
			seiscientos veintiuno	621	six hundred (and) twenty-one
			mil/un mil	1,000	a/one thousand
			un millón	1,000,000	a/one million

Colors
Colores

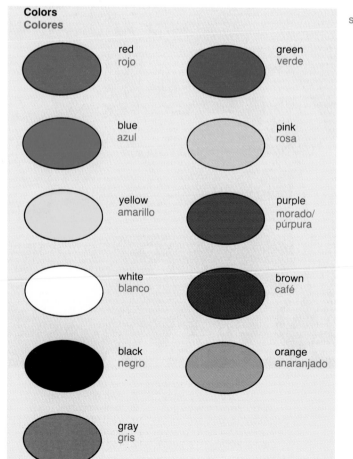

red
rojo

green
verde

blue
azul

pink
rosa

yellow
amarillo

purple
morado/
púrpura

white
blanco

brown
café

black
negro

orange
anaranjado

gray
gris

Two numbers occur after words in the index: the first refers to the page where the word is illustrated and the second to the item number of the word on that page. For example, above [ə bŭv⁄] **102** 2 means that the word *above* is the item numbered 2 on page 102. If only a bold number appears, then that word is part of the unit title or a subtitle.

The index includes a pronunciation guide for all the words illustrated in the book. This guide uses symbols commonly found in dictionaries for native speakers. These symbols, unlike those used in transcription systems such as the International Phonetic Alphabet, tend to preserve spelling and so should help you to become more aware of the connections between written English and spoken English.

Consonants

[b] as in **back** [băk]
[ch] as in **cheek** [chēk]
[d] as in **date** [dāt]
[dh] as in **the** [dh]
[f] as in **face** [fās]
[g] as in **gas** [găs]
[h] as in **half** [hăf]
[j] as in **jack** [jăk]

[k] as in **kite** [kīt]
[l] as in **leaf** [lēf]
[m] as in **man** [măn]
[n] as in **neck** [něk]
[ng] as in **ring** [rĭng]
[p] as in **pack** [păk]
[r] as in **rake** [rāk]
[s] as in **sand** [sănd]

[sh] as in **shell** [shěl]
[t] as in **tape** [tāp]
[th] as in **three** [thrē]
[v] as in **vine** [vīn]
[w] as in **waist** [wāst]
[y] as in **yam** [yăm]
[z] as in **zoo** [zoo]
[zh] as in **measure** [mězh⁄ ər]

Vowels

[ā] as in **bake** [bāk]
[ă] as in **back** [băk]
[ä] as in **bar** [bär]
[ē] as in **beat** [bēt]
[ĕ] as in **bed** [běd]
[ë] as in **bear** [bër]

[ī] as in **lime** [līm]
[ĭ] as in **lip** [lĭp]
[ï] as in **beer** [bïr]
[ō] as in **post** [pōst]
[ŏ] as in **box** [bŏks]
[ö] as in **claw** [klö]
      or **for** [för]

[oo] as in **cool** [kool]
[ŏŏ] as in **book** [bŏŏk]
[ow] as in **cow** [kow]
[oy] as in **boy** [boy]
[ŭ] as in **cut** [kŭt]
[ü] as in **curb** [kürb]
[ə] as in **above** [ə bŭv⁄]

All pronunciation symbols used are alphabetical except for the schwa [ə], which is the most frequent vowel sound in English. If you use it appropriately in unstressed syllables, your pronunciation will sound more natural.

You should note that an umlaut ([¨]) calls attention to the special quality of vowels before [r]. (The sound [ö] can also represent a vowel not followed by [r] as in *claw*.) You should listen carefully to native speakers to discover how these vowels actually sound.

Stress

This guide also follows the system for marking stress used in many dictionaries for native speakers.
   (1) Stress is not marked if a word consisting of a single syllable occurs in isolation.
   (2) Where stress is marked, two levels are distinguished:
      a bold accent [⁄] is placed after each syllable with primary stress,
      a light accent [⁄] is placed after each syllable with secondary stress.

Syllable Boundaries

Syllable boundaries are indicated by a single space.

NOTE: The pronunciation used in this index is based on patterns of American English. There has been no attempt to represent all of the varieties of American English. Students should listen to native speakers to hear how the language actually sounds in a particular region.

above [ə bŭv′] **102** 2

abdomen [ăb′də mən] **4** 14

accelerator [ăk sĕl′ə rā′tər] **50** 27

accordion [ə kör′dē ən] **98** 28

accountant [ə kown′tənt] **86** 18

acorn [ā′körn] **61** 33b

acorn squash [ā′körn skwŏsh′] **7** 28

across [ə krös′] **103** 6

actor [ăk′tər] **99** 19

actress [ăk′trəs] **99** 20

acute angle [ə kyōōt′ăng′gəl] **79** 8

address [ă′drĕs] **46** 11

adjectives [ăj′ĭk tĭvz] **24, 25**

aerial tramway [ër′ē əl trăm′wā] **55** 31

Africa [ă′frĭ kə] **70** 4

after-shave lotion [ăf′tər shāv lō′shən] **23** 21

ailments [āl′mənts] **40**

air conditioner [ër′kən dĭ′shə nər] **32** 11

air filter [ër′fĭl′tər] **51** 52

Air Force [ër′förs′] **48** 19

air mattress [ër′mă′trəs] **91** 26

air pump [ër′ pŭmp′] **53** 13

air travel [ër′ tră′vəl] **56**

aircraft [ër′krăft′] **57**

aircraft carrier [ër′krăft kăr′yər] **48** 4

aircraft types [ër′krăft tīps′] **57**

(airmail) envelope [ër′māl ĕn′və lōp] **46** 16

airman [ër′mən] **48** 20

airport check-in [ër′pört chĕk′ĭn] **56**

aisle [ī′əl] **14** 10, **56** 23

Alabama [ăl′ə bă′mə] **72** 1

alarm clock [ə lärm′ klŏk] **32** 8

Alaska [ə lăs′kə] **72** 2

alcohol [ăl′kə höl′] **39** 22

alligator [ăl′ə gā′tər] **65** 8

almond(s) [ö′mənd(z)] **9** 31

Alps [ălps] **70** 44

Amazon River [ă′mə zŏn rĭv′ər] **71** 59

ambulance [ăm′byə ləns] **42** 6

amphibians [ăm fĭ′bē ənz] **65**

ammunition [ăm′yə nĭsh′ən] **48**

anchor [ăng′kər] **58** 24

Andes [ăn′dēz] **71** 43

ankle [ăng′kəl] **5** 49

animals [ăn′ə məlz] **62-69**

ant [ănt] **63** 12

Antarctic Ocean [ănt ärk′ tĭk ō′shən] **70** 14

Antarctica [ănt ärk′tĭ kə] **70** 7

anteater [ănt′ē′tər] **66** 5

antenna [ăn tĕn′ə] **51** 46, **62** 1b

antler [ănt′lər] **67** 35a

apartment house [ə pärt′mənt hows′] **45** 23

apex [ā′pĕks] **79** 21

Appalachian Mountains [ăp′ə lā′chē ən mown′ tənz] **71** 41

apple [ă′pəl] **8** 2

apricot [ăp′rə kŏt′] **9** 25

apron [ā′prən] **16** 6

aquatic mammals [ə kwŏ′tĭk mă′məlz] **68**

Arabian Sea [ə rā′bē ən sē′] **70** 30

arc [ärk] **79** 16

architect [är′kə tĕkt′] **86** 8

Arctic [ärk′tĭk] **70** 8

Arizona [ăr′ə zō′nə] **72** 3

Arkansas [är′kən sö′] **72** 4

arm [ärm] **4** 6, **100** 20

armadillo [är′mə dĭl′ō] **66** 2

armed forces [ärmd′ för′səz] **48**

armpit [ärm′pĭt′] **4** 10

armrest [ärm′rĕst′] **50** 3

Army [är′mē] **48** 15

around [ə rownd′] **103** 2

artery [är′tə rē] **5** 69

artichoke [är′tə chōk′] **6** 11

artist [är′təst] **86** 3

arts [ärts] **86**

ashtray [ăsh′trā′] **16** 29

Asia [ā′zhə] **70** 5

asparagus [ə spăr′ə gəs] **6** 18

asteroid [ăs′tə royd′] **74** 20

astronaut [ăs′trə nŏt′] **75** 5

at [ăt] **102** 1

Atacama Desert [ăt′ə kŏ′mə dĕz′ərt] **71** 50

athletic supporter [ăth lĕ′tĭk sə pör′tər] **22** 4

atlas [ăt′ləs] **47** 20

attachments [ə tăch′mənts] **35** 17

attendant [ə tĕn′dənt] **39** 8, **53** 12

audience [ö′dē əns] **99** 15

audio [ö′dē ō′] **100**

aunt [ănt] **3** 6

Australia [ö strāl′yə] **70** 6

author [ö′thər] **47** 8

automatic transmission [ö′ tə măt′ĭk trănz mĭ′shən] **50**

avocado [ăv′ə kŏ′dō] **9** 33

away from [ə wā′ frŭm] **103** 5

axe [ăks] **42** 14

baboon [bă bōōn′] **69** 19

baby [bā′bē] **2** 5

baby carriage [bā′bē kăr′ĭj] **45** 27

baby lotion [bā′bē lō′shən] **33** 6

baby powder [bā′bē pow′dər] **33** 7

baby wipes [bā′bē wīps′] **33** 8

baby's room [bā′bēz rōōm′] **33**

back [băk] **4** 11, **23** 19

backache [băk′āk′] **40** 8

backboard [băk′börd′] **92** 19

backhoe [băk′hō′] **82** 26

backpack [băk′păk′] **19** 4

backseat [băk′sēt′] **50** 32

backyard [băk′yärd′] **27**

back-up light [băk′əp līt′] **50** 30

bacon [bā′kən] **10** 11, **18**, 33

badge [băj] **43** 5

Baffin Bay [băf′ən bā′] **70** 16

bag [băg] **12** 8, **15** 25, **21** 35

baggage [băg′ĭj] **56** 8

bake [bāk] **31** 14

baked beans [bākt′ bēnz′] **18** 3

baked goods [bākt gōōdz′] **14** 11

baked potato [bākt′ pə tā′tō] **18** 20

baker [bā′kər] **84** 8

bakery [bā′kə rē] **44** 6

balance beam [băl′əns bēm′] **94** 24

balcony [băl′kə nē] **99** 14

(bale of) hay [bāl′ əv hā′] **81** 13

ball [böl] **5** 52

ballet [bă lā′] **99**

ballfields [böl′fēldz′] **93**

ballpoint pen [böl′poynt pĕn′] **76** 22

Baltic Sea [böl′tĭk sē′] **70** 22

bananas [bə nă′nəz] **9** 20

Band-Aid [bănd′ ād′] **39** 4

band shell [bănd′ shĕl′] **87** 2

bandage [băn′dĭj] **39** 24

banister [băn′ə stər] **28** 11

banjo [băn′jō′] **98** 5

banking [băng′kĭng] **86**

bar [bär] **13** 18, **16** 24

bar stool [bär′stool′] **16** 25

barber [bär′bər] **84** 3

Barents Sea [băr′ənts sē′] **70** 23

barge [bärj] **58** 12

bark [bärk] **61** 35c

barn [bärn] **81** 5

barnyard [bärn′yärd′] **81** 8

barrel [băr′əl] **48** 23

barricade [băr′ə kād′] **82** 21

bartender [bär′těn′dər] **16** 21

base [bās] **79** 7, **93** 6

baseball [bās′böl′] **92**

baseball diamond [bās′böl dī′mənd]
93

baseline [bās′līn′] **95** 4

basin [bā′sən] **39** 16

basket [băs′kət] **92** 20

basketball [băs′kət böl′] **92**, **92** 21

bass [bās] **98** 10

bass guitarist [bās′gə tär′əst] **99** 23

bassoon [bă soon′] **98** 14

bat [băt] **66** 4, **92** 5

batboy [băt′boy′] **93** 18

bath mat [băth′ măt′] **34** 12

bath towel [băth′ tow′əl] **34** 24

bathing suit [bā′dhĭng soot′] **90** 18

bathing trunks [bā′ dhĭng trŭngks′]
91 33

bathrobe [băth′ rōb] **22** 20

bathroom [băth′ room′] **34**

bathtub [băth′ tŭb′] **34** 11

baton [bə tŏn′] **99** 9

batter [băt′ ər] **92** 7, **93** 14

battery [băt′ə rē] **51** 54

batting helmet [băt′ĭng hěl′mət] **92** 6

battleship [băt′əl shĭp′] **48** 5

Bay of Bengal [bā′ əv běn göl′] **70** 32

bayonet [bā′ ə nět′] **48** 24

bays [bāz] **70**

beach [bēch] **90**

beach ball [bēch′ böl′] **90** 11

beach chair [bēch′ chër′] **90** 20

beach towel [bēch′ tow′ əl] **90** 15

beach umbrella [bēch′ əm brěl′ə]
90 21

beads [bēdz] **23** 7

beak [bēk] **64** 3a

beaker [bē′ kər] **78** 23

beard [bĭrd] **4** 39

bears [bërz] **69**

beat [bēt] **31** 8

Beaufort Sea [bō′ fərt sē′] **70** 15

beaver [bē′vər] **66** 12

bed [běd] **32** 21

bed rest [běd′ rěst′] **41** 1

bedroom [běd′room′] **32**

bedspread [běd′sprěd′] **32** 23

bee [bē] **63** 19

beef [bēf] **10** 1

beef stew [bēf′ stoo′] **18** 14

beer [bĭr] **16** 23

beet(s) [bēts] **7** 33

beetle [bē′təl] **63** 10

behind [bə hīnd′] **102** 9

below [bə lō′] **102** 3

belt [bělt] **20** 16

bench [běnch] **43** 16, **44** 14, **78** 24,
87 10

beret [bə rā′] **19** 22

Bering Sea [bër′ĭng sē′] **70** 34

berries [bër′ēz] **8**

between [bə twēn′] **102** 4

beverages [běv′rə jəz] **14** 14

bib [bĭb] **33** 20

bicycle [bī′sĭ kəl] **52** 15

big [bĭg] **24** 8

(Big Dipper) constellation
[bĭg′dĭ′pər kŏn stə lā′shən] **74** 3

big toe [bĭg′ tō′] **5** 53

bike stand [bīk′ stănd′] **52** 14

biker [bī′kər] **90** 4

bikes [bīks] **52**

(bikini) panties [bə kē′ nē păn′ tēz]
22 11

bill [bĭl] **64** 24a

bin [bĭn] **15** 16

binding [bīn′ dĭng] **95** 16

binoculars [bə nŏk′ yə lərs] **90** 7

birch [bürch] **61** 32

birds [bürdz] **64**

biscuit [bĭs′ kət] **18** 27

bison [bī′ sən] **67** 19

bit [bĭt] **37** 43a

black bear [blăk′ bër′] **69** 21

black bean(s) [blăk′ bēn(z)′] **6** 14

black eye [blăk′ ī′] **40** 5

Black Sea [blăk′ sē′] **70** 26

blackberries [blăk′ bër′ ēz] **8** 12

bladder [blă′ dər] **5** 72

blade [blād] **94** 27

blanket [blăng′ket] **32** 20

blazer [blā′zer] **20** 2

bleach [blēch] **35** 26

blender [blěn′dər] **30** 12

blimp [blĭmp] **57** 5

blinds [blīndz] **32** 12

block [blŏk] **33** 32

blouse [blows] **21** 34

blue jay [bloo′ ja′] **64** 8

(blue) jeans [bloo′ jēnz′] **19** 6

blueberries [bloo′bër′ēz] **8** 14

blueprints [bloo′ prĭnts′] **82** 6

blush [blŭsh] **23** 32

board [börd] **82** 16

boarding [bör′ dĭng] **56**

boarding pass [bör′dĭng păs′] **56** 18

boardwalk [börd′wök′] **90** 1

body [bŏ′dē] **4**

boil [boyl] **31** 16

bollard [bŏl′ ərd] **58** 26

bolt [bōlt] **37** 38

bomb [bŏm] **48** 3

bomber [bŏm′ ər] **48** 2

bongos [bŏng′ gōz] **98** 22

book [book] **13** 17

(book of) matches [book′ əv mă′ chəz]
16 28

bookcase [book′ kās] **28** 22, **83** 20

bookstore [book′ stör] **45** 18

boom [boom] **59** 7

booth [booth] **16** 9

boots [boots] **19** 21, **21** 32

bottle [bŏt′ əl] **12** 3, **33** 17

bottle opener [bŏt′ əl ō′ pə nər] **30** 6

bounce [bowns] **97** 11

bow [bō] **98** 7a

bow [bow] **58** 5

bowl [bōl] **13** 23

bowling [bōl′ĭng] **94**

bowling ball [bōl′ĭng böl′] **94** 6

box [bŏks] **13** 12

box seat [bŏks′ sēt′] **99** 11

box spring [bŏks′ sprĭng′] **32** 18

boxer shorts [bŏk′ sər shörts′] **22** 2

boxing [bŏk′ sĭng] **94**

boy's frame [boyz′ frām′] **52** 11

bra(ssiere) [brŏ]/[brə zïr′] **22** 13

brace [brās] **36** 9

bracelet [brās′lət] **23** 9

brain [brān] **5** 57

brake [brāk] **50** 26, **52** 17

brake light [brāk′līt′] **50** 29

branch [brănch] **61** 35a

brass [brăs] **98**

bread [brĕd] **14** 12

bread and butter plate
  [brĕd′ ənd bŭt′ ər plāt′] **29** 11

break [brāk] **31** 7

breast [brĕst] **11** 21

bricks [brĭks] **82** 12

bridle path [brīd′ əl păth′] **87** 7

briefcase [brēf′kās′] **21** 37

briefs [brēfs] **22** 12

broccoli [brŏk′ ə lē] **6** 2

broil [broyl] **31** 13

broiler [broy′lər] **30** 33

broken bone [brō′kən bōn′] **40** 15

broom [brōōm] **35** 7

brother [brŭdh′ər] **3** 9

brother-in-law [brŭdh′ ər ən lö′] **3** 11

bruise [brōōz] **40** 17

brush [brŭsh] **76** 18

brussels sprouts [brŭs′ əl sprowts′] **6** 4

bucket [bŭk′ət] **35** 15

bucket seat [bŭk′ ət sēt′] **50** 16

buckle [bŭk′əl] **20** 17

bud [bŭd] **60** 18a

buffet [bə fā′] **29** 29

builder [bĭl′dər] **82** 5

building number [bĭl′dĭng nŭm′ bər]
  45 24

bulb [bŭlb] **60** 8a

bull [bŏŏl] **67** 34

bulldozer [bŏŏl′dō′ zər] **82** 27

bullet [bŏŏl′ĭt] **48** 26

bulletin board [bŏŏl′ ĭ tən börd′] **76** 7

bumper [bŭm′pər] **33** 5

bun [bŭn] **18** 7

bunch [bŭnch] **8** 1

Bunsen burner [bŭn′sən bür′ nər]
  78 20

buoy [bōō′ē]/[boy] **58** 16

bureau [byŏŏr′ō] **32** 9

burn [bürn] **17** 14, **40** 18

burner [bür′nər] **30** 29

bus [bŭs] **53** 20, **54**

bus driver [bŭs′drī′vər] **54** 3

bus stop [bŭs′stŏp′] **44** 13

busboy [bŭs′boy′] **16** 3

bushes [bŏŏsh′ əz] **61** 41

business workers [bĭz′nəs wür′kərz] **86**

butcher [bŏŏ′chər] **84** 13

butter [bŭt′ər] **18** 18

buttercup [bŭt′ ər kŭp′] **60** 17

butterfly [bŭt′ ər flī′] **63** 3

buttocks [bŭt′əks] **4** 15

button [bŭt′ən] **20** 3, **101** 9

buttonhole [bŭt′ ən hōl′] **101** 8

C-clamp [sē′klămp′] **36** 2

cab driver [kăb′drī′ vər] **55** 26

cabbage [kăb′ĭj] **6** 3

cabin [kăb′ĭn] **56** 19

cabin cruiser [kăb′ĭn krōō′ zər] **59** 16

cabinet [kăb′ə nət] **30** 22

cable [kā′bəl] **52** 23

cable car [kā′bəl kär′] **55** 32

cactus [kăk′təs] **61** 40

calculator [kăl′kyə lā′ tər] **83** 19,
  100 34

calendar [căl′ ən dər] **83** 9

calf [kăf] **4** 20, **67** 31

California [kăl′ ə för′ nyə] **72** 5

call card [köl′kärd′] **47** 6

call number [köl′ nŭm′bər] **47** 7

call slip [köl′slĭp′] **47** 12

camel [kăm′əl] **67** 33

camera [kăm′ər ə] **100** 8

cameraperson [kăm′ ər ə pür′ sən] **86** 10

camisole [kăm′ ə sōl′] **22** 9

camp stove [kămp′stōv′] **89** 25

camper [kăm′pər] **53** 16

campfire [kămp′fīr′] **89** 31

camping [kăm′pĭng] **89**

can [kăn] **12** 10

can opener [kăn′ ō′ pə nər] **30** 4

canary [kə nër′ ē] **64** 14

candle [kăn′dəl] **29** 27

candlestick [kăn′dəl stĭk′] **29** 28

canister [kăn′ ə stər] **30** 15

canned goods [kănd′ gŏŏdz′] **14** 13

cannon [kăn′ ən] **48** 11

canoe [kə nōō′] **59** 2

cantaloupe [kăn′ tə lōp′] **9** 36

canyon [kăn′ yən] **88** 3

cap [kăp] **19** 2, **21** 43, **92** 11

capsule [kăp′ səl] **41** 5

car [kär] **54** 9

card catalog [kärd′ kăt′ ə lög] **47** 4

cardigan [kär′dĭ gən] **21** 26

cardinal [kärd′nəl] **64** 11

cargo [kär′gō] **58** 10

cargo area [kär′gō ër′ ē ə] **57** 12

cargo bay [kär′gō bā′] **75** 9

cargo door [kär′gō dör′] **57** 13

Caribbean Sea [kăr′ ə bē′ ən sē′]
  70 20

carpenter [kär′pən tər] **85** 2

carpenter's rule [kär′ pən tərz rōōl′]
  36 1

carrot(s) [kăr′ ət(s)] **7** 32

carry [kăr′ē] **26** 16

carry-on bag [kăr′ē ŏn băg′] **56** 2

cars [kärz] **50-51**

carton [kär′tən] **12** 1

cartridge needle [kär′trĭj nē′ dəl]
  100 19

carve [kärv] **31** 6

cash register [kăsh′rĕ′ jə stər] **15** 21

cashew(s) [kăsh′ ōō(z)] **9** 27

cashier [kă shïr′] **15** 22

Caspian Sea [kăs′pē ən sē′] **70** 27

casserole dish [kăs′ ə rōl dĭsh′] **30** 14

cassette [kə sĕt′] **100** 26

cassette deck [kə sĕt′ dĕk′] **100** 22

cast [kăst] **39** 5

cat [kăt] **68** 4

catch [kăch] **96** 4

catcher [kăch′ ər] **92** 2, **93** 16

catcher's mask [kăch′ərz măsk′] **92** 3

catcher's mitt [kăch′ərz mĭt′] **92** 4

caterpillar [kăt′ər pĭl′ər] **63** 1

cattle [kăt′ əl] **81** 20

Caucasus [kö′kə səs] **71** 45

cauliflower [kŏl′ ə flow′ ər] **6** 1

ceiling [sē′ lĭng] **28** 2

ceiling fan [sē′ lĭng făn′] **28** 1

celery [sĕl′ ə rē] **6** 10

cello [chĕl′ o] **98** 9

cement [sə mĕnt′] **82** 10

cement mixer [sə mĕnt′ mĭk′ sər] **82** 25

cement truck [sə mĕnt′ trŭk′] **49** 13

center [sĕn′ tər] **79** 13, **93** 27

center divider [sĕn′ tər də vī′ dər] **53** 18, **82** 24

center fielder [sĕn′ tər fēl′ dər] **93** 2

center lane [sĕn′ tər lān′] **53** 6

centerboard [sĕn′ tər börd′] **59** 6

centipede [sĕn′ tə pēd′] **63** 22

chain [chān] **23** 5, **52** 18

chair [chër] **29** 17

chalk [chök] **76** 10

chalk tray [chök′ trā′] **76** 9

chalkboard [chök′ börd′] **76** 5

chandelier [shăn′ də lïr′] **29** 3

change (the sheets) [chānj′ dhə shēts′] **38** 13

changing table [chān′ jĭng tā′ bəl] **33** 9

charcoal briquettes [chär′ kōl brĭ kĕts′] **27** 23

chart [chärt] **39** 10

check [chĕk] **15** 27, **16** 14

checked [chĕkt] **24** 18

checkout counter [chĕk′ owt kown′ tər] **15** 26

checkout desk [chĕk′ owt dĕsk′] **47** 2

cheerleaders [chïr′ lē′ dərz] **93** 20

cheek [chēk] **4** 35

cherries [chër′ ēz] **9** 19

cherry picker [chër′ ē pĭk′ ər] **82** 18

chest [chĕst] **4** 12

chest of drawers [chĕst′ əv drörz′] **32** 30

chestnut(s) [chĕs′ nŭt(s)] **9** 32

chick [chĭk] **64** 22

chicken [chĭk′ ən] **11** 24, **64** 23

child's seat [chīldz′ sēt′] **50** 33

children [chĭl′ drən] **2** 7

chills [chĭlz] **40** 4

chimney [chĭm′ nē] **27** 9

chimpanzee [chĭm păn′ zē] **69** 16

chin [chĭn] **4** 3

china [chī′ nə] **29** 1

china closet [chī′ nə klŏz′ ət] **29** 2

chipmunk [chĭp′ mŭnk] **66** 6

chop [chŏp] **26** 11, **31** 11

chops [chŏps] **10** 9, **10** 15

chorus [kör′ əs] **99** 18

(chrysanthe)mum [krə săn′ thə məm]/[mŭm] **60** 4

cigarette [sĭg′ ə rĕt′] **16** 31

circle [sür′ kəl] **79** 11

circuit breaker [sür′ kət brā′ kər] **35** 5

circular saw [sür′ kyə lər sö′] **36** 20

circumference [sür kŭm′ fə rəns] **79** 17

citrus fruits [sĭ′ trəs frōōts′] **8**

city [sĭt′ ē] **44-45**

clam(s) [klăm(z)] **11** 32

clamp [klămp] **78** 7

clarinet [klăr′ə nĕt′] **98** 16

clasp [klăsp] **23** 17

classroom [klăs′ rōōm′] **76**

claw [klö] **62** 13a, **68** 2a

clean [klēn] **24** 6, **26** 2

cleanser [klĕn′ zər] **35** 9

clear [klïr] **17** 6

cliff [klĭf] **89** 21

clip-on earring [klĭp′ ŏn ïr′ ĭng] **23** 15

clock [klŏk] **76** 2

close (v) [klōz] **77** 5

closed [klōzd] **24** 16

closet [klŏz′ ət] **32** 3

cloth diaper [klöth′ dī′ pər] **33** 13

clothes [klōz] **19-24**

clothesline [klōz′ līn′] **35** 19

clothespins [klōz′ pĭnz′] **35** 20

cloudy [klow′ dē] **25** 2

clove [klōv] **7** 25a

cloverleaf [klō′ vər lēf′] **53** 4

clubs [klŭbz] **95** 5

clutch [klŭch] **50** 25

coach [kōch] **93** 21

coal [kōl] **80** 7

coal mine [kōl′ mīn′] **80** 6

coaster [kō′ stər] **16** 27

coat [kōt] **19** 24, **42** 13

cob [kŏb] **6** 12a

cobra [kō′ brə] **65** 11

cockpit [kŏk′ pĭt′] **56** 13

cockroach [kŏk′ rōch′] **63** 9

cocktail lounge [kŏk′ tāl lownj′] **16**

cocktail waitress [kŏk′ tāl wā′ trəs] **16** 32

cocoon [kə kōōn′] **63** 2

coconut [kō′ kə nŭt′] **8** 3

coffee [kö′ fē] **18** 35

coffeemaker [kö′ fē mā′ kər] **30** 31

coffeepot [kö′ fē pŏt′] **29** 18

coffee table [kö′ fē tā′ bəl] **28** 26

coins [koynz] **13** 26

colander [kŏl′ ən dər] **30** 7

cold [kōld] **25** 10, **40** 11

cold water faucet [kōld′ wö tər fö′ sət] **34** 18

collar [kŏl′ ər] **20** 20

colonial-style house [kə lō′ nē əl stīl hows′] **27**

Colorado [kŏl′ ə rŏd′ ō] **72** 6

column [kŏl′ əm] **50** 13

comb [kōm] **32** 6

combine (n) [kŏm′ bīn] **81** 17

comet [kŏm′ ət] **74** 2

comforter [kŭm′ fər tər] **32** 22

command module [kə mănd′ mŏj′ ōōl] **75** 8

communication satellite [kə myōō′ nə kā shən săt′ ə līt] **75** 2

commuter [kə myōō′ tər] **55** 17

commuter train [kə myōō′ tər trān′] **55** 14

compact disc (CD) [kŏm′ păkt dĭsk′]/[sē′ dē′] **100** 27

compact disc player [kŏm′ păkt dĭsk′ plā′ ər] **100** 28

computer [kəm pyōō′ tər] **76** 8, **83** 16, **100**

computer programmer [kəm pyōō′ tər prō′ grăm ər] **86** 16

conductor [kən dŭk′ tər] **54** 7, **99** 8

cone [kōn] **61** 34b, **79** 28, **82** 19

conga [kŏng′ gə] **98** 20

Congo River [kŏng′ gō rĭv′ ər] **71** 62

Connecticut [kə nĕ′ tĭ kət] **72** 7

constellation [kŏn′ stə lā′ shən] **74** 3

construction [kən strŭk′ shən] **82**

(construction) boots [kən strŭk′ shən bōōts′] **21** 32

construction site [kən strŭk⁄ shən sīt⁄] **82**

construction worker
[kən strŭk⁄ shən wür⁄ kər] **82** 14

container [kən tā⁄nər] **12** 2, **58** 7

(container)ship [kən tā⁄ nər shĭp⁄] **58** 9

containers [kən tā⁄ nərz] **12**

continents [kŏn⁄ tə nənts] **70**

control tower [kən trōl⁄ tow⁄ər] **57** 20

conveyor belt [kən vā⁄ər bĕlt] **15** 23,
56 12

cook (n) [kŏŏk] **16** 1

cook (v) [kŏŏk] **17** 4

cookie [kŏŏk⁄ ē] **18** 22

cool [kŏŏl] **25** 9

cooler [kŏŏ⁄ lər] **91** 41

cooling tower [kŏŏ⁄lĭng tow⁄ər] **80** 16

copilot [kō⁄pī lət] **56** 16

cord [körd] **32** 26a, **54** 1

(corduroy) pants [kör⁄ də roy pănts⁄]
21 27

core [kör] **8** 2b, **80** 14

cork [körk] **16** 18

corkscrew [körk⁄ skrŏŏ⁄] **16** 17

corn [körn] **6** 12, **60** 24

corner [kör⁄ nər] **44** 3

corral [kə răl⁄] **81** 24

cosmetics [kŏz mĕt⁄ ĭks] **23**

cotton balls [kŏt⁄ ən bölz⁄] **39** 23

cotton swab [kŏt⁄ ən swŏb⁄] **33** 10

counter [kown⁄ tər] **30** 27

court [kört] **43**, **94** 13

court officer [kört⁄ ö⁄ fə sər] **43** 19

court reporter [kört⁄ rə pör⁄ tər] **43** 14

cousin [kŭz⁄ən] **3** 7

cow [kow] **67** 32

cowboy [kow⁄ boy⁄] **81** 21

cowgirl [kow⁄ gürl⁄] **81** 22

crab(s) [kră b(z)] **11** 36, **62** 9

cradle [krā⁄ dəl] **33** 26

cranberries [krăn⁄ bĕr⁄ ēz] **8** 13

crane [krān] **58** 6

creamer [krē⁄ mər] **29** 24

crew [krŏŏ] **75** 12

(crewneck) sweater
[krŏŏ⁄ nĕk swĕt⁄ ər] **19** 7

crib [krĭb] **33** 4

criket [krĭk⁄ ət] **63** 5

crime [krīm] **43**

crochet [krō shā⁄] **101** 28

crochet hook [krō⁄ shā⁄ hŏŏk⁄] **101** 29

crocus [krō⁄ kəs] **60** 9

cross-country skiing
[krös⁄ kŭn trē skē⁄ ĭng] **94**

crosswalk [krös⁄ wök⁄] **44** 4

crow [krō] **64** 3

crutch [krŭch] **39** 7

cube [kyŏŏb] **79** 27

cubicle [kyŏŏ⁄ bə kəl] **83** 5

cucumber(s) [kyŏŏ⁄ kŭm bər(z)] **7** 20

cuff links [kŭf⁄ lĭnks⁄] **23** 12

cup [kŭp] **13** 19, **29** 20

curb [kürb] **45** 26

curtain [kür⁄ tən] **32** 10, **99** 1

curtain rings [kür⁄ tən rĭngz⁄] **34** 2

curtain rod [kür⁄ tən röd⁄] **34** 1

curve [kürv] **79** 3

cushion [kŏŏsh⁄ ən] **28** 24

customer [kŭs⁄ tə mər] **15** 17

cut (v) [kŭt] **31** 9

cut (n) [kŭt] **40** 16

cutting board [kŭt⁄ ĭng börd⁄] **30** 26

cylinder [sĭl⁄ ĭn dər] **79** 26

cymbals [sĭm⁄ bəlz] **98** 18

daffodil [dăf⁄ ə dĭl] **60** 8

dairy cow [dër⁄ ē kow⁄] **81** 11

dairy farm [dër⁄ ē färm⁄] **81**

dairy products [dër⁄ ē prŏd⁄ ŭkts] **14** 4

daisy [dā⁄ zē] **60** 5

dam [dăm] **80** 18

dance [dăns] **99**

dancer [dăn⁄ sər] **99** 3

dark [därk] **24** 10

dashboard [dăsh⁄ börd⁄] **50** 19

date [dāt] **9** 23

daughter [dö⁄ tər] **3** 15

deck [dĕk] **27** 5, **58** 22

deer [dïr] **67** 26

defendant [də fĕn⁄ dənt] **43** 23

defense attorney [də fĕns⁄ ə tür⁄ nē]
43 22

Delaware [dĕl⁄ ə wăr⁄] **72** 8

deli counter [dĕl⁄ ē kown⁄ tər] **14** 1

delivery boy [də lĭv⁄ ə rē boy⁄] **85** 10

delivery person [də lĭv⁄ ə rē pür⁄ sən]
49 10

dental care [dĕn⁄ təl kër⁄] **39**

dentist [dĕn⁄ tĭst] **39** 17

department store [də pärt⁄ mənt stör⁄]
44 5

depth [dĕpth] **79** 33

derrick [dĕr⁄ ĭk] **80** 2

deserts [dĕz⁄ ərts] **71**

desk [dĕsk] **28** 14, **76** 16, **83** 13

detective [də tĕk⁄ tĭv] **43** 2

diagonal [dī ăg⁄ ə nəl] **79** 20

diameter [dī ăm⁄ ə tər] **79** 12

dictionary [dĭk⁄ shə nër⁄ ē] **47** 24

diesel fuel [dē⁄ zəl fyŏŏ⁄ əl] **80** 34

dig [dĭg] **26** 3

dime [dīm] **13** 29

dinghy [dĭng⁄ ē] **59** 18

dining room [dī⁄ nĭng rŏŏm⁄] **29**

dipstick [dĭp⁄ stĭk⁄] **51** 58

dirt bike [dürt⁄ bīk⁄] **52** 8

disc jockey (DJ) [dĭsk⁄ jŏk⁄ ē]/[dē⁄ jā]
86 9

dirty [dür⁄ tē] **24** 5

dish drainer [dĭsh⁄ drā⁄ nər] **30** 2

dish towel [dĭsh⁄ tow⁄ əl] **30** 18

dishwasher [dĭsh⁄ wŏsh⁄ ər] **30** 1

dishwashing liquid
[dĭsh⁄ wŏsh ĭng lĭ⁄ kwĭd] **30** 10

disposable diaper
[dĭs pō⁄ zə bəl dī⁄ pər] **33** 12

dissection kit [dĭ sĕk⁄ shən kĭt⁄] **78** 33

dive [dīv] **97** 14

dock [dŏk] **58** 28

doctor [dŏk⁄ tər] **39** 11

dogs [dögz] **69**

dogwood [dög⁄ wŏŏd⁄] **61** 28

doll [dŏl] **33** 28

doll house [dŏl⁄ hows⁄] **33** 25

dollar bills [dŏl⁄ər bĭlz⁄] **13** 25

dolly [dŏl⁄ ē] **56** 6

dolphin [dŏl⁄ fĭn] **68** 13

donkey [dŏng⁄ kē] **67** 23

door handle [dör⁄ hăn⁄ dəl] **50** 4

door lock [dör⁄ lŏk⁄] **50** 1

doorman [dör⁄ mən] **85** 11

down [down] **103** 3

down vest [down⁄ vĕst⁄] **19** 12

dragonfly [drăg⁄ ən flī⁄] **63** 4

drain [drān] **34** 9

drainpipe [drān⁄ pīp⁄] **27** 18

drapes [drāps] **28** 23

draw [drö] **77** 11

drawer [drör] **47** 5

dress [drĕs] **20** 22

dried fruits [drīd′ frōōts′] **9**

drill [drĭl] **39** 15

drink [drĭngk] **17** 2

drive [drīv] **97** 15

driveway [drīv′ wā′] **27** 1

drugstore [drŭg′ stör′] **45** 22

drum [drŭm] **98** 19

drummer [drŭm′ər] **99** 27

drumsticks [drŭm′ stĭks′] **98** 19a

dry [drī] **25** 14, **38** 9

dryer [drī′ər] **35** 24

duck [dŭk] **11** 25, **64** 25

(duck) pond [dŭk′ pŏnd′] **87** 8

dugout [dŭg′ owt′] **93** 13

dump truck [dŭmp′ trŭk′] **49** 14

dust [dŭst] **38** 15

dustpan [dŭst′ păn′] **35** 8

eagle [ē′ gəl] **64** 5

ear [ïr] **4** 34

(ear of) corn [ïr′ əv körn′] **6** 12

earmuffs [ïr′ mŭfs′] **19** 10

earrings [ïr′ ĭngz] **23** 1

Earth [ürth] **74** 8, **13**

east [ēst] **71** 73

East China Sea [ēst′ chī′ nə sē′]
    70 38

eat [ēt] **17** 1

eel [ēl] **65** 4

egg [ĕg] **18** 32, **64** 13

egg roll [ĕg′ rōl′] **18** 25

eggplant [ĕg′ plănt′] **7** 21

elbow [ĕl′ bō] **4** 8

electric drill [ĭ lĕk′ trĭk drĭl′] **37** 43

electric guitar [ĭ lĕk′ trĭk gĭ tär′]
    99 26

electric generator
    [ĭ lĕk′ trĭk gĕn′ ə rā tər] **80** 21

electrical tape [ĭ lĕk′ trĭ kəl tāp′]
    37 34

electrician [ĭ lĕk trĭ′ shən] **85** 6

electricity [ĭ lĕk trĭs′ ĭ tē] **80** 32

electronics [ĭ lĕk trŏn′ ĭks] **100**

elephant [ĕl′ ə fənt] **66** 17

elevator [ĕl′ ə vā′ tər] **45** 17, **80** 9

elm [ĕlm] **61** 36

embroidery [ĕm broi′ də rē] **101** 27

emergency brake [ĭ mür′ jən sē brāk′]
    50 15

emery board [ĕm′ ə rē börd′] **23** 24

encyclopedia [ĕn sī′ klə pē′ dē ə] **47** 25

end table [ĕnd′ tā′ bəl] **28** 29

end zone [ĕnd′ zōn′] **93** 23

energy [ĕn′ ər jē] **80**

engagement ring [ĕn gāj′ mənt rĭng′]
    23 3

engine [ĕn′ jən] **51, 52** 32

engineer [ĕn′ jə nïr′] **55** 15

enter [ĕn′ tər] **77** 14

entrance ramp [ĕn′ trəns rămp′] **53** 21

envelope [ĕn′ və lōp′] **46** 16, **83** 31

equator [ĭ kwā′ tər] **71** 70

erase [ĭ rās′] **77** 3

eraser [ĭ rā′ sər] **76** 11

escarole [ĕs′ kə rōl′] **6** 7

esophagus [ĭ sŏf′ ə gəs] **5** 61

eucalyptus [yōō′ kə lĭp′ təs] **61** 27

Europe [yōor′ əp] **70** 3

examining table [ĭg zăm′ ə nĭng tā′ bəl]
    39 6

exhaust pipe [ĭg zöst′ pīp′] **52** 33

exit ramp [ĕg′ zĭt rămp′] **53** 2

exit sign [ĕg′ zĭt sīn′] **53** 24

Express Mail (package)
    [ĭk sprĕs′ māl păk′ ĭj] **46** 23

extension cord [ĭk stĕn′ shən körd′]
    36 5

eye [ī] **5**

eye drops [ī′ drŏps′] **41** 10

eye shadow [ī′ shă′ dō] **23** 30

eyebrow [ī′ brow′] **5** 44

eyebrow pencil [ī′ brow pĕn′ səl]
    23 26

eyelashes [ī′ lăsh′ əz] **5** 46

eyelid [ī′ lĭd′] **5** 45

eyeliner [ī′ lī′ nər] **23** 33

fabric softener [făb′ rĭk sö′ fə nər]
    35 27

face [fās] **4** 1

face guard [fās′ gärd′] **92** 15

factory work [făk′ tə rē würk′] **85**

fairway [fĕr′ wā′] **95** 12

fall [föl] **96** 7

Fall [föl] **26**

family [făm′ ə lē] **3**

family restaurant [făm′ ə lē rĕs′ tər ənt]
    16

fan belt [făn′ bĕlt′] **51** 53

fare [fĕr] **55** 21

fare box [fĕr′ bŏks′] **54** 5

farmhouse [färm′ hows′] **81** 3

farmer [fär′ mər] **81** 7

farming [fär′ mĭng] **81**

fashion designer [făsh′ ən də zī′ nər]
    86 6

father [fŏdh′ ər] **3** 5

faucet [fö′ sĭt] **34** 17, 18

fawn [fön] **67** 27

feather [fĕdh′ ər] **64** 7a

feather duster [fĕdh′ ər dŭs′ tər] **35** 2

fence [fĕns] **81** 9

fender [fĕn′ dər] **52** 10

ferry [fĕr′ ē] **58** 17

fever [fē′ vər] **40** 2

field [fēld] **81** 16

fields and courses [fēldz′ ənd kör′ səz]
    95

fig [fĭg] **9** 21

fighter plane [fī′ tər plān′] **48** 1

file cabinet [fīl′ kăb′ ə nət] **83** 21

file clerk [fīl′ klürk′] **83** 23

file folder [fīl′ fōl′ dər] **83** 22

filet [fĭ lā′] **11** 28

fill [fĭl] **26** 9

film [fĭlm] **100** 10, **100** 17

filter paper [fĭl′ tər pā′ pər] **78** 16

fin [fĭn] **65** 3b

finger [fĭng′ gər] **4** 25

fingernail [fĭng′ gər nāl′] **4** 23

fingerprints [fĭng′ gər prĭnts′] **43** 24

finish line [fĭn′ ĭsh līn′] **95** 21

fire [fīr] **28** 9, **42** 5

fire engine [fīr′ ĕn′ jən] **42** 2

fire escape [fīr′ ə skāp′] **42** 4

fire extinguisher
    [fīr′ ĭk stĭng′ gwĭ shər] **42** 11

fire fighter [fīr′ fī′ tər] **42** 10

fire hydrant [fīr′ hī′ drənt] **42** 9

fire truck [fīr′ trŭk′] **42** 3

firefighting [fīr′ fī′ tĭng] **42**

firefly [fīr′ flī′] **63** 17

fireplace [fīr′ plās′] **28** 8

first baseman [fürst′ bās′ mən] **93** 8

first quarter [fürst′ kwör′ tər] **74** 23

fish [fĭsh] **11** 26, **65**

fisherman [fĭsh′ ər mən] **58** 2

fishing [fĭsh′ ĭng] **88**

fishing boat [fĭsh′ ĭng bōt′] **58** 1

fishing line [fĭsh′ ĭng lĭn′] **88** 8

fishing net [fĭsh′ ĭng nĕt′] **88** 9

fishing rod [fĭsh′ ĭng rŏd′] **88** 7

flag [flăg] **76** 1, **82** 20, **95** 9

flame [flām] **29** 26, **78** 21

flamingo [flə mĭng′ gō] **64** 29

flanker [flăng′ kər] **93** 31

flannel shirt [flăn′ əl shürt′] **19** 3

flare [flër] **51** 41

flash [flăsh] **100** 7

flashlight [flăsh′ līt′] **35** 3

flask [flăsk] **78** 2

(flat) sheet [flăt′ shēt′] **32** 19

flatbed [flăt′ bĕd′] **49** 18

flight attendant [flīt′ ə tĕn′ dənt] **56** 20

flight deck [flīt′ dĕk′] **75** 10

flight engineer [flīt′ ĕn jə nïr′] **56** 17

flipper [flĭp′ ər] **68** 12a

flippers [flĭp′ ərz] **91** 36

floor [flör] **32** 29

Florida [flör′ ə də] **72** 9

florist [flör′ ĭst] **84** 11

flounder [flown′ dər] **65** 7

flowers [flow′ ərz] **60**

flute [floot] **99** 13

fly [flī] **63** 18

flying mammal [flī′ ĭng mă′ məlz] **66**

foal [fōl] **67** 22

foggy [fŏg′ ē] **25** 12

fold [fōld] **38** 1

food [food] **6-18**

foot [foot] **5**

football [foot′ böl′] **92**, **92** 13

football field [foot′ böl fēld′] **93**

forceps [för′ səps] **78** 28

forearm [för′ ärm′] **4** 9

forehead [för′ hĕd′] **4** 32

forelegs [för′ lĕgz′] **66** 3d

foreman [för′ mən] **85** 13

fork [förk] **29** 12

forklift [förk′ lĭft′] **58** 4

foul line [fowl′ līn′] **93** 9

foundation [fown dā′ shən] **82** 11

four-door hatchback [för′ dör hăch′ băk]
51

fox [fŏks] **68** 6

fractions [frăk′ shənz] **79**

frame [frām] **28** 4

frame backpack [frām′ băk′ păk] **89** 28

freezer [frē′ zər] **14** 3, **30** 20

freezing [frē′ zĭng] **25** 11

french fries [frĕnch′ frīz′] **18** 28

French horn [frĕnch′ hörn′] **98** 26

fried chicken [frīd′ chĭk′ ən] **18** 29

Frisbee™ [frĭz′ bē] **90** 13

frog [frŏg] **65** 17

from [frŭm] **103** 10

front bumper [frŭnt′ bŭm′ pər] **51** 51

frozen foods [frō′ zən foodz′] **14** 2

fruit and vegetable market
[froot′ ənd vĕj′ tə bəl mär′ kət] **45** 28

fruit tree [froot′ trē′] **81** 2

fruits [froots] **8**

fry [frī] **31** 15

frying pan [frī′ ĭng păn′] **30** 5

fuel truck [fyoo′ əl trŭk′] **49** 3

full moon [fool′ moon′] **74** 24

full slip [fool′ slĭp′] **22** 10

fullback [fool′ băk′] **93** 34

funnel [fŭn′ əl] **78** 17

fuselage [fyoo′ sə lŏj′] **57** 14

galaxy [găl′ək sē] **74** 1

Ganges River [găn′ jēz rĭv′ ər] **71** 67

gangway [găng′ wā′] **58** 20

garage [gə rŏj′] **27** 2

garbage can [gär′ bĭj kăn′] **35** 31

garbage truck [gär′ bĭj trŭk′] **49** 6

garden hose [gär′ dən hōs′] **27** 14

gardenia [gär dēn′ yə] **60** 14

gardener [gärd′ nər] **85** 3

garlic [gär′ lĭk] **7** 25

garment bag [gär′ mənt băg′] **56** 1

garter belt [gär′ tər bĕlt′] **22** 14

(garter) snake [gär′ tər snāk′] **65** 9

gas gauge [găs′ gāj′] **50** 9

gas pump [găs′ pŭmp′] **53** 14

gas tank [găs′ tănk′] **50** 34

gas(oline) [găs′ ə lēn′] **80** 28

(gauze) bandage [göz′ băn′ dĭj] **39** 24

gauze pads [göz′ pădz′] **39** 25

gavel [găv′ əl] **43** 12

gear [gïr] **89** 27

gear changer [gïr′ chān′ jər] **52** 22

gearshift [gïr′ shĭft′] **50** 17

geometrical figures
[jē′ ə mĕ′ trĭ kəl fĭg′ yərz] **79**

Georgia [jör′ jə] **72** 10

geyser [gī′ zər] **80** 5

gibbon [gĭb′ ən] **69** 15

gill [gĭl] **65** 3c

giraffe [jə răf′] **67** 29

girdle [gür′ dəl] **22** 15

girl [gürl] **2** 9

girl's frame [gürlz′ frām′] **52** 3

give [gĭv] **17** 9

glass [glăs] **12** 20

glasses [glăs′ əz] **21** 44

glider [glī′ dər] **57** 4

globe [glōb] **47** 19

glove [glŭv] **92** 12, **94** 11, **94** 15

glove compartment
[glŭv′ kəm pärt′ mənt] **50** 20

gloves [glŭvz] **19** 1

glue [gloo] **37** 33, **76** 17

goal [gōl] **92** 25

goalie [gōl′ ē] **92** 24

goalpost [gōl′ pōst′] **93** 35

goat [gōt] **67** 28

Gobi Desert [gō′ bē dĕz′ ərt] **71** 54

golf [gŏlf] **94**

golf bag [gŏlf′ băg′] **95** 7

golf ball [gŏlf′ böl′] **94** 7

golf cart [gŏlf′ kärt′] **95** 8

golf course [gŏlf′ körs′] **95**

golfer [gŏl′ fər] **94** 10

goose [goos] **64** 26

gooseberries [goos′ bĕr′ ēz] **8** 11

gopher [gō′ fər] **66** 8

gorilla [gə rĭl′ ə] **69** 17

graduated cylinder
[grăj′ oo ā tĭd sĭl′ ən dər] **78** 25

grains [grānz] **60**

granddaughter [grănd′ dö′ tər] **2** 11

grandfather [grănd′ fŏ′ dhər] **3** 2

grandmother [grănd′ mŭ′ dhər] **3** 1

grandparents [grănd păr′ ənts] **2** 10

grandson [grănd′ sŭn′] **2** 12

grapefruit [grăp′ frōot′] **8** 7

grapes [grāps] **8** 1

graph paper [grăf′ pā′ pər] **78** 11

grass [grăs] **27** 15

grasses [grăs′ əz] **60**

grasshopper [grăs′ hŏp′ ər] **63** 6

grate [grāt] **31** 2

Great Sandy Desert
   [grāt′ săn′ dē děz′ ərt] **71** 55

green [grēn] **95** 10

greengrocer [grēn′ grō′ sər] **84** 7

grill [grĭl] **27** 22, **88** 12

grizzly bear [grĭz′ lē bër′] **69** 23

groceries [grō′ sə rēz] **15** 24

ground beef [grownd′ bēf′] **10** 2

grounding plug [grown′ dĭng plŭg′]
   36 7

guitar [gĭ tär′] **98** 11

Gulf of Alaska [gŭlf′ əv ə lăs′kə]
   70 17

Gulf of Guinea [gŭlf′ əv gĭn′ ē] **70** 25

Gulf of Mexico [gŭlf′ əv měk sə kō]
   70 19

gulfs [gŭlfs] **70**

gun [gŭn] **43** 7

gun turret [gŭn′ tür′ ət] **48** 12

gutter [gŭt′ ər] **27** 10, **94** 3

gymnast [jĭm′ nəst] **94** 23

gymnastics [jĭm năs′ tĭks] **94**

hacksaw [hăk′ sö′] **36** 18

hair [hër] **4** 30

hair dryer [hër′ drī′ ər] **34** 26

hairbrush [hër′ brŭsh′] **32** 7

hairdresser [hër′ drĕs′ ər] **84** 10

half (1/2) [hăf] **79** 30

half slip [hăf′ slĭp′] **22** 8

halfback [hăf′ băk′] **93** 33

hall [höl] **76** 12

ham [hăm] **10** 12

hamburger [hăm′ bür′ gər] **18** 9

hammer [hăm′ ər] **36** 13

hammock [hăm′ ək] **27** 11

hamper [hăm′ pər] **34** 28

hand [hănd] **4**

hand brake [hănd′ brāk′] **52** 24

hand grenade [hănd′ grə nād′] **48** 29

hand towel [hănd′ tow′ əl] **34** 23

hand truck [hănd′ trŭk′] **87** 4

handball [hănd′ böl′] **94**, **94** 12

handcuffs [hănd′ kŭfs′] **43** 4

handicrafts [hăn′ dē krăfts′] **101**

handlebars [hăn′ dəl bärz′] **52** 2

hang [hăng] **38** 6

hang glider [hăng′ glī′ dər] **57** 6

hangar [hăng′ ər] **57** 17

hanger [hăng′ ər] **32** 2

hard hat [härd′ hăt′] **21** 28, **82** 4

harmonica [här mŏn′ ə kə] **98** 30

harness [här′ nəs] **89** 22

harp [härp] **98** 6

hat [hăt] **19** 18

hatchback [hăch′ băk′] **51** 43

hatchet [hăch′ ət] **36** 17

Hawaii [hə wŏ′ ē] **72** 11

hawk [hök] **64** 7

hay [hā] **81** 13

hazelnut(s) [hā′ zəl nŭt(s)′] **9** 30

head [hĕd] **4**, **37** 42a

(head of) cauliflower
   [hĕd′ əv köl ə flow′ ər] **6** 1

head protector [hĕd prə tĕk′ tər] **94** 14

headache [hĕd′ āk′] **40** 6

headboard [hĕd′ börd′] **32** 14

headlights [hĕd′ līts′] **51** 48

headphones [hĕd′ fōnz′] **100** 29

headrest [hĕd′ rĕst′] **50** 35

headset [hĕd′ sĕt′] **83** 2

heart [härt] **5** 64

heat [hēt] **80** 27

heating pad [hē′ tĭng păd′] **41** 3

hedge clippers [hĕj′ klĭp′ ərz] **27** 29

heel [hēl] **5** 50, **20** 5

heels [hēlz] **20** 25

height [hīt] **79** 34

helicopter [hĕl′ ə kŏp′ tər] **57** 2

helmet [hĕl′ mət] **42** 12, **52** 7, **92** 14

hem [hĕm] **101** 11

hem binding [hĕm′ bīn′ dĭng] **101** 12

herb(s) [ürb(z)] **6** 9

(herd of) cattle [hürd′ əv kăt′ əl] **81** 20

high [hī] **24** 11

high blood pressure [hī′ blŭd prĕsh′ ər]
   40 10

high chair [hī′ chër′] **16** 8

high heels [hī′ hēlz′] **20** 25

highway travel [hī′ wā trăv′ əl] **53**

hikers [hī′ kərz] **88** 2

hiking boots [hī′ kĭng bōots′] **19** 9

hill [hĭl] **88** 4

Himalayas [hĭm′ ə lā′ əz] **70** 47

hind legs [hīnd′ lĕgz′] **66** 3b

hip [hĭp] **4** 16

hippopotamus [hĭp′ ə pŏt′ ə məs]
   66 14

hit [hĭt] **96** 1

hitchhiker [hĭch′ hī′ kər] **53** 9

hockey stick [hŏk′ ē stĭk′] **92** 18

hog [hög] **66** 30

hold [hōld] **17** 12, **58** 8

hole [hōl] **94** 8

holly [hŏl′ ē] **61** 37

holster [hōl′ stər] **43** 8

home plate [hōm′ plāt′] **93** 15

honeydew melon
   [hŭn′ ē dōo mĕl′ ən] **9** 35

hood [hōod] **51** 47

hoof [hōof] **66** 35b

hoofed mammals [hōoft′ măm′ əlz] **66**

hook [hōok] **32** 1, **36** 16

hook and eye [hōok′ ənd ī′] **101** 14

horn [hörn] **50** 12, **52** 5, **66** 16a

horse [hörs] **66** 21

horse racing [hörs′ rā′ sĭng] **94**

horse-drawn carriage
   [hörs′ drön kăr′ ĭj] **54** 33

horseback rider [hörs′ băk rī′ dər]
   87 6

horses [hörs′ əz] **81** 23

hose [hōz] **42** 8, **50** 57

hot [hŏt] **25** 7

hot air balloon [hŏt′ ër bə lōon′] **57** 1

hot dog [hŏt′ dög′] **18** 2

hot water faucet [hŏt′ wŏt ər fö′ sət]
   34 17

house plants [hows′ plănts′] **60** 39

household items [hows′ hōld ī′ təmz]
   15 15

household services
   [hows′ hōld sür′ və səz] **85**

housekeeper [hows′ kē′ pər] **85** 8

houses [how′ zəz] **27**

housework [hows′ würk′] **38**

Huang River [hwöng′ rĭv′ər] **71** 68

hubcap [hŭb′ kăp′] **50** 36

Hudson Bay [hŭd′ sən bā′] **70** 18

human body [hyōō′ mən bŏd′ ē] **4**

hummingbird [hŭm′ ĭng bürd′] **64** 2

hump [hŭmp] **67** 33a

husband [hŭz′ bənd] **2** 3, **3** 12

hyacinth [hī′ ə sĭnth] **60** 10

hyena [hī ē′ nə] **68** 30

hypotenuse [hī pŏt′ ə nōōs′] **79** 24

ice cream cone [īs′ krēm cōn′] **18** 36

ice hockey [īs′ hŏk′ ē] **92**

ice pack [īs′ păk′] **41** 4

ice skates [īs′ skāts′] **19** 15

ice skating [īs′ skā′ tĭng] **94**

ice tray [īs′ trā′] **30** 21

icy [ī′ sē] **25** 16

Idaho [ī′ də hō′] **72** 12

ignition [ĭg nĭsh′ ən] **50** 14

iguana [ĭ gwŏ′ nə] **65** 13

Illinois [ĭl′ ə noy′] **72** 13

in [ĭn] **102** 7

in front of [ĭn frŭnt′ əv] **102** 6

in-box [ĭn′ bŏks] **83** 12

(index) finger [ĭn′ dĕks fĭng′ gər] **4** 25

Indian Ocean [ĭn′ dē ən ō′ shən′] **70** 13

Indiana [ĭn′ dē ăn′ ə] **72** 14

individual sports
    [ĭn′ də vĭj′ ōō əl spörts′] **94**

infection [ĭn fĕk′ shən] **40** 14

inflatable raft [ĭn flā′ tə bəl răft′] **59** 20

information desk
    [ĭn′ fər mā′ shən dĕsk′] **47** 22

injection [ĭn jĕk′ shən] **41** 8

injuries [ĭn′ jə rēz] **40**

insect bite [ĭn′ sĕkt bīt′] **40** 3

insects [ĭn′ sĕkts] **63**

instep [ĭn′ stĕp′] **5** 51

instruments [ĭn′ strə mənts]
    39 13, **56** 14, **98**

internal organs [ĭn tür′ nəl ör′ gənz] **5**

intersection [ĭn′ tər sĕk′ shən] **44** 11

interstate highway
    [ĭn′ tər stāt hī′ wā] **53** 1

intestines [ĭn tĕs′ tənz] **5** 67

into [ĭn′ tōō] **103** 12

Iowa [ī′ ə wə] **72** 15

iris [ī′ rəs] **5** 47, **60** 11

iron (n) [ī′ ərn] **35** 12

iron (v) [ī′ ərn] **38** 11

ironing board [ī′ ər nĭng börd′] **35** 13

jack [jăk] **32** 26b, **50** 38

jacket [jăk′ ət] **19** 17, **21** 33

jackhammer [jăk′ hăm′ər] **82** 22

jail [jāl] **43** 1

janitor [jăn′ə tər] **85** 9

jar [jär] **12** 9

jaw [jö] **4** 38

jeans [jēnz] **19** 6

jeep [jēp] **48** 9

jelly [jĕl′ ē] **18** 31

jellyfish [jĕl′ ē fĭsh′] **62** 12

jet engine [jĕt′ ĕn′ jən] **57** 11

jet fuel [jĕt′ fyōō′ əl] **80** 31

(jet) plane [jĕt′ plān′] **57** 18

jeweller [jōō′ ə lər] **84** 12

jewelry [jōō′ əl rē] **23**

jewelry box [jōō′ əl rē bŏks′] **32** 4

jigsaw [jĭg′ sö] **36** 3

jockey [jŏk′ ē] **94** 21

jogging path [jŏg′ ĭng păth′] **87** 9

judge [jŭj] **43** 10

jukebox [jōōk′ bŏks′] **16** 12

jump [jŭmp] **96** 8

jungle gym [jŭng′ əl jĭm′] **87** 17

Jupiter [jōō′ pə tər] **74** 15

jury [jōōr′ ē] **43** 21

jury box [joor′ ē bŏks′] **43** 20

kangaroo [kăng′ gə rōō′] **66** 3

Kansas [kăn′ zəs] **72** 16

Kara Sea [kär′ə sē′] **70** 31

kayak [kī′ ăk] **59** 17

Kentucky [kĕn tŭk′ ē] **72** 17

ketchup [kĕch′ əp] **16** 4

kettledrum [kĕt′ əl drŭm′] **98** 21

keyboard [kē′ börd′] **98** 1a, **100** 33

keyboard player [kē′ börd plā′ ər] **99** 22

kickstand [kĭk′ stănd′] **52** 9

kidney [kĭd′ nē] **5** 70

kidney bean(s) [kĭd′ nē bēn(z)′] **6** 13

kitchen [kĭch′ ən] **30**

kite [kīt] **91** 22

kitten [kĭt′ ən] **68** 5

knee [nē] **4** 19

knee socks [nē′ sŏks′] **22** 16

knife [nīf] **29** 15

knitting [nĭt′ ĭng] **101** 22

knitting needle [nĭt′ ĭng nē′ dəl] **101** 25

knuckle [nŭk′ əl] **4** 22

koala [kō ŏl′ ə] **66** 1

label [lā′ bəl] **46** 21

lacrosse [lə krös′] **92**

lacrosse stick [lə krös′ stĭk′] **92** 16

ladder [lăd′ ər] **42** 1, **82** 8

ladybug [lā′ dē bŭg′] **63** 14

lamb [lăm] **10** 13, **67** 24

lamp [lămp] **28** 28

lampshade [lămp′ shād′] **28** 27

landing gear [lăn′ dĭng gïr′] **57** 15

lane [lān] **94** 4

lantern [lăn′ tərn] **88** 29

lapel [lə pĕl′] **20** 1

Laptev Sea [lăp′ tĕv sē′] **70** 33

last quarter [lăst′ kwör′ tər] **74** 25

launchpad [lönch′ păd′] **75** 15

laundry [lön′ drē] **35** 28

laundry basket [lön′ drē băs′ kət] **35** 29

laundry detergent [lön′ drē də tür′ jənt]
    35 25

lawn mower [lön′ mō′ ər] **27** 12

lead guitarist [lēd′ gĭ tär′ ĭst] **99** 25

leaf [lēf] **60** 36a

leave [lēv] **77** 13

left fielder [lĕft′ fēl′ dər] **93** 1

left guard [lĕft′ gärd′] **93** 26

left lane [lĕft′ lān′] **53** 5

left tackle [lĕft′ tăk′ əl] **93** 25

leg [lĕg] **4** 17, **10** 14, **11** 20

(legal) pad [lē′ gəl păd′] **83** 26

lemon [lĕm′ ən] **8** 9

Lena River [lē′ nə rĭv′ər] **71** 66

length [lĕngth] **79** 36

lens [lĕnz] **100** 6

leopard [lĕp′ərd] **68** 1

letter [lĕt′ər] **46** 7

letter carrier [lĕt′ər kăr′ yər] **46** 3

lettuce [lĕt′ əs] **6** 6

level [lĕv′ əl] **82** 3

librarian [lī brĕr′ ē ən] **47** 23

library card [lī′ brĕr ē kärd′] **47** 3

library clerk [lī′ brĕr ē klürk′] **47** 1

license plate [lī′ səns plāt′] **50** 28

lid [lĭd] **30** 9

life jacket [līf′ jăk′ ət] **59** 1

life preserver [līf′ prə zür′ vər] **90** 9

lifeboat [līf′ bōt′] **58** 19, **90** 10

lifeguard [līf′gärd′] **90** 6
lifeguard chair [līf′gärd chër′] **90** 8
light (v) [līt] **17** 13
light (adj) [līt] **24** 9
light switch [līt′swĭch′] **32** 25
lightbulb [līt′bŭlb′] **35** 22
lighter [lī′tər] **16** 30
lighthouse [līt′hows′] **58** 14
lily [lĭl′ē] **60** 3
lima bean(s) [lī′mə bēn(z)′] **6** 16
lime [līm] **8** 10
line [līn] **58** 25
lines [līnz] **79**
linesman [līnz′mən] **82** 17
lion [lī′ən] **68** 3
lip [lĭp] **4** 43
lipstick [lĭp′stĭk′] **23** 29
liquor (bottle) [lĭk′ər bŏt′əl] **16** 22
listen [lĭs′ən] **77** 6
little finger [lĭt′əl fĭng′gər] **4** 28
little league baseball [lĭt′əl lēg bās′böl] **92**
Little Leaguer [lĭt′əl lēg′ər] **92** 8
little toe [lĭt′əl tō′] **5** 55
liver [lĭv′ər] **5** 65
livestock [līv′stŏk′] **81** 12
living quarters [lĭv′ĭng kwör′tərz] **75** 11
living room [lĭv′ĭng rōōm′] **28**
lizard [lĭz′ərd] **65** 15
llama [lŏm′ə] **66** 15
loaf [lōf] **12** 7
loafer [lō′fər] **21** 42
lobby [lŏb′ē] **44** 2
lobster [lŏb′stər] **11** 30, **62** 13
lock [lŏk] **52** 13
locker [lŏk′ər] **76** 6
locksmith [lŏk′smĭth′] **85** 4
log [lög] **28** 10
long [löng] **24** 2
long johns [löng′jŏnz′] **22** 7
long sleeve [löng′slēv′] **20** 15
loose [lōōs] **24** 4
(loose-leaf) paper [lōōs′lēf pā′pər] **76** 13
loudspeaker [lowd′spē′kər] **76** 3
Louisiana [lōō ē ′ zē ăn′ə] **72** 18
lounge chair [lownj′chër′] **27** 24

low [lō] **24** 12
lunar eclipse [lōō′nər ĭ klĭps′] **74** 6
lunar module [lōō′nər mŏj′ōōl] **75** 7
lunch box [lŭnch′bŏks′] **20** 31
lunch truck [lŭnch′trŭk′] **49** 8
lung [lŭng] **5** 63
machine gun [mə shēn′gŭn′] **48** 25
magazine [măg′ə zēn′] **47** 16
magnet [măg′nət] **78** 27
magnifying glass [măg′nə fī ĭng glăs′] **78** 15
magnolia [măg nōl′yə] **61** 29
mail [māl] **46** 2
mail slot [māl′slŏt′] **46** 13
mail truck [māl′trŭk′] **46** 5
mailbag [māl′băg′] **46** 4
mailbox [māl′bŏks′] **46** 1
Maine [mān] **72** 19
maintenance [mān′tə nəns] **85**
make (the bed) [māk′dhə bĕd′] **38** 8
makeup [māk′ŭp′] **23**
mallet [măl′ĭt] **36** 11
mammals [măm′əlz] **66-69**
man [măn] **2** 2
manager [măn′ĭ jər] **83** 18
mandolin [măn′də lĭn′] **98** 4
mane [mān] **66** 21a
mango [măng′gō] **8** 5
manhole [măn′hōl′] **45** 32
mantel [măn′təl] **28** 7
mantis [măn′tĭs] **63** 7
manual transmission [măn′yōō əl trănz mĭsh′ən] **50**
map [măp] **70**
maple [mā′pəl] **61** 38
marigold [măr′ə gōld′] **60** 6
marine [mə rēn′] **48** 18
Marines [mə rēnz′] **48** 17
Mars [märz] **74** 14
Maryland [mër′ə lənd] **72** 20
mascara [mă skăr′ə] **23** 28
mashed potatoes [măsht′pə tā tōz] **18** 17
mask [măsk] **91** 35
Massachusetts [măs′ə chōō′sĭts] **72** 21
mast [măst] **59** 8
mat [măt] **50** 22

matches [măch′əz] **16** 28
material [mə tĭr′ē əl] **101** 4
math [măth] **79**
mattress [mă′trəs] **32** 17
measurement [mĕzh′ər mənt] **79**
meat [mēt] **10**
meatballs [mēt′bölz′] **18** 11
mechanic [mə kăn′ĭk] **84** 2
media [mē′dē ə] **86**
medical care [mĕd′ə kəl kër′] **39**
medicine [mĕd′ə sən] **41**
medicine chest [mĕd′ə sən chĕst′] **34** 14
medicine dropper [mĕd′ə sən drŏp′ər] **78** 26
Mediterranean Sea [mĕd′ĭ tə rā′nē ən sē′] **70** 24
melon [mĕl′ən] **9** 35
menu [mĕn′yōō] **16** 7
Mercury [mür′kyə rē] **74** 11
merry-go-round [mĕr′ē gō rownd′] **87** 5
message pad [mĕs′ĭj păd′] **83** 25
messenger [mĕs′ən jər] **86** 19
metal detector [mĕt′əl də tĕk′tər] **56** 10
meteor [mē′tē ər] **74** 5
meter [mē′tər] **55** 23
mezzanine [mĕz′ə nēn′] **99** 13
Michigan [mĭsh′ə gən] **72** 22
microfilm [mī′krə fĭlm′] **47** 13
microfilm reader [mī′krə fĭlm rē′dər] **47** 14
microscope [mī′krə skōp′] **78** 30
microwave oven [mī′krə wāv ŭv′ən] **30** 23
middle finger [mĭd′əl fĭng′gər] **4** 26
milk [mĭlk] **14** 5
Minicam™ [mĭn′ē kăm′] **100** 2
Minnesota [mĭn′ə sō′tə] **72** 23
mirror [mĭr′ər] **32** 5
Mississippi [mĭs′ə sĭp′ē] **72** 24
Mississippi River [mĭs′ə sĭp′ē rĭv′ər] **71** 58
Missouri [mĭ zōōr′ē] **73** 25
mitt [mĭt] **27** 20
mittens [mĭt′ənz] **19** 11

mixed vegetables [mĭkst′ věj′ tə bəlz] **18** 16

mixing bowl [mĭk′ sĭng bōl′] **30** 24

mobile [mō′ bēl] **33** 2

model [mŏd′ əl] **86** 5

Mojave Desert [mō hŏv′ ē děz′ ərt] **71** 48

money [mŭn′ ē] **12**

money order [mŭn′ ē ôr′ dər] **46** 18

monitor [mŏn′ ə tər] **100** 32

monkey [mŭng′ ke] **69** 14

monkey wrench [mŭng′ kē rěnch′] **36** 12

monorail [mŏn′ ə rāl′] **55** 29

Montana [mŏn tăn′ ə] **73** 26

Moon [mōon] **74** 9

mooring [mōor′ ĭng] **59** 19

moose [mōos] **67** 35

mop [mŏp] **35** 6

(mop) refill [mŏp′ rē′ fĭl] **35** 11

mortar [môr′ tər] **48** 28

mosquito [mə skē′ tō] **63** 13

motel [mō tĕl′] **90** 3

moth [mŏth] **63** 21

mother [mŭdh′ ər] **3** 4

motor oil [mōt′ ər oyl′] **80** 33

motor scooter [mōt′ ər skōo′ tər] **52** 29

motorboat [mōt′ ər bōt′] **59** 13

motorcycle [mōt′ ər sī′ kəl] **52** 30, **53** 19

mountain [mown′ tən] **89** 19

mountain climbing [mown′ tən klīm′ ĭng] **89**

mountain ranges [mown′ tən rān′ jəz] **71**

mouse [mows] **66** 9

mousetrap [mows′ trăp′] **35** 32

mouth [mowth] **4** 2

mover [mōo′ vər] **49** 12

movie camera [mōo′ vē kăm′ ə rə] **100** 15

moving van [mōo′ vĭng văn′] **49** 11

mow [mō] **26** 6

mum [mŭm] **60** 4

muscle [mŭs′ əl] **5** 62

mushroom(s) [mŭsh′ rōom(z)] **7** 30

music [myōo′ zĭk] **99**

musical comedy [myōo′ zə kəl kŏm′ ə dē] **99**

musical instruments [myōo′ zə kəl ĭn′ strə mənts] **98**

musician [myōo zĭsh′ ən] **99** 10

mussel(s) [mŭs′ əl(z)] **11** 34, **62** 3

mustache [mŭs′ tăsh] **4** 40

mustard [mŭs′ tərd] **18** 1

nail [nāl] **37** 41

nail clippers [nāl′ klĭp′ ərz] **23** 31

nail polish [nāl′ pŏl′ ĭsh] **23** 25

nailbrush [nāl′ brŭsh′] **34** 20

napkin [năp′ kĭn] **29** 14

natural gas [năch′ ər əl găs′] **80** 29

Navy [nā′ vē] **48** 13

Nebraska [nə brăs′ kə] **73** 27

neck [něk] **4** 4

necklace [něk′ lĭs] **23** 6

nectarine [něk′ tə rēn′] **8** 17

needle [nē′ dəl] **39** 26, **60** 34a, **101** 18

needlecrafts [nē′ dəl krăfts′] **101**

needlepoint [nē′ dəl poynt′] **101** 26

neighborhood parks [nā′ bər hŏod pärks′] **87**

nephew [něf′ yōo] **3** 13

Neptune [něp′ tōon] **74** 18

nest [něst] **64** 31

net [nět] **92** 23

Nevada [nə văd′ ə] **73** 28

new [nōo] **24** 13

New Hampshire [nōo′ hămp′ shər] **72** 29

New Jersey [nōo′ jûr′ ze] **73** 30

New Mexico [nōo′ měk′ sə kō] **73** 31

new moon [nōo′ mōon′] **74** 26

New York [nōo′ yörk′] **73** 32

newscaster [nōoz′ kăs′ tər] **86** 2

newspaper [nōoz′ pā′ pər] **21** 48

newsstand [nōoz′ stănd′] **45** 30

next to [někst′ tōo] **102** 11

nickel [nĭk′ əl] **13** 28

niece [nēs] **3** 14

Niger River [nī′ jər rĭv′ ər] **71** 61

night table [nīt′ tā′ bəl] **32** 27

nightgown [nīt′ gown′] **22** 21

nightstick [nīt′ stĭk′] **43** 9

Nile River [nīl′ rĭv′ ər] **71** 63

nipple [nĭp′ əl] **33** 18

north [nörth] **71** 71

North America [nörth′ ə mër′ ə kə] **70** 1

North Atlantic [nörth′ ăt lăn′ tĭk] **70** 11

North Carolina [nörth′ kăr ə lī′ nə] **73** 33

North Dakota [nörth′ də kō′ tə] **73** 34

North Pacific [nörth′ pə sĭf′ ĭk] **70** 9

North Sea [nörth′ sē′] **70** 21

nose [nōz] **4** 36, **57** 8

nostril [nŏs′ trĭl] **4** 37

nozzle [nŏz′ əl] **42** 17

nuclear reactor [nōo′ klē ər rē ăk′ tər] **80** 13

nurse [nûrs] **39** 19

nut [nŭt] **37** 39

nuts [nŭts] **9**

oak [ōk] **61** 33

oar [ör] **59** 22

oarlock [ör′ lŏk′] **59** 21

oats [ōts] **60** 23

Ob River [ŏb′ rĭv′ ər] **71** 64

oboe [ō′bō] **98** 15

obtuse angle [ŏb tōos′ ăng′ gəl] **79** 5

occupations [ŏk′ yə pā′ shənz] **84-86**

ocean liner [ō′ shən lī′ nər] **58** 27

oceans [ō′ shənz] **70**

octopus [ōk′ tə pəs] **62** 6

office [ö′ fĭs] **83**

office building [ö′ fĭs bĭl′ dĭng] **44** 1

officer [ö′ fĭ sər] **86** 13

Ohio [ō hī′ ō] **73** 35

oil [oyl] **38** 12

oil well [oyl′ wěl′] **80** 1

ointment [oynt′ mənt] **41** 9

Oklahoma [ō′ klə hō′ mə] **73** 36

old [ōld] **24** 14

on [ŏn] **102** 5

on top of [ŏn tŏp′ əv] **102** 10

onion(s) [ŭn′ yən(z)] **7** 31

open [ō′ pən] **24** 15, **31** 3

optician [ŏp tĭsh′ ən] **84** 9

oral hygienist [ör′ əl hī jē′ nĭst] **39** 14

orange [ör′ ĭnj] **8** 8

orangutan [ə răng′ ə tăn′] **69** 18

orbit [ör′ bĭt] **74** 21

orchard [ör′ chərd] **81** 1

orchestra [ör′ kə strə] **99** 6

orchestra seating [ör′ kə strə sēt′ ĭng]
  99 12

orchid [ör′ kĭd] **60** 12

order [ör′ dər] **17** 5

Oregon [ör′ ə gən] **73** 37

organ [ör′ gən] **98** 29

ostrich [ŏs′ trĭch] **64** 12

otter [ŏt′ ər] **68** 10

out of [owt′ əv] **103** 7

outboard motor [owt′ börd mō′ tər]
  59 12

outer space [owt′ər spās′] **74**

outlet [owt′ lət] **36** 6

oval [ō′ vəl] **79** 18

oven [ŭv′ ən] **30** 32

over [ō′ vər] **103** 8

overalls [ō′ vər ölz′] **21** 30

overcoat [ō′ vər kōt′] **19** 20

overhead projector
  [ō′ vər hĕd prə jĕk′ tər] **76** 27

overpass [ō′ vər păs′] **53** 3

owl [owl] **64** 6

oyster(s) [oy′ stər(z)] **11** 33, **62** 2

pacifier [păs′ ə fī′ ər] **33** 22

pack [păk] **13** 16

package [păk′ ĭj] **12** 4, **46** 19

pad [păd] **83** 26

paddle [păd′ əl] **59** 3, **94** 18

pail [pāl] **90** 16

paint (v) [pānt] **26** 1

paint (n) [pānt] **37** 31

paintbrush [pānt′ brŭsh′] **37** 30

Painted Desert [pān′ təd dez′ ərt] **71** 49

painter [pān′ tər] **85** 7

painting [pān′ tĭng] **28** 5

(pair of) scissors [pĕr′ əv sĭz′ ərz]
  101 17

pajamas [pə jŏm′ əz] **22** 19

palm [pŏm] **4** 29, **61** 26

pan [păn] **37** 28

pancakes [păn′ kāks′] **18** 5

pancreas [pang′ krē əs] **5** 71

panda [păn də] **69** 20

panel truck [păn′ əl trŭk′] **49** 9

pansy [păn′ zē] **60** 2

panties [păn′ tēz] **22** 11

pants [pănts] **21** 27

pantyhose [păn′ tē hōz′] **22** 5

papaya [pə pī′ yə] **8** 6

paper [pā′ pər] **76** 13

paper clips [pā′ pər klĭps′] **83** 28

paper towels [pā′ pər tow′əlz] **35** 23

parachute [păr′ ə shōōt′] **48** 6

parakeet [păr′ ə kēt] **64** 15

parallel lines [păr′ ə lĕl līnz′] **79** 4

paramedic [păr′ ə mĕd′ ĭk] **42** 7

Parana River [păr′ ə nŏ′ rĭv′ ər] **71** 60

parents [păr′ ənts] **2** 6

park [pärk] **87**

park ranger [pärk′ rān′ jər] **88** 5

parka [pär′ kə] **19** 8

parking lights [pär′ kĭng līts′] **51** 49

parking garage [pär′ kĭng gə rŏj′]
  45 19

parking meter [pär′ kĭng mē′ tər]
  45 20

parrot [păr′ ət] **64** 16

part [pärt] **4** 31

pass [păs] **96** 5

passenger [păs′ ĭn jər] **55** 25

passenger car [păs′ ĭn jər kär′] **53** 15

pasture [păs′ chər] **81** 6

patient [pā′shənt] **39** 20

patio [păt′ ē ō′] **27** 17

pattern [păt′ ərn] **101** 7

pattern piece [păt′ ərn pēs′] **101** 6

paw [pö] **69** 29a

pay [pā] **17** 7

pea(s) [pē(z)] **6** 17

peach [pēch] **9** 37

peacock [pē′ kŏk′] **64** 18

peak [pēk] **89** 20

peanut(s) [pē′ nŭt(s)′] **9** 28

pear [pĕr] **8** 18

pedal [pĕd′ əl] **39** 18, **52** 19

pedestrian [pə dĕs′ trē ən] **44** 12

peel (n) [pēl] **9** 20a

peel (v) [pēl] **31** 5

pegboard [pĕg′ börd′] **36** 15

pelican [pĕl′ ə kən] **64** 24

pencil [pĕn′ səl] **76** 24

pencil eraser [pĕn′ səl ə rā′ sər] **76** 21

pencil sharpener
  [pĕn′ səl shär′ pə nər] **76** 20, **83** 30

Pennsylvania [pĕn səl vān′ yə] **73** 38

penny [pĕn′ ē] **13** 27

penguin [pĕn′ gwĭn] **64** 27

people [pē′ pəl] **2**

pepper shaker [pĕp′ ər shā′ kər] **29** 9

pepper(s) [pĕp′ ər(z)] **7** 22

percussion [pər kŭsh′ ən] **98**

perfume [pür′ fyōōm] **23** 27

periodicals section
  [pĭr′ ē ŏd′ ə kəlz sĕk′ shən] **47** 15

periscope [pĕr′ ə skōp′] **48** 8

perpendicular lines
  [pür′ pən dĭk′ yə lər līnz′] **79** 2

Persian Gulf [pür′ zhən gŭlf′] **70** 28

personal computer (PC)
  [pür′ sə nəl kŭm pyōō′ tər]/
  [pē′ sē′] **100** 31

personnel [pür′ sə nĕl′] **48**

petal [pĕt′ əl] **60** 18b

petri dish [pēt′ rē dĭsh′] **78** 3

petunia [pə tōōn′ yə] **60** 7

pharmacist [fär′ mə sĭst] **84** 1

phases of the moon
  [fā′ zəz əv dhə mōōn′] **74**

pheasant [fĕz′ ənt] **64** 19

Phillips screwdriver
  [fĭl′ ĭps skrōō′ drī vər] **37** 25

phone [fōn] **32** 26

photocopier [fō′ tə kŏp′ ē ər] **83** 24

photocopy machine
  [fō tə kŏp ē mə shēn′] **47** 18

photographer [fə tŏg′ rə fər] **86** 4

photography [fə tŏg′ rə fē] **100**

piano [pē ăn′ ō] **98** 1

piccolo [pĭk′ ə lō′] **98** 12

pick (v) [pĭk] **26** 7

pick (n) [pĭk] **98** 11a

pickup truck [pĭk′ ŭp trŭk′] **49** 4

pickax [pĭk′ ăks′] **82** 13

pickle [pĭk′ əl] **18** 8

picnic area [pĭk′ nĭk ër′ ē ə] **88**

picnic basket [pĭk′ nĭk băs′ kət] **88** 13

picnic table [pĭk′ nĭk tā′ bəl] **88** 15

piece [pēs] **12** 22

pier [pĭr] **58** 3

pierced earring [pïrst′ ïr′ ĭng] **23** 16

pigeon [pĭj′ ən] **64** 1

pill [pĭl] **41** 7

pillow [pĭl′ ō] **32** 16

pillowcase [pĭl′ ō kās′] **32** 15

pilot [pī′ lət] **56** 15

pin [pĭn] **23** 8, **94** 5, **101** 20

pincushion [pĭn′ kŏŏsh′ ən] **101** 3

pine [pīn] **60** 34

pineapple [pīn′ ăp′ əl] **8** 4

ping-pong [pĭng′ pŏng′] **94**

ping-pong ball [pĭng′ pŏng bŏl′] **94** 19

pinking shears [pĭng′ kĭng shïrz′]
   101 5

pipe [pīp] **16** 26, **35** 18

pipette [pī pĕt′] **78** 14

pit [pĭt] **8** 37a

pitcher [pĭch′ ər] **29** 4, **93** 12

pitcher's mound [pĭch′ ərz mownd′]
   93 11

pitchfork [pĭch′ förk′] **81** 14

pizza [pēt′ sə] **18** 30

plaid [plăd] **24** 22

plane [plān] **57** 18

planets [plăn′ əts] **74**

plant (v) [plănt] **26** 4

plants (n) [plănts] **60**

plate [plāt] **29** 13

plateau [plă tō′] **88** 1

platform [plăt′ förm′] **54** 11

playground [plā′ grownd′] **87** 15

playpen [plā′ pĕn′] **33** 30

pleasure boating [plĕzh′ ər bō′ tĭng] **59**

pliers [plī′ ərz] **36** 19

plug [plŭg] **37** 43d

plum [plŭm] **9** 34

plumber [plŭm′ ər] **85** 1

plunger [plŭn′ jər] **35** 14

Pluto [ploo′ tō] **74** 19

pocket [pŏk′ ət] **21** 41

pod [pŏd] **6** 17a

podium [pō′ dē əm] **99** 7

poinsettia [poyn sĕt′ē ə] **60** 15

poison ivy [poy′ zən ī′ vē] **61** 45

poison oak [poy′ zən ōk′] **61** 43

poison sumac [poy′ zən soo′ măk]
   61 44

poisonous plants [poy′ zə nəs plănts′]
   61

polar bear [pōl′ ər bër′] **69** 22

pole [pōl] **94** 34, **95** 14

police officer [pə lēs′ öf′ ə sər] **43** 6

police station [pə lēs′ stā′ shən] **43**

polish [pŏl′ ĭsh] **38** 3

polka dot [pō′ kə dŏt′] **24** 19

pond [pŏnd] **87** 8

pony [pō′ nē] **67** 20

poplar [pŏp′ lər] **61** 30

porch [pörch] **27** 6

pork [pörk] **10** 6

pork chops [pörk′ chŏps′] **18** 15

port [pört] **58**

porter [pör′ tər] **56** 5

porthole [pört′ hōl′] **58** 21

post [pōst] **23** 18

post office [pōst′ öf′ ĭs] **44** 9, **46**

postal worker [pōs′ təl wür′ kər] **46** 14

postcard [pōst′ kärd′] **46** 17

postmark [pōst′ märk′] **46** 9

pot [pŏt] **30** 13

pot holder [pŏt′ hōl′ dər] **30** 34

potato chips [pə tā′ tō chĭps′] **18** 4

potato(es) [pə tā′ tō(z)] **7** 23

potty [pŏt′ ē] **33** 33

pouch [powch] **66** 3c

pouched mammals [powcht′ măm′ əlz]
   66

poultry [pōl′ trē] **10**

pour [pör] **31** 4

power lines [pow′ ər līnz′] **80** 24

power sander [pow′ ər săn′ dər] **37** 26

power saw [pow′ ər sö′] **27** 25

power station [pow′ ər stā′ shən] **80** 20

prepositions [prep′ ə zĭ′ shənz]
   102, **103**

primates [prī′ māts] **69**

print [prĭnt] **24** 21

printer [prĭn′ tər] **83** 4

printout [prĭnt′ owt′] **83** 8

prints [prĭnts] **100** 11

prism [prĭz′ əm] **78** 1

private jet [prī′ vət jĕt′] **57** 3

produce [prŏd′ oos] **14** 9

programs [prō′ grămz] **99** 17

projector [prə jĕk′ tər] **100** 16

propane gas [prō′ pān găs′] **80** 30

propeller plane [prə pĕl′ ər plān′] **57** 7

prosecuting attorney
   [prŏ′ sə kyoo tĭng ə tür′ nē] **43** 17

prune [proon] **9** 22

public library [pŭb′ lĭk lī′ brër ē] **47**

public transportation
   [pŭb′ lĭk trăns pər tā′ shən] **54**

public telephone [pŭb′ lĭk tĕl′ ə fōn]
   44 7

puck [pŭk] **92** 17

pump [pŭmp] **13** 14, **52** 21

pumpkin [pŭmp′ kĭn] **7** 26

punishment [pŭn′ ĭsh mənt] **43**

pupil [pyoo′ pəl] **5** 48

puppy [pŭp′ ē] **69** 27

purse [pürs] **20** 23

push [pŏŏsh] **26** 12

putter [pŭt′ ər] **94** 9

puzzle [pŭz′ əl] **33** 31

pyramid [pïr′ ə mĭd′] **79** 25

quantities [kwŏn′ tə tēz] **12**

quarter [kwör′ tər] **11** 18, **13** 30,
   79 31

quarterback [kwör′ tər băk′] **93** 32

quill [kwĭl] **66** 11a

quilting [kwĭl′ tĭng] **101** 32

rabbit [răb′ ĭt] **66** 13

raccoon [ră koon′] **68** 7

race track [rās′ trăk′] **95**

(racing) handlebars
   [rā′ sĭng hăn′ dəl bärz] **52** 2

rack [răk] **47** 17, **78** 8

racket [răk′ ĭt] **94** 2

racquet [răk′ ĭt] **94** 29

racquetball [răk′ ĭt bŏl′] **94** 30

radiator [rā′ dē āt′ ər] **51** 56

radio [rā′ dē ō′] **50** 18

radish(es) [răd′ ĭsh (əz)] **7** 29

radius [rā′ dē əs] **79** 14

raft [răft] **89** 16

rafters [răf′ tərz] **82** 1

rafting [răf′ tĭng] **89**

rags [răgz] **35** 4

rain boots [rān′ boots′] **19** 25

raincoat [rān′ kōt′] **21** 38

rainy [rān′ ē] **25** 1

raise (one's hand) [rāz′ wŭnz hănd′]
   77 1

raisin(s) [rā′ zən(z)] **9** 24

rake (v) [rāk] **26** 10

rake (n) [rāk] **27** 30

ranch [rănch] **81**

ranch house [rănch′ hows′] **27**

ranching [rănch′ ĭng] **81**

rapids [răp′ ĭdz] **89** 17

rash [răsh] **40** 1

raspberries [răz′ bër′ ēz] **8** 16

rat [răt] **66** 7

rattle [răt′ əl] **33** 21

rattlesnake [răt′ əl snāk′] **65** 10

razor [rā′ zər] **23** 20

razor blades [rā′ zər blādz′] **23** 23

read [rēd] **77** 4

real estate agent [rēl′ ə stāt ā′ jənt]
  85 5

rear bumper [rïr′ bŭm′ pər] **50** 42

rearview mirror [rïr′ vyōō mïr′ ər]
  50 7

receipt [rə sēt′] **15** 20, **55** 24

receiver [rə sē′ vər] **100** 21

receptionist [rə sĕp′ shə nəst] **86** 17

recliner [rə klī′ nər] **28** 16

records [rĕk′ ərdz] **100** 23

rectangle [rĕk′ tăng′ gəl] **79** 19

Red Sea [rĕd′ sē′] **70** 29

redwood [rĕd′ wŏŏd′] **61** 25

(reel of) film [rēl′ əv fĭlm′] **100** 17

referee [rĕf′ ə rē′] **93** 22, **94** 16

reference section
  [rĕf′ ə rəns sĕk′ shən] **47** 21

(reference) librarian
  [rĕf′ ə rəns lī brër′ e ən] **47** 23

refill [rē′ fĭl′] **35** 11

refinery [rə fī′ nə rē] **80** 12

reflector [rə flĕk′ tər] **52** 25

refreshment stand
  [rə frĕsh′ mənt stănd′] **90** 2

refrigerator [rə frĭj′ ə rā′ tər] **30** 19

reins [rānz] **94** 22

relationships [rə lā′ shən shĭps′] **2**

remedies [rĕm′ ə dēz] **41**

remote control [rə mōt′ kən trōl′]
  28 17

repair [rə për′] **38** 10

repairperson [rə për′ pür′ sən] **84** 5

reporter [rə pör′ tər] **86** 11

reptiles [rĕp′ tĭlz] **65**

rescue [rĕs′ kyōō] **42**

restaurant [rĕs′ tə rənt] **16**

retriever [rə trē′ vər] **69** 26

return address [rə türn′ ă drĕs′] **46** 8

rhinoceros [rī nŏs′ ə rəs] **66** 16

Rhode Island [rōd′ ī′ lənd] **73** 39

rice [rīs] **60** 21

ride [rīd] **97** 13

rider [rī′ dər] **54** 6

rifle [rī′ fəl] **48** 21

right angle [rīt′ ăng′ gəl] **79** 23

right fielder [rīt′ fēl′ dər] **93** 3

right guard [rīt′ gärd′] **93** 28

right lane [rīt′ lān′] **53** 7

right tackle [rīt′ tăk′ əl] **93** 29

right triangle [rīt′ trī′ ăng gəl] **79** 22

rind [rīnd] **8** 8b

ring(s) [rĭng(z)] **23** 2, **74** 16a, **94** 17

ring binder [rĭng′ bīn′ dər] **76** 14

ring finger [rĭng′ fĭng′ gər] **4** 27

ring stand [rĭng′ stănd′] **78** 19

rink [rĭngk] **94** 25

Rio Grande River [rē′ ō grănd′ rĭv′ ər]
  71 57

rivers [riv′ ərz] **71**

road sign [rōd′ sīn′] **53** 23

road work [rōd′ würk′] **82**

roadrunner [rōd′ rŭn′ ər] **64** 32

roast [rōst] **10** 3, **10** 8

roasting pan [rōs′ tĭng păn′] **30** 17

robes [rōbz] **43** 11

robin [rŏb′ in] **64** 9

rock group [rŏk′ grōōp′] **99**

rocket [rŏk′ ət] **75** 13

rocks [rŏks] **88** 11

rocking chair [rŏk′ ĭng chër′] **33** 16

Rocky Mountains [rŏk′ ē mown′ tənz]
  71 40

rodents [rō′ dənts] **66**

roll [rōl] **12** 11, **18** 19

(roll of) film [rōl′ əv fĭlm′] **100** 10

roller [rōl′ ər] **37** 29

rolling pin [rōl′ ĭng pĭn′] **30** 25

rolodex [rōl′ ə dĕks′] **83** 14

rooster [rōō′ stər] **64** 21

roof [rōōf] **27** 4

root [rōōt] **60** 35d

rope [rōp] **89** 23

rose [rōz] **60** 18

rotor [rō′ tər] **57** 2a

rough [rŭf] **95** 6

router [row′ tər] **37** 37

row [rō] **47** 11, **81** 18

rowboat [rō′ bōt′] **59** 23

Rub′ al Khali Desert
  [rōōb′ ăl kŏl′ ē dĕz′ ərt] **71** 52

rubber tubing [rŭb′ ər tōōb′ ĭng] **78** 18

rudder [rŭd′ ər] **59** 5

rug [rŭg] **32** 28

ruler [rōō′ lər] **76** 23

run [rŭn] **96** 6

rung [rŭng] **82** 9

runner [rŭn′ ər] **91** 23, **94** 31

runway [rŭn′ wā′] **57** 19

saddle [săd′ əl] **94** 20

safety glasses [săf′ tē glăs′ əz] **78** 12

safety goggles [săf′ tē gŏg′ əlz] **94** 28

safety pin [săf′ tē pĭn′] **33** 11

Sahara Desert [sə hër′ ə dĕz′ ərt]
  71 51

sail [sāl] **59** 9

sailboard [sāl′ börd′] **59** 15

sailboat [sāl′ bōt′] **59** 4

sailor [sāl′ ər] **48** 14

salad bowl [săl′ əd bōl′] **29** 25

salad dressing [săl′ əd drĕs′ ĭng] **18** 12

salamander [săl′ ə măn′ dər] **65** 14

salesperson [sālz′ pür′ sən] **86** 12

salt shaker [sölt′ shā′ kər] **29** 10

sand (v) [sănd] **26** 14

sand (n) [sănd] **90** 31

sand dunes [sănd′ dōōnz′] **90** 12

sand trap [sănd′ trăp′] **95** 11

sandal [săn′ dəl] **20** 19

sandbox [sănd′ bŏks′] **87** 13

sandcastle [sănd′ kăs′ əl] **91** 32

sandpaper [sănd′ pā′ pər] **37** 27

sandwich [sănd′ wĭch] **16** 16

sanitation worker
  [săn ə tā′ shən wür′ kər] **49** 7

Saturn [săt′ ərn] **74** 16

saucepan [sös′ păn′] **30** 8

saucer [sö′ sər] **29** 21

sausage [sö′ sĭj] **10** 7

saw [sö] **36** 8

saxophone [săk′ sə fōn′] **98** 24

scaffolding [skăf′ əl dĭng] **82** 7

scale [skāl] **14** 7, **34** 32, **78** 4

scallop(s) [skăl′ əp(s)] **11** 35, **62** 10

scarecrow [skër′ krō′] **81** 19

scarf [skärf] **19** 19

scenery [sē′ nə rē] **99** 2

school [skool] **76, 77**

science lab [sī′ əns lăb′] **78**

scissors [sĭz′ərz] **101** 17

scoreboard [skör′ börd′] **93** 19

scorpion [skör′ pē ən] **63** 8

scouring pad [skowr′ ĭng păd′] **30** 11

scrape [skrāp] **26** 15

scraper [skrāp′ ər] **36** 14

screen [skrēn] **27** 19, **100** 14

screw [skroo] **37** 42

screwdriver [skroo′ drī′ vər] **37** 24

scrub [skrŭb] **38** 2

scuba tank [skoo′ bə tăngk′] **91** 37

sea gull [sē′ gŭl′] **64** 4

sea horse [sē′ hörs′] **65** 1

Sea of Japan [sē′ əv jə păn′] **70** 36

Sea of Okhotsk [sē′ əv ō kŏtsk′]
    70 35

seafood [sē′ food′] **10**

seal [sēl] **68** 12

seam [sēm] **101** 10

seas [sēz] **70**

seat [sēt] **52** 16, **54** 2

seat belt [sēt′ bĕlt′] **50** 23

second baseman [sĕk′ ənd bās′ mən]
    93 7

secretary [sĕk′ rə tër′ ē] **83** 11

section [sĕk′ shən] **8** 8a, **79** 15

security [sə kyoor′ ə tē] **56**

security guard [sə kyoor′ ə tē gärd′]
    56 9, **86** 14

sedan [sə dăn′] **51**

seed [sēd] **8** 8c

seesaw [sē′ sö′] **87** 18

serve [sürv] **17** 3, **96** 2

service area [sür′ vəs ër′ ē ə] **53** 11

sevice court [sür′ vəs kört′] **95** 1

service line [sür′ vəs līn′] **95** 3

set (the table) [sĕt′ dhə tā′ bəl] **17** 8

sewing [sō′ ĭng] **101**

sewing machine [sō′ ĭng mə shēn′]
    101 1

shade [shād] **33** 1

shaft [shăft] **80** 10

shampoo [shăm poo′] **34** 8

shank [shănk] **37** 43b

shark [shärk] **65** 5

shaving cream [shā′ vĭng krēm′] **23** 22

sheep [shēp] **67** 25, **81** 10

sheet [shēt] **32** 19

sheet music [shēt′ myoo′ zĭk] **98** 2

shelf [shĕlf] **14** 6, **47** 26

shell [shĕl] **48** 27, **62** 1a, **65** 18a,
    90 40

shellfish [shĕl′ fĭsh′] **11**

shepherd [shĕp′ ərd] **69** 28

shingle [shĭng′ gəl] **82** 2

ship [shĭp] **58** 9

shirt [shürt] **21** 46

shock absorbers [shŏk′ əb zör′ bərz]
    52 31

shoe [shoo] **21** 49

shoelace [shoo′ lās′] **20** 7

shoot [shoot] **97** 16

shop worker [shŏp′ wür′ kər] **85** 12

shopping bag [shŏp′ ĭng băg′] **20** 18

shopping basket [shŏp′ ĭng băs′ kət]
    14 8

shopping cart [shŏp′ ĭng kärt′] **15** 19

short [shört] **24** 1

short sleeve [shört′ slēv′] **20** 21

shorts [shörts] **20** 14

shortstop [shört′ stŏp′] **93** 5

shoulder [shōl′ dər] **4** 5, **53** 22

(shoulder) bag [shōl′ dər băg′] **21** 35

shovel (n) [shŭv′ əl] **27** 31, **82** 15,
    90 17

shovel (v) [shŭv′ əl] **26** 13

shower cap [show′ ər kăp′] **34** 3

shower curtain [show′ ər kür′ tən] **34** 5

shower head [show′ ər hĕd′] **34** 4

shrimp [shrĭmp] **11** 31, **62** 8

shutter [shŭt′ ər] **27** 8

shuttle car [shŭt′ əl kär′] **80** 8

side [sīd] **79** 10

side mirror [sīd′ mïr′ ər] **50** 2

sideburn [sīd′ bürn′] **4** 33

sidewalk [sīd′ wök′] **45** 25

Sierra Madre [sē ër′ ə mö′ drē] **71** 42

silo [sī′ lō] **81** 4

silverware [sĭl′ vər wër′] **29** 22

simple animals [sĭm′ pəl ăn′ ə məlz] **62**

singer [sĭng′ ər] **99** 24

sink [sĭngk] **34** 19

sister [sĭs′ tər] **3** 10

sister-in-law [sĭs′ tər ən lö′] **3** 8

six-pack [sĭks′ păk′] **13** 13

skate (n) [skāt] **94** 26

skate (v) [skāt] **97** 9

skein [skān] **101** 24

ski [skē] **95** 17

ski boot [skē′ boot′] **95** 15

ski cap [skē′ kăp′] **19** 16

ski lift [skē′ lĭft′] **95** 18

ski slope [skē′ slōp′] **95**

skier [skē′ ər] **94** 35

skis [skēz] **94** 33

skin [skĭn] **9** 37b

skirt [skürt] **21** 36

skunk [skŭngk] **68** 8

slacks [slăks] **20** 4

sleeping bag [slē′ pĭng băg′] **89** 26

sleepwear [slēp′ wër′] **22**

slice (n) [slīs] **13** 21

slice (v) [slīs] **31** 10

slide [slīd] **78** 31, **87** 12

slide projector [slīd′ prə jĕk′ tər]
    100 13

slides [slīdz] **100** 12

sling [slĭng] **39** 3

slippers [slĭp′ərz] **22** 18

slug [slŭg] **62** 4

small [smöl] **24** 7

smoke [smōk] **42** 15

smoke detector [smōk′ də tĕk′ tər]
    33 15

smokestack [smök′ stăk′] **58** 18,
    80 22

snacks [snăks] **14** 18

snail [snāl] **62** 1

snake [snāk] **65** 9

snap [snăp] **101** 13

sneakers [snē′ kərz] **20** 11

snorkel [snör′ kəl] **91** 34

snow plow [snō′ plow′] **49** 5

snowy [snō′ e] **25** 3

soap [sōp] **34** 15

soap dish [sōp′ dĭsh′] **34** 6

soccer [sŏk′ ər] **92**

soccer ball [sŏk′ ər böl′] **92** 26

socks [sŏks] **22** 17

sofa [sō**/** fə] **28** 25

soft drink [söft**/** drĭngk**/**] **16** 11

softball [söft**/** böl**/**] **92, 92** 10

solar collector [sō**/** lər kə lĕk**/** tər] **80** 17

solar eclipse [sō**/** lər ĭ klĭps**/**] **74** 10

solar system [sō**/** lər sĭs**/** təm] **74**

soldier [sōl**/** jər] **48** 16

sole [sōl] **20** 6

solid [sŏl**/** əd] **24** 20

solid figures [sŏl**/** əd fĭg**/** yərz] **79**

son [sŭn] **3** 16

Sony Walkman [sō**/** nē wök**/** mən] **100** 30

sore throat [sör**/** thrōt**/**] **40** 12

south [sowth] **71** 72

South America [sowth**/** ə mër**/** ə kə] **70** 2

South Atlantic [sowth**/** ăt lăn**/** tək] **70** 12

South Carolina [sowth**/** kăr ə lī**/** nə] **73** 40

South China Sea [sowth**/** chi**/** nə sē **/**] **70** 39

South Dakota [sowth**/** də kō**/** tə] **73** 41

South Pacific [sowth pə sĭf**/** ək] **70** 10

space probe [spās**/** prōb] **75** 4

space program [spās**/** prō**/** grăm] **75**

space shuttle [spās**/** shŭt**/** əl] **75** 14

space station [spās**/** stā**/** shən] **75** 1

space suit [spās**/** sōōt**/**] **75** 6

spacecraft [spās**/** krăft**/**] **75**

spaghetti [spə gĕt**/** ē] **18** 10

spaniel [spăn**/** yəl] **69** 24

spare ribs [spër**/** rĭbz**/**] **10** 10

spare tire [spër**/** tīr**/**] **51** 39

sparrow [spăr**/** ō] **64** 10

spatula [spăch**/**ə lə] **27** 21

speaker [spē**/** kər] **28** 21, **100** 24

speed limit sign [spēd**/** lĭm ət sīn**/**] **53** 8

speedometer [spə dŏm**/**ə tər] **50** 10

spider [spī**/** dər] **63** 16

spinach [spĭn**/** əch] **6** 8

spinal cord [spī**/** nəl körd**/**] **5** 58

spiral notebook [spī**/** rəl nōt**/** bŏok] **76** 15

split [splĭt] **11** 17

split end [splĭt**/** ĕnd**/**] **93** 24

spoke [spōk] **52** 26

sponge [spŭnj] **34** 7

(sponge) mop [spŭnj**/** mŏp**/**] **35** 6

(spool of) thread [spōōl**/** əv thrĕd**/**] **101** 2

spoon [spōōn] **29** 8

sports car [spörts**/** kär**/**] **53** 17

sports [spörts] **92-97**

spotlight [spŏt **/** līt**/**] **99** 4

sprain [sprān] **40** 13

spray can [sprā**/** kăn**/**] **13** 24

spray starch [sprā**/** stärch**/**] **35** 21

spread [sprĕd] **17** 11

Spring [sprĭng] **26**

sprinkler [sprĭng**/** klər] **27** 13, **87** 14

sprocket [sprŏk**/** ət] **52** 20

square [skwër] **79** 9

squid [skwĭd] **62** 5

squirrel [skwür**/** əl] **66** 10

stage [stāj] **99** 5

staircase [stër**/** kās] **28** 12

stake [stāk] **89** 30

stamp [stămp] **46** 10

stands [stăndz] **93** 10

staple remover [stāp**/** əl rə moo**/** vər] **83** 29

stapler [stāp**/** lər] **83** 27

star [stär] **74** 4

starfish [stär**/** fĭsh**/**] **62** 7

starting gate [stär**/** tĭng gāt**/**] **95** 20

station [stā**/** shən] **55** 18

station wagon [stā**/** shən wăg**/** ən] **50**

steak [stāk] **10** 5, **11** 29, **18** 21

steam [stēm] **31** 12

steamer [stēm**/** ər] **30** 3

steering wheel [stĭr**/** ĭng wēl**/**] **50** 8

stem [stĕm] **8** 2a, **60** 1a

step [stĕp] **28** 13

stepladder [stĕp**/** lăd**/** ər] **35** 1

stereo cassette player [stĕr**/** ē ō kə sĕt plā **/** ər] **100** 25

stereo system [stĕr**/** ē ō sĭs**/** təm] **28** 20

stern [stürn] **58** 11

stethoscope [stĕth**/** ə skōp**/**] **39** 9

stewing meat [stoo**/** ĭng mēt] **10** 4

stick [stĭk] **12** 5

stick shift [stĭk**/** shĭft**/**] **50** 24

sting [stĭng] **63** 8a

stingray [stĭng**/** rā**/**] **65** 6

stir [stür] **31** 1

stitch [stĭch] **101** 19

stitches [stĭch**/** əz] **39** 21

stockings [stŏk**/** ĭngz] **22** 6

stomach [stŭm**/** ək] **5** 66

stomachache [stŭm**/** ək āk**/**] **40** 7

stool [stōōl] **78** 34

stopper [stŏp**/** ər] **34** 10, **78** 10

stork [störk] **64** 30

stove [stōv] **30** 30

straight line [strāt**/** līn**/**] **79** 1

(strand of) beads [strănd**/** əv bēdz**/**] **23** 7

strap [străp] **54** 8

straw [strö] **16** 10

strawberry [strö**/** bër**/** ē] **8** 15

strawberry shortcake [strö**/** bër ē shört**/** kāk] **18** 26

stream [strēm] **88** 6

street [strēt] **45** 31

street cleaner [strēt**/** klē**/** nər] **49** 1

street sign [strēt**/** sīn**/**] **44** 8

streetcar [strēt**/** kär**/**] **55** 30

streetlight [strēt**/** līt**/**] **45** 29

stretch [strĕch] **95** 19

stretch bandage [strĕch**/** băn**/** dĭj] **40** 13a

stretcher [strĕch**/** ər] **39** 12

stretchie [strĕch**/** ē] **33** 19

string [strĭng] **46** 20, **98** 10a

string bean(s) [strĭng**/** bēn(z)**/**] **6** 15

strings [strĭngz] **98**

striped [strīpt] **24** 17

stroller [strō**/** lər] **33** 14

student [stōō**/** dənt] **76** 19

stuffed animal [stŭft**/** ăn ə məl] **33** 27

subject [sŭb**/** jəkt] **47** 10

submarine [sŭb**/** mə rēn**/**] **48** 7

subway [sŭb**/** wā**/**] **54**

subway station [sŭb**/** wā stā**/** shən] **44** 16

sugar (packet) [shŏog**/** ər păk**/** ət] **16** 13

sugar bowl [shŏog**/** ər bōl**/**] **29** 23

sugarcane [shŏog**/** ər kān**/**] **60** 20

suitcase [sōōt**/** kās**/**] **56** 7

Summer [sŭm**/** ər] **26**

sun [sŭn] **74** 7, **80** 3

sunbather [sŭn′ bā′ dhər] **90** 19

sundae [sŭn′ dē] **18** 23

sunflower [sŭn′ flŏw′ ər] **60** 19

sunglasses [sŭn′ glăs′ əz] **90** 14

sunny [sŭn′ ē] **25** 4

(sunnyside-up) egg
   [sŭn′ ē sīd ŭp′ ĕg′] **18** 32

sunroof [sŭn′ rōof′] **51** 44

suntan lotion [sŭn′ tăn lō′ shən] **91** 39

supermarket [sōo′ pər mär′ kət] **14**

surf [sürf] **97** 12

surfboard [sürf′ börd′] **91** 25

surgery [sür′ jə rē] **41** 2

suspect [sŭs′ pĕkt] **43** 3

swan [swŏn] **64** 28

sweatband [swĕt′ bănd′] **20** 12

sweater [swĕt′ ər] **19** 7, **19** 13, **19** 23

sweatpants [swĕt′ pănts′] **20** 10

sweatshirt [swĕt′ shürt′] **20** 8

sweep [swēp] **38** 7

swimmer [swĭm′ ər] **91** 28

swing [swĭng] **33** 24

swings [swĭngz] **87** 16

switch [swĭch] **37** 43c

switchboard [swĭch′ börd′] **83** 3

switchboard operator
   [swĭch′ börd ŏp′ ə rā tər] **83** 1

swordfish [sörd′ fĭsh′] **65** 3

synthesizer [sĭn′ thə sī′ zər] **99** 21

syringe [sə rĭnj′] **39** 27

syrup [sĭr′ əp] **18** 6

T-shirt [tē′ shürt′] **21** 29

table [tā′ bəl] **29** 7

tablecloth [tā′ bəl klöth′] **29** 16

tablet [tăb′ lət] **41** 6

taco [tŏ′ kō] **18** 24

tadpole [tăd′ pōl′] **65** 16

tail [tāl] **57** 10, **65** 3a, **66** 3a

taillight [tāl′ līt′] **50** 31

tailor [tā′ lər] **84** 6

take [tāk] **17** 10

takeoff [tāk′ ŏf′] **57**

Takla Makan Desert
   [tŏk′ lə mə kŏn′ dĕz′ ərt] **71** 53

tambourine [tăm′ bə rēn′] **98** 17

tank [tăngk] **48** 10

tank top [tăngk′ tŏp′] **20** 13

tanker [tăngk′ ər] **58** 15

tap [tăp] **16** 20

tape [tāp] **46** 22

tape measure [tāp′ mĕzh′ ər] **36** 21,
   101 15

taxi [tăk′ sē] **55**

taxi stand [tăk′ sē stănd′] **55** 28

taxicab [tăk′ sē kăb′] **55** 27

tea [tē] **16** 15

teacher [tē′ chər] **76** 4

teakettle [tē′ kĕt′ əl] **30** 28

team sports [tēm′ spörts′] **92**

teapot [tē′ pŏt′] **29** 19

tear [tër] **77** 9

teddy bear [tĕd′ ē bër′] **33** 3

tee [tē] **95** 13

telephone [tĕl′ ə fōn′] **83** 15

telescope [tĕl′ ə skōp′] **74** 22

television [tĕl′ ə vĭzh′ ən] **28** 18, **100** 5

teller [tĕl′ ər] **86** 15

temperature [tĕm′ pər ə chər] **25** 6

Tennessee [tĕn′ ə sē′] **73** 42

tennis [tĕn′ əs] **94**

tennis ball [tĕn′ əs böl′] **94** 1

tennis court [tĕn′ əs kört′] **95**

tent [tĕnt] **89** 24

tentacle [tĕn′ tə kəl] **62** 12a

terminal [türm′ ə nəl] **51** 55, **58** 29

terminal building [türm′ ə nəl bĭl′ dĭng]
   57 16

termite [tür′ mīt] **63** 11

terrier [tĕr′ ē ər] **69** 25

test tube [tĕst′ tōob′] **78** 9

Texas [tĕk′ səs] **73** 43

textbook [tĕkst′ bŏok′] **76** 26

theater [thē′ ə tər] **99**

thermometer
   [thər möm′ ə tər] **25** 5, **78** 22

thermos [thür′ məs] **88** 14

thigh [thī] **4** 18, **11** 19

thimble [thĭm′ bəl] **101** 21

third (1/3) [thürd] **79** 32

third baseman [thürd′ bās′ mən] **93** 4

thorn [thörn] **60** 18c

thread [thrĕd] **37** 42b, **101** 2

three-piece suit [thrē′ pēs sōot] **21** 40

throat [thrōt] **5** 59

through [thrōo] **103** 1

throw [thrō] **97** 10

thumb [thŭm] **4** 24

thumbtack [thŭm′ tăk′] **76** 25

ticket [tĭk′ ət] **55** 16, **56** 4

ticket window [tĭk′ ət wĭn′ dō] **55** 19

tie (n) [tī] **21** 47

tie (v) [tī] **77** 12

tie clip [tī′ klĭp′] **23** 14

tie pin [tī′ pĭn′] **23** 13

tiger [tī′ gər] **68** 2

tight [tīt] **24** 3

tighten [tī′ tən] **38** 4

tight end [tīt′ ĕnd′] **93** 30

tights [tīts] **19** 14

tile [tīl] **34** 27

timer [tī′ mər] **78** 13

timetable [tīm′ tă′ bəl] **55** 20

tip [tĭp] **55** 22

tire [tīr] **50** 37, **52** 28

tissues [tĭsh′ ōoz] **32** 13

title [tī′ təl] **47** 9

to [tōo] **103** 9

toast [tōst] **18** 34

toaster [tōs′ tər] **30** 16

toe [tō] **5** 54

toenail [tō′ nāl′] **5** 56

toilet [toy′ lət] **34** 29

toilet brush [toy′ lət brŭsh′] **34** 31

toilet paper [toy′ lət pā′ pər] **34** 30

toiletries [toy′ lə trēz′] **23**

token booth [tō′ kən bōoth′] **54** 13

tollbooth [tōl′ bōoth′] **53** 27

tomato(es) [tə mā′ tō(z)] **7** 19

tongs [tŏngz] **78** 29

tongue [tŭng] **4** 41

tongue depressor [tŭng′ də prĕs′ ər]
   40 12a

toolbox [tōol′ bŏks′] **36** 23

toolshed [tōol′ shĕd′] **27** 28

tooth [tōoth] **4** 42

toothache [tōoth′ āk′] **40** 9

toothbrush [tōoth′ brŭsh′] **34** 21

toothless mammals [tōoth′ ləs măm′ əlz]
   66

toothpaste [tōoth′ pāst′] **34** 16

tortoise [tör′ təs] **65** 18

tossed salad [töst′ săl′ əd] **18** 13

touch [tŭch] **77** 2

touring handlebars
[tŏŏr′ ĭng hăn′ dəl bärz] **52** 12
tow truck [tō′ trŭk] **49** 2
toward [törd] **103** 4
towel rack [tow′ əl răk′] **34** 25
towrope [tō′ rōp′] **59** 11
toy chest [toy′ chĕst′] **33** 29
track [trăk] **54** 10, **94** 32
track and field [trăk′ ənd fēld′] **94**
tractor [trăk′ tər] **81** 15
tractor trailer [trăk′ tər trā′ lər] **49** 15
traffic cop [trăf′ ək kŏp′] **44** 10
traffic light [trăf′ ək līt′] **45** 21
trailer [trā′ lər] **53** 10
train [trān] **55**
training wheels [trān′ ĭng wēlz′] **52** 1
transcript [trăn′ skrĭpt] **43** 15
transfer [trăns′ fər] **54** 4
transformer [trăns för′ mər] **80** 25
transmission towers
[trănz mĭsh′ ən tow′ ərz] **80** 23
transportation [trăns′ pər tā′ shən] **54**
transporter [trăns′ pör tər] **49** 17
trash basket [trăsh′ băs′ kət] **44** 15
trash can [trăsh′ kăn′] **87** 11
travel agent [trăv′ əl ā′ jənt] **84** 4
traveler [trăv′ ə lər] **56** 3
tray [trā] **16** 33
tray table [trā′ tā′ bəl] **56** 22
treatments [trēt′ mənts] **41**
tree [trē] **61** 35
trees [trēz] **60**
triangle [trī′ ăng′ gəl] **79** 6
tricycle [trī′ sĭ kəl] **52** 6
trigger [trĭg′ ər] **48** 22
tripod [trī′ pod] **100** 9
trim [trĭm] **26** 8
trombone [trŏm bōn′] **98** 23
trough [tröf] **81** 25
trout [trowt] **65** 2
trowel [trow′ əl] **27** 27
truck [trŭk] **49**, **53** 25
truck driver [trŭk′ drī′ vər] **49** 16
trumpet [trŭm′ pət] **98** 25
trunk [trŭngk] **51** 40, **61** 35b, **66** 17a
tub [tŭb] **12** 6
tuba [tōō′ bə] **98** 27
tube [tōōb] **13** 15, **91** 29

tugboat [tŭg′ bōt′] **58** 13
tulip [tōō′ ləp] **60** 1
turkey [tür′ kē] **10** 23, **64** 20
turnip [tür′ nəp] **7** 34
turn signal lever [türn′ sĭg nəl lĕ′ vər] **50** 11
turn signal lights [türn′ sĭg nəl līts′] **51** 50
turnstile [türn′ stīl′] **54** 12
turntable [türn′ tā′ bəl] **100** 18
turtle [tür′ təl] **65** 12
(turtleneck) sweater
[tür′ təl nĕk swĕ′ tər] **19** 13
tusk [tŭsk] **66** 17b
TV antenna [tē′ vē ăn tĕn′ ə] **27** 3
tweezers [twē′ zərz] **78** 32
twig [twĭg] **61** 33a
(two-door) sedan [tōō′ dör sə dăn′] **51**
type [tīp] **77** 10
typewriter [tīp′ rī′ tər] **83** 10
typing chair [tī′ pĭng chër′] **83** 17
typist [tī′ pəst] **83** 6
U.S. mailbox [yōō′ ĕs māl′ bŏks] **46** 6
U.S. Postal System
[yōō′ ĕs pōs′ təl sĭs təm] **46**
ukulele [yōō′ kə lā′ lē] **98** 3
umbrella [ŭm brĕl′ ə] **20** 24
umpire [ŭm′ pīr] **92** 1, **93** 17
uncle [ŭng′ kəl] **3** 3
under [ŭn′ dər] **102** 8
underpants [ŭn′ dər pănts′] **22** 3
undershirt [ŭn′ dər shürt′] **22** 1
underwear [ŭn′ dər wër′] **22**
uniform [yōō′ nə förm′] **21** 45, **92** 9
United States of America
[yōō nī′ təd stāts′ əv əmër′ ə kə] **72**
universe [yōō′ nə vürs′] **74**
up [ŭp] **103** 11
upper arm [ŭp′ ər ärm′] **4** 7
Urals [yōōr′ əlz] **71** 46
uranium rods [yōō rā′ nē əm rŏdz′] **80** 15
Uranus [yōōr′ ə nəs] **74** 17
usher [ŭsh′ ər] **99** 16
Utah [yōō′ tö] **73** 44
utility pole [yōō tĭl′ ə tē pōl′] **80** 26
utility room [yōō tĭl′ ə tē rōōm′] **35**

(V-neck) sweater [vē′ nĕk swĕt′ ər] **19** 23
vacuum [văk′ yōōm] **38** 14
vacuum cleaner [văk′ yōōm klē′ nər] **35** 16
valve [vălv] **52** 27
van [văn] **53** 26
vase [vās] **28** 6
VCR (videocassette recorder)
[vē′ sē är′]/
[vĭd′ ē ō kə sĕt′ rə kör′ dər] **100** 4
vegetables [vĕj′ tə bəlz] **6**
vehicles and equipment
[vē′ ə kəlz ənd ə kwĭp′ mənt] **48**
vein [vān] **5** 68
vendor [vĕn′ dər] **87** 3
vent [vĕnt] **50** 21
Venus [vē′ nəs] **74** 12
verbs [vürbz] **17**, **26**, **31**, **38**, **77**, **96**
Vermont [vür mŏnt′] **73** 45
vest [vĕst] **21** 39
video [vĭd′ē ō] **100**
video camera [vĭd′ ē ō kăm′ ə rə] **100** 1
videocassette (tape)
[vĭd′ ē ō kə sĕt′ tāp′] **100** 3
vine [vīn] **61** 42
viola [vē ōl′ ə] **98** 8
violet [vī′ ə lət] **60** 16
violin [vī ə lĭn′] **98** 7
Virginia [vər jĭn′ yə] **73** 46
vise [vīs] **37** 36
visor [vĭz′ ər] **50** 5
volleyball [vŏl′ ē böl′] **92**, **92** 22
waders [wā′ dərz] **88** 10
waist [wāst] **4** 13
waiter [wā tər] **16** 5
waitress [wā′ trəs] **16** 2
walk [wök] **77** 8
walker [wök′ ər] **33** 23
wall [wöl] **28** 3
wall unit [wöl′ yōō′ nət] **28** 19
wall-to-wall carpeting
[wöl′ tə wöl kär′ pə tĭng] **28** 15
wallet [wöl′ ət] **20** 9
walnut(s) [wöl′ nət(s)] **9** 29
walrus [wöl′ rŭs] **68** 11
warm [wörm] **25** 8

wash [wǒsh] **38** 16

washcloth [wǒsh′klöth′] **34** 22

washer [wǒsh′ ər] **37** 40

washing machine
[wǒsh′ ĭng mə shēn′] **35** 30

Washington [wǒsh′ĭng tən] **73** 47

wasp [wǒsp] **63** 20

wastepaper basket
[wāst′ pā pər bǎs′ kət] **34** 13

watch [wǒch] **23** 10

watchband [wǒch′bǎnd′] **23** 11

water (n) [wǒt′ ər] **42** 16, **91** 30

water (v) [wǒt′ ər] **26** 5

water fountain [wǒt′ ər fown′ tən]
87 19

water glass [wǒt′ ər glǎs′] **29** 6

waterfall [wǒt′ər föl] **80** 11, **89** 18

water-skier [wǒt′ər skē′ ər] **59** 10

watercress [wǒt′ər krěs′] **6** 5

watering can [wǒt′ər ĭng kǎn′] **27** 16

watermelon [wǒt′ər měl′ ən] **9** 26

wave [wāv] **91** 24

weapon [wěp′ənz] **48**

weather [wědh′ər] **25**

weather forecaster
[wědh′ər för′ kǎst ər] **86** 1

weather satellite [wědh′ər sǎt′ ə līt]
75 3

weaving [wē′ vĭng] **101** 30

web [wěb] **63** 15

wedding ring [wěd′ĭng rĭng′] **23** 4

weights [wāts] **78** 5

west [wěst] **71** 74

West Virginia [wěst′ vər jĭn′ yə] **73** 48

wet [wět] **25** 15

wet suit [wět′ sōot′] **91** 38

whale [wāl] **68** 9

wheat [wēt] **60** 22

wheat farm [wēt′ färm′] **81**

(wheat) field [wēt′ fēld′] **81** 16

wheel [wēl] **52** 4

wheelbarrow [wēl′ bǎr′ ō] **27** 32,
82 23

wheelchair [wēl′ chër′] **39** 2

whistle [wĭs′ əl] **90** 5

whole [hōl] **11** 27, **79** 29

whole (chicken) [hōl′ chĭk′ ən] **11** 16

width [wĭdth] **79** 35

wife [wīf] **2** 4

willow [wĭl′ ō] **61** 31

wind [wĭnd] **80** 4

windbreaker [wĭnd′ brā′ kər] **19** 5

windlass [wĭnd′ ləs] **58** 23

windmill [wĭnd′ mĭl′] **80** 19

window [wĭn′ dō] **27** 7, **46** 15

window cleaner [wĭn′ dō klē′ nər]
35 10

windpipe [wĭnd′ pīp′] **5** 60

windshield [wĭnd′ shēld′] **51** 45

windshield wiper [wĭnd′ shēld wī′ pər]
50 6

windsurfer [wĭnd′ sür′ fər] **59** 14

windy [wĭn′ dē] **25** 13

wine [wīn] **16** 19

wine glass [wīn′ glǎs′] **29** 5

wing [wĭng] **11** 22, **57** 9, **63** 4a,
64 1a

Winter [wĭn′ tər] **26**

wipe [wīp] **38** 5

wire [wīr] **37** 35

wire mesh screen [wīr′ měsh skrēn′]
78 6

Wisconsin [wĭs kǒn′ sən] **73** 49

witness [wĭt′ nəs] **43** 13

witness stand [wĭt′ nəs stǎnd′] **43** 18

wolf [woolf] **69** 29

woman [woom′ən] **2** 1

wood [wood] **36** 4

wood plane [wood′ plān′] **37** 32

woodpecker [wood′ pěk′ ər] **64** 17

woods [woodz] **89** 32

woodwinds [wood′ wĭndz′] **98**

wool [wool] **101** 23

word processor [würd′ prǒ′ sěs ər]
83 7

work gloves [würk′ glŭvz′] **27** 26

workbench [würk′ běnch′] **36** 22

workshop [würk′ shǒp′] **36**

world [würld] **70**

worm [würm] **62** 11

wrench [rěnch] **36** 10

wrist [rĭst] **4** 21

write [rīt] **77** 7

writer [rī′ tər] **86** 7

Wyoming [wī ō′ mĭng] **73** 50

X ray [ěks′ rā′] **39** 1

X ray screener [ěks′ rā skrē′ nər] **56** 11

xylophone [zī′ lə fōn′] **98** 31

yam [yǎm] **7** 24

Yangtze River [yǎng′ sē rĭv′ ər] **71** 69

yarn [yärn] **101** 31

Yellow Sea [yěl′ ō sē′] **70** 37

Yenisey River [yěn′ ə sā′ rĭv′ ər]
71 65

Yukon River [yōo′ kǒn rĭv′ ər] **71** 56

zebra [zē′ brə] **66** 18

zinnia [zĭn′ ē ə] **60** 13

zip code [zĭp′ kōd′] **46** 12

zipper [zĭp′ ər] **101** 16

zoo [zōo] **87** 1

zucchini [zōo kē′ nē] **7** 27

a (la cancha de golf) **103** 9

a (la colina) **103** 11

a cuadros **24** 18

a través de (el faro) **103** 1

abajo (del gato blanco) **102** 3

abarrotes **15** 24

abdomen **4** 14

abedul **61** 32

abeja **63** 19

abierto **24** 15

abogado defensor **43** 22

abordaje **56**

abrelatas **30** 4

abrigo **19** 24, **42** 13

abrigo de invierno **19** 8

abrir **31** 3

abuela **3** 1

abuelo **3** 2

abuelos **2** 10

acampando **89**

accesorios **35** 17

acebo **61** 37

aceitar **38** 12

aceite de motor **80** 33

acelerador **50** 27

acera **45** 25

acolchado (sustantivo) **101** 32

acomodador **99** 16

acoplado **49** 18

acordeón **98** 28

actividades al aire libre **88, 89**

actor **99** 19

actriz **99** 20

acumulador **51** 54

acusado **43** 23

aderezo **18** 12

Africa **70** 4

agalla **65** 3c

agarrar **17** 10, **96** 4

agarradera **30** 34, **54** 8

agente de bienes raíces **85** 5

agente de viajes **84** 4

agrifolio **61** 37

agua **42** 16, **91** 30

aguacate **9** 33

aguantar **17** 12

aguaviva **62** 12

aguijón **63** 8a

el águila **64** 5

aguja **39** 26, **61** 34a, **101** 18

aguja de cartucho **100** 19

aguja de gancho **101** 29

aguja de tejer **101** 25

agujeta **20** 7

aire acondicionado **32** 11

ajo **7** 25

ajolote **65** 16

al otro lado de (el agua) **103** 6

ala **11** 22, **57** 9, **63** 4a, **64** 1a

ala extrema **93** 24, **93** 30

Alabama **72** 1

alacena de loza **29** 2

alacrán **63** 8

álamo **61** 30

Alaska **72** 2

albaricoque **9** 25

albóndigas **18** 11

alcachofa **6** 11

alcancía de cuota **54** 5

alcantarilla **45** 32

alce **67** 35

alcohol **39** 22

aleta **65** 3b

aletas **91** 36

alfiler **101** 20

alfiler de corbata **23** 13

alfiletero **101** 3

alfombra **32** 28, **50** 22

alfombra (de baño) **34** 12

alfombrado (de pared a pared) **28** 15

algodón **39** 23

algodoncito **33** 10

alijadora **36** 14

alicate **36** 19

alimentos congelados **14** 2

alimentos de mar Mariscos **11** C

alimentos preparados comunes **18**

almeja(s) **11** 32, **62** 3

almendra(s) **9** 31

almíbar **18** 6

almidón en lata rociadora **35** 21

almohada **32** 16

Alpes **71** 44

alpinismo **89**

alrededor de (el faro) **103** 2

alta presión sanguínea **40** 10

alto **24** 11

altoparlante **76** 3, **100** 24

altura **79** 34

alunizaje **75** B

ama de llaves **85** 8

amarrar **77** 12

Amazonas **71** 59

ambulancia **42** 6

ametralladora **48** 25

amortiguadores **52** 31

amplificador de microfilm **47** 14

anacardo(s) **9** 27

ancho **79** 35

el ancla **58** 24

anclaje **59** 19

andadera **33** 23

anador **33** 23

Andes **71** 43

anfibios y reptiles **65** B

anguila **65** 4

ángulo agudo **79** 8

ángulo obtuso **79** 5

ángulo recto **79** 23

anillo(s) **23** 2, **74** 16a

anillo de boda **23** 4

anillo de compromiso **23** 3

animal de peluche **33** 27

Animales sencillos **62**

anotador **43** 14

Antártica **70** 7

Antártico **70** 14

antebrazo **4** 9

antena **51** 46, **62** 1b

antena de televisión **27** 3

anteojos **21** 44

anular **4** 27

anzar **97** 10

apagador **32** 25

aparador **29** 29

aparejo **89** 22

apartamentos **45** 23

ápice **79** 21

apio **6** 10

apretado **24** 3

apretar **38** 4

arándano agrios **8** 13
arándano azules **8** 14
araña **63** 16
arandela **37** 40
árbitro **92** 1, **93** 17, **93** 22, **94** 16
árbol **61** 35
árbol frutal **81** 2
árboles **61**
arbustos **61** 41
arce **61** 38
archivero **83** 21
archivista **83** 23
archivo **83** 22
arco **79** 16, **98** 7a
arcón **15** 16
ardilla **66** 10
ardillita **66** 6
el área de carga **57** 12
área de juego **87** 15
área de picnic **88**
área de servicios **53** 11
área habitacional **75** 11
área postal **46** 12
área verde **95** 10
área verde y plana **95** 12
arena **91** 31
arenoso **71** 55
arete de broche **23** 16
arete de presión **23** 15
aretes **23** 1
Arizona **72** 3
Arkansas **72** 4
arma **43** 7
Armada **48** 15
armadillo **66** 2
armario **29** 2, **76** 6
armas y munición **48** C
armazón **80** 2
aros para cortina **34** 2
arquitecto **86** 8
arreglista **99** 22
arrojar **97** 10
arroyuelo **88** 6
arroz **60** 21
arteria **5** 69
Artico **70** 8
artículos de tocador y maquillaje **23** B

artículos del hogar **15** 15
el, la artista **86** 3
asado **10** 3, **18** 14
asador **30** 33
asar **31** 13
ascensor **45** 17
ascensor de esquíes **95** 18
Asia **70** 5
asiento **16** 25, **52** 16, **54** 2
asiento deportivo **50** 16
asiento para niño **50** 33
asiento trasero **50** 32
asistente **53** 12
asoleadera **27** 5
aspiradora **35** 16
aspirar **38** 14
asta **67** 35a
asteroide **74** 20
astil **37** 43b
astronauta **75** 5
Atacama **71** 50
atajador derecho **93** 29
atajador izquierdo **93** 25
Atlántico del norte **70** 11
Atlántico del sur **70** 12
atlas **47** 20
atletismo **94**
atrás **23** 19
audífonos **100** 29, **83** 2
audio **100** D
auditorio **99** 15
auriculares **83** 2
Australia **70** 6
autobús **54** A, **53** 20
autor **47** 8
avellana(s) **9** 30
aventar **97** 10
Aves **64**
aves de corral **11** B
el avestruz **64** 12
aviador **48** 20
avión de caza **48** 1
avión de motor **57** 7
aviones **57**
avispa **63** 20
axila **4** 10
ayudante **39** 8, **53** 12

ayudante de camarero **16** 3
azafrán croco **60** 9
azúcar (paquetito de) **16** 13
azucarera **29** 23
azucena **60** 3
azulejo **34** 27
babero **33** 20
babosa **62** 4
baboso **62** 4
Bahía Baffin **70** 16
Bahía de Bengala **70** 32
Bahía del Hudson **70** 18
el bailarín **99** 3
la bailarina **99** 3
bajada **95** C
bajo **24** 12, **98** 10, **99** 23
bajón **98** 14
bala **48** 26
balcón **27** 6, **99** 14
balde **90** 16
ballena **68** 9
el ballet **99** A
balón **92** 21, **92** 26
baloncesto **92**
balsa **89** 16
banca **44** 14, **87** 10
banco **43** 16, **78** 34, **93** 13
banda **15** 23, **20** 12, **56** 12
banda (del ventilador) **51** 53
bandeja **16** 33, **37** 28
bandeja de asar **30** 17
bandera **76** 1, **95** 9
banderín **95** 9
bañera **34** 11
banjo **98** 5
el, la bañista **90** 19
el baño **34**
banqueta **45** 25
baqueta **43** 8
bar **16** B, **16** 24
barba **4** 39
barbilla **4** 3
barcaza **58** 12
barco de carga **58** 9
barco de guerra **48** 5
barco tanque **58** 15
barquillo **18** 36

barquillo de nieve **18** 36

barra de balance **94** 24

barra de pan **12** 7

barra **13** 18, **16** 24

barranca **89** 21

barredora **49** 1

barrer **38** 7

barrita **12** 5

báscula **34** 32

base **79** 7, **93** 6, **93** 15

basinica **33** 33

bastilla **101** 12

basurero **34** 13, **35** 31, **44** 15, **87** 11

bata **43** 11

bata (de baño) **22** 20

bata de noche **22** 21

bate **92** 5

batea **12** 6

bateador **92** 7, **93** 14

batería **51** 54

baterista **99** 27

batir **31** 8

batuta **99** 9

baúl **51** 40

baúl de juguetes **33** 29

bayas **8**

bayoneta **48** 24

bebé **2** 5

bebedero **81** 25, **87** 19

beber **17** 2

bebidas **14** 14

becerro **67** 31

béisbol **92**

bellota **61** 33b

berenjena **7** 21

berro **6** 5

betabel(es) **7** 33

biberón **33** 17

la biblioteca pública **47**

bibliotecaria **47** 23

bicicleta(s) **52** , **52** 15

bicicleta de hombre **52** 11

bicicleta de mujer **52** 3

bicicleta para campo **52** 8

biftec **10** 5

bigote **4** 40

billete(s) **13** 25

billete de transbordo **54** 4

billetera **20** 9

binoculares **90** 7

bisonte **67** 19

bisquet **18** 27

bisté **10** 5, **11** 29, **18** 21

blanqueador **35** 26

block (de papel) **83** 26

block para mensajes **83** 25

bloques **33** 32

blusa **21** 34

boca **4** 2, **62** 13a

bocadillos **15** 18

bocina **28** 21, **50** 12, **52** 5, **76** 3, **100** 24

bodega **58** 8

boina **19** 22

bola **5** 52

bola de boliche **94** 6

bola de frontón **94** 12

bola de frontón con raqueta **94** 30

bola de golf **94** 7

bola de ping-pong **94** 19

bola de tenis **94** 1

bolardo **58** 26

boleto **54** 4, **55** 16, **56** 4

boliche **94**

bolígrafo **76** 22

bolillos de tambor **98** 19a

bolla **59** 19

bolo **94** 5

bolos **94**

bolsa **12** 8, **15** 25, **21** 41, **66** 3c

bolsa de compras **20** 18

bolsa de correo **46** 4

bolsa de golf **95** 7

bolsa de hielo **41** 4

bolsa para dormir **89** 26

bolsillo **21** 41

bolso **21** 35, **20** 23

bolso de mano **56** 2

bomba de agua para incendios **42** 9

bomba de aire **53** 13

bomba de gasolina **53** 14

bomba **35** 14, **48** 3

bombardero **48** 2

bombero **42** 10

bombilla **35** 22

bongos **98** 22

bordado **101** 27

borde **53** 22

borrador **76** 11, **76** 21

borrar **77** 3

borrego **67** 24

borregos **81** 10

bosques **89** 32

bota de esquiar **95** 15

botalón **59** 7

botar **97** 11

botas **19** 21, **21** 32, **88** 10

botas de excursionismo **19** 9

botas de lluvia **19** 25

botavara **59** 7

bote **59** 18

bote de paseo **59** 16

bote de pesca **58** 1

bote de remo **59** 23

bote de vela **59** 4

bote salvavidas **58** 19, **90** 10

botecito **59** 18

botella **12** 3

(botella de) licor **16** 22

botiquín **34** 14

botón **20** 3, **60** 18a, **101** 9

botón de oro **60** 17

boxeo **94**

boya **58** 16

brazalete **23** 9

brazo **4** 6, **100** 20

brillo **30** 11

brincar **96** 8

brocha **37** 30, **76** 18

broche **23** 17

broche de corbata **23** 14

broche de presión **101** 13

brocoli **6** 2

bufanda **19** 19

búho **64** 6

bulbo **60** 8a

(bulto de) paja **81** 13

buque **58** 27

buró **32** 9

burro **67** 23

bustillo **22** 9

buzón **46** 1

buzón de los Estados Unidos **46** 6

cabalgar **97** 13

caballista **87** 6

caballito de San Pedro **63** 4

caballitos **87** 5

caballo **67** 21

caballo de mar **65** 1

caballos **81** 23

cabecera **32** 14

cabello **4** 30

cabeza **4** C, **37** 42a

(cabeza de) coliflor **6** 1

cabina **56** 19

cabina de mando **56** 13

cable **52** 23

cable eléctrico **37** 35

cacahuete(s) **9** 28

cacerola **30** 8, **30** 14, **37** 28

cachar **96** 4

cácher **92** 2, **93** 16

cachete **4** 35

cachorro **69** 27

cachucha **21** 43

cactus **61** 40

cadena **23** 5, **52** 18

cadera **4** 16

caer **96** 7

café **18** 35

cafetera **29** 18, **30** 31

caída de agua **80** 11

caja **13** 12, **15** 21, **58** 7

caja de fusibles **35** 5

caja de herramientas **36** 23

cajera **15** 22

cajero **15** 22, **86** 15

cajetilla **13** 16

cajón **47** 5

cajón de arena **87** 13

cajuela **51** 40

calabacita **7** 27

calabaza **7** 26

calabaza pequeña **7** 28

calamar **62** 5

calcetines **22** 17

calcetines largos **22** 16

calculadora **83** 19, **100** 34

caldero **30** 13

calefacción **80** 27

calendario **83** 9

caliente **25** 7

California **72** 5

calle **45** 31

caluroso **25** 8

calzón **22** 3

calzón largo **22** 7

calzoncillo **22** 3

calzoncillo boxer **22** 2

cama **32** 21

cámara **100** 8

cámara de cine **100** 15

cámara de video **100** 1

camarógrafo **86** 10

camarón **11** 31, **62** 8

cambiar (las sábanas) **38** 13

cambio de velocidades **50** 17

camello **67** 33

camilla **39** 12

caminar **77** 8

camino de harradura **87** 7

camino entarimado **90** 1

camión **49** 9, **53** 25

camión de la basura **49** 6

camión de correo **46** 5

camión de mudanza **53** 26

camión de volteo **49** 14

camionero **49** 16

camiones **49**

camioneta **49** 4, **50** C

camioneta cuatro puertas **51** E

camioneta de lonchar **49** 8

camisa **21** 46

camisa de franela **19** 3

camiseta **22** 1

camiseta manga corta **21** 29

camiseta sin mangas **20** 13

camisola **22** 9

camisón **22** 21

campista central **93** 2

campista delantero **93** 5

campista derecho **93** 3

campista izquierdo **93** 1

campo **93** 5

campo de fútbol **93** B

campo de golf **95** B

campos de juego **93**

campos y canchas de juego **95**

canal **94** 3

canal de tizas **76** 9

canalizador **37** 37

canario **64** 14

canasta **15** 16, **92** 20

canasta de compras **14** 8

canasta de día de campo **88** 13

canasto **34** 28

canasto de lavandería **35** 29

cancha **94** 13

cancha de tenis **95** A

candelero **29** 28

candil **29** 3

caneva **101** 26

cangrejo **62** 9

canguro **66** 3

canoa **59** 2

canoa de los esquimales **59** 17

cantante **99** 24

cantina **16** B

cantina rodante **49** 8

cantinero **16** 21

caña de azúcar **60** 20

caña de pesca **88** 7

cañón **48** 11, **48** 23, **88** 3

capa de agua **21** 38

el, la capataz **85** 13

capota **51** 47

cápsula **41** 5

capullo **63** 2

cara **4** 1

caracol **62** 1, **91** 40

carapacho **65** 18a

carbón **27** 23, **80** 7

cárcel **43** 1

cardenal **64** 11

careta **91** 35, **92** 15

carga **58** 10

cargar **26** 16

carne **10** A

carne, aves, y mariscos **10**, **11**

carne de puerco **10** 6

carne de res **10** 1

carne molida **10** 2

carne para cocido **10** 4

carnicero **84** 13

Carolina del norte **73** 33

Carolina del sur **73** 40

carpeta **76** 14

carpintero **85** 2

carreras de caballo **94**

carreta tirada por caballos **55** 33

(carrete de) hilo **101** 2

carretera interestatal **53** 1

carretilla **27** 32

carril **54** 10, **94** 4

carril central **53** 6

carril de entrada **53** 21

carril de salida **53** 2

carril derecho **53** 7

carril izquierdo **53** 5

carrito de bebé **33** 14

carrito de compras **15** 19

carrito de equipaje **56** 6

carrito de golf **95** 8

carrito manual **87** 4

carro bombas **42** 2

carro casa **53** 16

carro de bomberos **42** 3

carro de ferrocarríl **54** 9

carro de mudanza **49** 11

carro de pasajeros **53** 15

carro deportivo **53** 17

carro para bebé **45** 27

carro tanque de bomberos **42** 2

carro tanque **49** 3

carros **50** , **51**

carta **46** 7

cartera **20** 9, **20** 23

(carterita de) cerillos **16** 28

carterita **13** 17

cartero **46** 3

cartón **12** 1

casa de campaña **89** 24

casa de energía **80** 20

casa de fuerza **80** 20

casa de granja **81** 3

casa de muñecas **33** 25

casa de rancho **27** A

casa estilo colonial **27** B

casa-remolque **53** 10

casas **27**

cascada **80** 11, **89** 18

cáscara **8** 8b, **9** 3a, **9** 37b

casco **21** 28, **42** 12, **52** 7, **92** 14

casco del bateador **92** 6

casco protector **94** 14

caseta **16** 9

caseta de cobro **53** 27

caseta de taxis **55** 28

casilla **54** 13

casquillo **48** 27

cassette **100** 26

castaña(s) **9** 32

castillo de arena **91** 32

castor **66** 12

catálogo **47** 4

catarina **63** 14

catsup **16** 4

cazuela **30** 17

cebolla(s) **7** 31

cebra **66** 18

ceja **5** 44

cello **98** 9

cenicero **16** 29

centavo **13** 27

centro **8** 2b, **79** 13, **93** 27

cepillo de baño **34** 31

cepillo de dientes **34** 21

cepillo de madera **37** 32

cepillo de pelo **32** 7

cepillo para uñas **34** 20

cerca **81** 9

cerdo **10** 6, **67** 30

cerebro·**5** 57

cerezas **9** 19

cerillos **16** 28

cerrado **24** 16

cerrajero **85** 4

cerrar **77** 5

cervato **67** 27

cerveza **16** 23

cerveza de barril **20** 16

césped **27** 15

chabacano **9** 25

chaleco **21** 39

chaleco de plumas de ganso **19** 12

chaleco salvavidas **59** 1

chamarra **19** 17

chamarra de invierno **19** 8

champú **34** 8

chancletas **22** 18

chango **69** 14

chapa **43** 5

chapa de matrícula **50** 28

chapaletas **91** 36

chapulín **63** 6

chaqueta **19** 17

charola **16** 33

charola para cubitos de hielo **30** 21

chavito prieto **13** 27

cheque **15** 27

chícharo(s) **6** 17

chico **24** 7

chimenea **27** 9, **28** 8, **58** 18, **80** 22

chimpancé **69** 16

china **8** 8

chinero **29** 2

chiringa **91** 22

chivo **67** 28

chofer **49** 16, **54** 3

chopo **61** 30

chorizo **10** 7

chorrera **87** 12

chorrito **87** 14

chuletas **10** 15

chuletas de puerco **10** 9, **18** 15

chupón **33** 22

ciclista **90** 4

ciempiés **63** 22

cierre **101** 16

cigarillo **16** 31

cigarro **16** 31

cigüeña **64** 30

cilindro **79** 26

cilindro graduado **78** 25

cinta **20** 12, **46** 22, **100** 3, **100** 26

cinta de aislar **37** 34

cinta de medir **36** 21

cinta métrica **101** 15

cintas **100** 25

cintura **4** 13

cinturón **20** 16

cinturón de seguridad **50** 23

círculo **79** 11

circunferencia **79** 17

ciruela **9** 34

ciruela pasa **9** 23

cirugía **41** 2

cisne **64** 28

la ciudad **44, 45**

clarabolla **58** 21

clarinete **98** 16

claro **24** 9

clases de aviones **57** A

clavelón **60** 6

clavija **37** 43d

clavija de tierra **36** 7

clavo **37** 41

claxon **50** 12, **52** 5

cliente **15** 17

closet **32** 3

clutch **50** 25

cobertor acolchado **32** 22

cobija **32** 20

cobra **65** 11

coche **54** 9

coches **50, 51**

la cocina **30**

cocinar **17** 4

cocinar a vapor **31** 12

cocinero **16** 1

coco **8** 3

cocodrilo **65** 8

cocuyo **63** 2

código postal **46** 12

codo **4** 8

cohete **75** 13

cojín **28** 24

cojincillo de restregar **30** 11

col **6** 3

cola **57** 10, **65** 3a, **66** 3a

coladera **30** 7

colador **30** 7

colcha **32** 23

colchón **32** 17

colchón de aire **91** 26

colchón de muelles **32** 18

colchón protector **33** 5

colector solar **80** 17

coles pequeñas **6** 4

colgar **38** 6

colibrí **64** 2

colina **88** 4

collar **23** 6

collar de cuentas **23** 7

colmillo **66** 17b

colocar **17** 8

Colorado **72** 6

colorados **6** 13

colorete **23** 32

columpio **33** 24

columpios **87** 16

combate del fuego y rescate **42**

combustible diesel **80** 34

combustible para jet **80** 31

comedia musical **99** B

el comedor **29**

comer **17** 1

cometa **74** 2, **91** 22

cómoda **32** 30

compartimento de equipaje **56** 21

comprador **15** 17

compra **15** 24

compuerta trasera **51** 43

computadora **76** 8, **83** 16

computadoras **100** E

concha **62** 1a, **62** 10, **65** 18a, **91** 40

conductor **54** 3, **54** 7, **99** 8

conejo **66** 13

conexión **32** 26b

confitería **15** 18

conga **98** 20

congelado (y resbaloso) **25** 16

congelador **14** 3, **30** 20

Congo **71** 62

conmutador **83** 3

Connecticut **72** 7

cono **61** 34b, **79** 28

constelación (Osa Mayor) **74** 3

contacto **36** 6

contador **86** 18

continentes **70**

contraventana **27** 8

control remoto **28** 17

copa de vino **29** 5

copiloto **56** 16

corazón **5** 64, **8** 2b

corbata **21** 47

corcho **16** 18, **61** 35c

cordero **10** 13, **67** 25

cordilleras **71**

cordón **20** 7, **32** 26a, **46** 20, **54** 1

cordón de pesca **88** 8

cornejo **61** 28

corneta francesa **98** 26

coro **99** 18

corral **81** 8, **81** 24

corral de juego **33** 30

correa **20** 16

correa de reloj **23** 11

correcaminos **64** 32

corredor **94** 31

corredores **91** 23

correo **46** 2

correr **96** 6

corta **24** 1

corta circuitos **35** 5

corta uñas **23** 31

cortada **40** 16

cortadora de césped (grama) **27** 12

cortar (v) **26** 11, **31** 6, **31** 9

cortar el césped **26** 6

cortar la grama **26** 6

corte **43** B

cortina **32** 10, **99** 1

cortina de baño **34** 5

cortinas **28** 23

cortinero **34** 1

cortinilla **33** 1

costillas **10** 10

costura **101** A, **101** 10

costurera **84** 6

cotonete **33** 10

cotorro **64** 16

crema de afeitar **23** 22

cremera **29** 24

crimen y castigo **43**

crin de caballo **67** 21a

crisantemo **60** 4

cruce **44** 11

cruce de trébol **53** 4

cuaderno de espiral **76** 15

cuadrado **79** 9

cuadrilátero **94** 17

cuadro **28** 4

cuadro médico **39** 10

el cuarto de servicios **35**
el cuarto del bebé **33**
cuarto menguante **74** 25
cubeta **35** 15, **90** 16
cubeta de hielo **30** 21
cubículo **83** 5
cubierta **58** 22
cubierta de vuelo **75** 10
cubito **90** 16
cubo **35** 15, **79** 27
cucaracha **63** 9
cuchara **29** 8
cuchara (de albañil) **27** 27
cuchillo **29** 15
cucubano **63** 17
cuello **4** 4, **20** 20
cuenta **16** 14
cuerda **46** 20, **58** 25, **89** 23, **98** 10a
cuerdo de remolque **59** 11
cuerno **66** 16a, **67** 35a
el cuerpo **4** A
el cuerpo humano **4, 5**
cuervo **64** 3
cuesto abajo de esquiar **95** C
cuidado médico y dental **39**
culebra **65** 9
cumbre **79** 21
cuna **33** 4
cuna mecedora **33** 26
cuñada **3** 8
cuñado **3** 11
cuneta **45** 26
cuota **55** 21
curita **39** 4
curva **79** 3
Dakota del norte **73** 34
Dakota del sur **73** 41
dar **17** 9
dátil **9** 22
de (la cancha de golf) **103** 10
dedo de enmedio **4** 26
debajo de (el escritorio) **102** 8
decoración **99** 2
de bolítas **24** 19
de cuadritos **24** 18
dedal **101** 21
dedo del pie **5** 54

dedo gordo del pie **5** 53
(dedo) pulgar **4** 24
defensa **52** 10
defensa delantera **51** 51
defensa derecha **93** 28
defensa izquierda **93** 26
defensa trasera **51** 42
delantal **16** 6
Delaware **72** 8
delfín **68** 13
delineador **23** 33
de lineas (rayitas) **24** 17
demandado **43** 23
dentista **39** 17
dentro de (el cajón) **102** 7
deportes en equipo **92**
deportes individuales **94**
depósito **15** 16
depresor de lengua **40** 12a
depunto **101** 26
desagüe **27** 10, **34** 9
desagüe de lluvia **27** 18
desarmador **37** 24
desarmador Phillips **37** 25
descansa brazo **50** 3
descanso en cama **41** 1
descripción de ropa **24**
descripción del clima **25**
desde (la cancha de golf) **103** 10
desembarcadero **58** 28
desengrapador **83** 29
desiertos **71**
deslizador de vela **59** 14
deslizador **57** 6
deslizarse **97** 12
despegue **57** B
despertador **32** 8
destapa caños **35** 14
destapador **30** 6
destello **100** 7
destornillador **37** 24
detective **43** 2
detector de humo **33** 15
detector de metales **56** 10
detergente **35** 25
detrás de (la silla) **102** 9
diagonal **79** 20

diamante de béisbol **93** A
diámetro **79** 12
dibujar **77** 11
diccionario **47** 24
diente **4** 42
diente de ajo **7** 25a
dinero **13**
dique **58** 28
dirección **46** 11
dirigible **57** 5
disc jockey **86** 9
disco compacto **100** 27
disco de (hule duro) hockey **92** 17
discos **100** 23
diseñador de moda **86** 6
diseño a cuadros **24** 22
disparar **97** 16
Distrito de Columbia **73** 51
división central **53** 18
divisor **53** 18
dobladillo **101** 11
doblar **38** 1
doctor **39** 11
documentación recibida **83** 12
dolor de cabeza **40** 6
dolor de espalda **40** 8
dolor de estómago **40** 7
dolor de garganta **40** 12
dolor de muela **40** 9
drenaje **34** 9
ducha **34** 4
dunas de arena **90** 12
durazno **9** 37
echar **31** 4
echar clavados **97** 14
eclipse lunar **74** 6
eclipse solar **74** 10
ecuador **71** 70
edificio de oficinas **44** 1
eje **50** 13
Ejército **48** 15
ejote(s) **6** 15
electricidad **80** 32
el, la electricista **85** 6
electrónica y fotografía **100**
elefante **66** 17
elevador **80** 9, **45** 17

elote **6** 12a

embrague **50** 25

embudo **78** 17

empeine **5** 51

empleado de biblioteca **47** 1

empleado de limpieza **49** 7, **85** 9

empleado postal **46** 14

empleados de negocios **86** C

empujar **26** 12

en (la ventana) **102** 1

en la playa **90**, **91**

enagua **22** 8

enarenar **26** 14

encendedor **16** 30

encender **17** 13

encendido **50** 14

enchufe **32** 26b, **36** 6

enciclopedia **47** 25

energía **80**,**80** A, **80** 24

enfermedades y heridas **40**

enfermera **39** 19

enfermero **42** 7

engrane **52** 20

engrapadora **83** 27

enredadera **61** 42

ensalada **18** 13

ensaladera **29** 25

entablado **90** 1

entero **79** 29

entero (color) **24** 20

entrada de carro **27** 1

entrar **77** 14

entre (los cojines) **102** 4

entrega de correo **46** A

entrenador **93** 21

entresuelo **99** 13

envase **12** 2

envases, cantidades, y dinero **12**, **13**

enyesado **39** 5

equipaje **56** 8

equipo (de alpinismo) **89** 27

escabroso **95** 6

escala **14** 7, **78** 4

escálamo **59** 21

escalera **28** 12, **35** 1, **42** 1

escalofrios **40** 4

escalón **28** 13

escalope **11** 35, **62** 10

escape **52** 33

escape de incendio **42** 4

escarabajo **63** 10

escenario **99** 5

esfera **47** 19

escoba **35** 7

escribir **77** 7

escribir a máquina **77** 10

escritor **86** 7

escritorio **28** 14, **76** 16, **83** 13

escuchar **77** 6

escudo **43** 5

escupidera **33** 33

escupidero **39** 16

escurridor **30** 2

esmalte para uñas **23** 25

esófago **5** 61

espacio exterior **74** A

espagueti **18** 10

espalda **4** 11

espantapájaros **81** 19

espárragos **6** 18

espátula **27** 21, **36** 14

espejo **32** 5

espejo lateral **50** 2

espejo retrovisor **50** 7

espina **60** 18c

espina dorsal **5** 58

espinaca **6** 8

esponja **34** 7

esposa **2** 4

esposas **43** 4

esposo **2** 3, **3** 12

esquí **95** 17

esquiador **59** 10, **94** 35

esquiando a campo traviesa **94**

esquina **44** 3

esquíes **94** 33

estaca **89** 30

estación **55** 18

estación de carga **58** 29

estación de policía **43** A

estación del metro **44** 16

estación del subterráneo **44** 16

estación espacial **75** 1

estacionamiento **45** 19

Los Estados Unidos **72**, **73**

estambre **101** 31

estampado **24** 21

estampilla **46** 10

estanque (de patos) **87** 8

estante **14** 6, **47** 17, **78** 8

estante de bicicleta **52** 14

este **71** 73

estéreo **28** 20

estetoscopio **39** 9

el, la estilista **84** 10

estómago **5** 66

estrella **74** 4

estuche de disección **78** 33

el, la estudiante **76** 19

estufa **30** 30

estufa de campamento **89** 25

etiqueta **46** 21

eucalipto **61** 27

Europa **70** 3

excavar **26** 3

excursionistas **88** 2

excusado **34** 29

explorador espacial **75** 4

extensible **23** 11

extensión **36** 5

extinguidor **42** 11

fagot **98** 14

faisán **64** 19

faja **22** 15

falcón **64** 7

falda **21** 36

familia de Mary Smith **3**

la familia **3**

farmacéutica **84** 1

farmacia **45** 22

faro **58** 14

fases de la luna **74** C

ficha de reclamo **47** 12

fiebre **40** 2

figuras geométricas **79** B

figuras sólidas **79** C

fila **47** 11, **81** 18

filete **11** 28

filtro **51** 52

fiscal acusador **43** 17

flama **29** 26, **78** 21

flamingo **64** 29

flanqueador **93** 31

flash **100** 7

flauta **98** 13

flojo **24** 4

flor de nochebuena **60** 15

flores **60**

Florida **72** 9

el florista **84** 11

flotador inflable **59** 20

foca **68** 12

foco **35** 22

fogata **89** 31

fondo entero **22** 10

foro **99** 5

fósforos **16** 28

fotocopiadora **47** 18, **83** 24

fotografía **100** B

fotógrafo **86** 4

fotos **100** 11

fracciones **79** D

fractura **40** 15

frambuesas **8** 16

frasco **12** 9, **78** 2

freir **31** 15

freno **50** 26, **52** 17

freno de emergencia **50** 15

freno manual **52** 24

frente **4** 32, **23** 18

frente a (la chimenea) **102** 6

fresa **8** 15

fresco **25** 9

frijoles cocidos **18** 3

frijol(es) negro(s) **6** 14

frío **25** 10

frisbee **90** 13

frontón con raqueta **94**

frontón de mano **94**

frutas **8**, **9**

frutas cítricas **8**

frutas pequeñas **8**

frutas secas **9**

frutas y legumbres **14** 9

fuego **28** 9, **42** 5

fuente **87** 19

fuentes de fuerza **80** A

fuera de (el agua) **103** 7

Fuerza Aérea **48** 19

funda **15** 25, **32** 15, **43** 8

fuselaje **57** 14

fútbol **92**, **92** 13

gabinete **30** 22

gafas **21** 44

gafas de sol **90** 14

gajo **8** 8a

galaxia **74** 1

galleta **18** 22

gallo **64** 21

ganado **81** 12

gancho **23** 18, **32** 1, **36** 16

gancho para ropa **32** 2

Ganges **71** 67

ganso **64** 26

garaje **27** 2

gardenia **60** 14

garganta **5** 59

garra **68** 2a, **69** 29a

gas natural **80** 29

gas propano **80** 30

gasolina **80** 28

gatillo **48** 22

gatito **68** 5

gato **51** 38, **68** 4

gaveta **47** 5

gaveta para guante **50** 20

gavetero **32** 30

gavetes **20** 7

gaviota **64** 4

gaza **39** 25

gemelos **90** 7

generador eléctrico **80** 21

género **101** 4

gente y parentesco **2**

Georgia **72** 10

gerente **83** 18

geyser **80** 5

gimnasia **94**

el, la gimnasta **94** 23

girafa **67** 29

girasol **60** 19

giro de postal **46** 18

gis **76** 10

Gobi **71** 54

gol **92** 25

golf **94**

golfista **94** 10

Golfo de Alaska **70** 17

Golfo de Guinea **70** 25

Golfo de México **70** 19

Golfo Pérsico **70** 28

golpe **40** 17

golpear **96** 1

goma **50** 37, **52** 28, **76** 21, **78** 18

gorila **69** 17

gorrión **64** 10

gorra **19** 2, **21** 43, **92** 11

gorro de baño **34** 3

gorro de esquiar **19** 16

gotas para los ojos **41** 10

gotera **27** 10

gotero **78** 26

grabadora **100** 22

gráfico **78** 11

grama **27** 15

granada (de mano) **48** 29

grande **24** 8

granero **81** 5

granja de trigo **81** B

granja lechera **81** A

la granja y el rancho **81**

granjero **81** 7

(granos de) avena **60** 23

grapadora **83** 27

gratinar **31** 2

grillo **63** 5

grosellas **8** 11

grúa **49** 2, **58** 6

grupo (musical) de Rock **99** C

guagua **54** A

guante **27** 20, **92** 12, **94** 11, **94** 15

guante del cácher **92** 4

guante entero **19** 11

guantera **50** 20

guantes **19** 1

guantes de trabajo **27** 26

el, la guarda **88** 5

el, la guarda parques **88** 5

el guardia de seguridad **56** 9

guardia de seguridad **86** 14

guarniciones **89** 22

guía **50** 8
guiar **97** 15
guineo **9** 20
guitarra **98** 11
guitarra eléctrica **99** 26
guitarrista principal **99** 25
gusano de seda **63** 1
haba(s) **6** 16
habichuela(s) **6** 13
habichuelas cocidas **18** 3
habichuela(s) tiernas **6** 15
hacer (la cama) **38** 8
hacha **36** 17, **42** 14
hacia (la cancha de golf) **103** 9
hacia (el hoyo) **103** 4
hacia abajo de (la colina) **103** 3
hacia arriba de (la colina) **103** 11
hacia dentro de (el hoyo) **103** 12
halcón **64** 7
hamaca **27** 11
hamburguesa **18** 9
el hangar **57** 17
harmónica **98** 30
harpa **98** 6
Hawaii **72** 11
hebilla **20** 17
helado **18** 36, **25** 11, **25** 16
helando **25** 11
hélice **57** 2a
helicóptero **57** 2
hermana **3** 10
hermano **3** 9
hervir **31** 16
hiedra venenosa **61** 45
hielera **91** 41
hiena **69** 30
hierba(s) **69**
hígado **5** 65
higienista bucal **39** 14
higo **9** 21
hija **3** 15
hijo **3** 16
(carrete de) hilo **101** 2
Himalayas **71** 47
hipopótamo **66** 14
hipotenusa **79** 24
hockey sobre hielo **92**

hogaza de pan **12** 7
hoja de música **98** 2
hoja **61** 36a, **94** 27
(hojas sueltas de) papel **76** 13
holgado **24** 4
hombre **2** 2
hombro **4** 5
hongo(s) **7** 30
horario **55** 20
hormiga **63** 12
hornear **31** 14
hornilla **30** 29
horno microondas **30** 23
horno **30** 32
horquilla **59** 21
hot dog **18** 2
hoyo **94** 8
Huang **71** 68
huellas digitales **43** 24
huerta **81** 1
hueso **9** 37a
huevo **64** 13
huevo estrellado **18** 32
humo **42** 15
Idaho **72** 12
iguana **65** 13
Illinois **72** 13
imán **78** 27
imperdibles **33** 11
impermeable **21** 38
impresiones **100** 11
impresora **83** 4
incendio **42** 5
Indiana **72** 14
índice **4** 25
Indico **70** 13
infección **40** 14
información **47** 22
ingeniero **55** 15
ingeniero de vuelo **56** 17
inodoro **34** 29
insectos **63**
insignia **43** 5
instrumentos **39** 13, **56** 14
instrumentos de cuerdas **98**
instrumentos de metal **98**
instrumentos de percusión **98**

instrumentos de viento **98**
instrumentos musicales **98**
interruptor **37** 43c
interruptor de luz **32** 25
intestinos **5** 67
invierno **26**
inyección **41** 8
Iowa **72** 15
iris **5** 47
jabón **34** 15
jabón de fregar **30** 10
jabón líquido para trastes **30** 10
jabonera **34** 6
jacinto **60** 10
jaiba(s) **11** 36
jalea **18** 31
jamón **10** 12
jardinero **85** 3
jarra **29** 4
jarrón **28** 6
jeep **48** 9
jeringa **39** 27
el jet **57** 18
jet privado **57** 3
(ji) tomate(s) **7** 19
jinete (profesional) **94** 21
jockey **94** 21
joroba **67** 33a
joyera **84** 12
joyería **23** A
joyería y cosméticos **23**
joyero **32** 4
juego de cubiertos **29** 22
juegos infantiles **87** 17
juey (es) **11** 36, **62** 9
juez **43** 10
juguetero **33** 29
junto a (la TV) **102** 11
Júpiter **74** 15
jurado **43** 21
Kansas **72** 16
Kentucky **72** 17
labio **4** 43
labor de gancho **101** 28
laboratorio de ciencias **78**
lacrosse **92**
lado **79** 10

lagartija **65** 15

lámpara **28** 28, **89** 29

lámpara (de mano) **35** 3

lana **101** 23

lancha **59** 18

lancha de motor **59** 13

lanchón **58** 12

langosta **11** 30, **62** 13

lanza agua **42** 17

lanzador **93** 12

lanzar **97** 10

lápiz **76** 24

lápiz labial **23** 29

lápiz para cejas **23** 26

larga **24** 2

largo **79** 36

las Fuerzas armadas **48**

lata rociadora **13** 24

lata **12** 10

latería **30** 15

lavabo **34** 19

lavadora **35** 30

lavandería **35** 28

lavamanos **34** 19

lavaplatos **30** 1

lavar **38** 16

levantar (la mano) **77** 1

lazo **58** 25

leche **14** 5

lechuga **6** 6, **6** 7

lechuza **64** 6

leer **77** 4

legumbres **6**, **7**

lejos de (el hoyo) **103** 5

Lena **71** 66

lengua **4** 41

lente **100** 6

lentes **21** 44

lentes de protección **94** 28

lentes de seguridad **78** 12

lentes para el sol **90** 14

leña **28** 10

león **68** 3

leopardo **68** 1

letrero **44** 8

letrero de carretera **53** 23

letrero de límite de velocidad **53** 8

letrero de salida **53** 24

libélula **63** 4

libra de pan **12** 7

librería **45** 18

librero **28** 22, **83** 20

librito **13** 17

libro (de texto) **76** 26

licuadora **30** 12

liguero **22** 14

lija **37** 27

lima **8** 10, **23** 24

limón **8** 9

limpia calles **49** 1

limpia parabrisas **50** 6

limpiador **50** 6

limpiador de esponja **35** 6

limpiador en polvo **35** 9

limpiamesas **16** 3

limpiar **17** 6, **26** 2, **38** 5

limpio **24** 6

línea de fuera **93** 9, **95** 4

línea del saque **95** 3

línea recta **79** 1

lineas **79** A

líneas de corriente **80** 24

líneas paralelas **79** 4

líneas perpendiculares **79** 2

linterna **89** 29

líquido limpia ventanas **35** 10

lirio **60** 11

listado **83** 8

llama **29** 26, **66** 15

llanta **50** 37, **52** 28

llanta de repuesto **51** 39

llanta inflable **91** 29

llave de perro **36** 10

llave de tuercas **36** 10

llave del agua caliente **34** 17

llave del agua fría **34** 18

llave inglesa **36** 12

llenar **26** 9

lluvioso **25** 1

lobo **69** 29

loción para bebé **33** 6

loción para después de afeitar **23** 21

loción para el sol **91** 39

locker **76** 6

locutor de noticiero **86** 2

lombriz **62** 11

lonchera **21** 31

longaniza **10** 7

loro **64** 16

loseta **34** 27

Louisiana **72** 18

loza **29** 1

luces delanteras **51** 48

luces direccionales **51** 50

luces para estacionarse **51** 49

luciérnaga **63** 17

luna **74** 9

luna llena **74** 24

luna nueva **74** 26

luneta **99** 12

lupa **78** 15

lustrar **38** 3

luz de reversa **50** 30

luz del freno **50** 29

luz trasera **50** 31

macana **43** 9

madeja **101** 24

madera **36** 4

madras **24** 22

madre **3** 4

maestra **76** 4

magnolia **61** 29

mahón **19** 6

Maine **72** 19

maíz **60** 24

malecón **58** 3

maleta **56** 7

maletera **51** 40

maletero **56** 5

maletín **21** 37

mamadera **33** 18

mameluco **21** 30

mamíferos I **66**, **67**

mamíferos II **68**, **69**

mamíferos acuáticos **68**

mamíferos de bolsa, sin dientes, y
 voladores **66**

mamíferos de pezuña **66**

(manada de) ganado **81** 20

mancuernas **23** 12

mandadero **86** 19

mandíbula **4** 38

mandolina **98** 4

mandril **69** 19

manejar **97** 15

manga corta **20** 21

manga larga **20** 15

mango **8** 5

manguera **27** 14, **42** 8, **51** 57

maní **9** 28

manija **50** 4

la mano **4** B

mantaraya **65** 6

mantel **29** 16

mantequilla **18** 18

mantis **63** 7

manubrios (de carreras) **52** 2

manubrios de viaje **52** 12

manzana **8** 2

mapa del mundo **70**, **71**

mapache **68** 7

máquina de coser **101** 1

máquina de escribir **83** 10

máquina de lavar platos **30** 1

Mar Amarillo **70** 37

Mar Arábigo **70** 30

Mar Báltico **70** 22

Mar Caribe **70** 20

Mar Caspiano **70** 27

Mar de Barents **70** 23

Mar de Beaufort **70** 15

Mar de Bering **70** 34

Mar de Kara **70** 31

Mar de Laptev **70** 33

Mar de Okhotsk **70** 35

Mar del Caribe **70** 20

Mar del Este de China **70** 38

Mar del Japón **70** 36

Mar del Norte **70** 21

Mar del Sur de China **70** 39

Mar Mediterráneo **70** 24

Mar Negro **70** 26

Mar Rojo **70** 29

marañón(es) **9** 27

maraquita **33** 21

maravilla **60** 6

marcador **55** 23

marco **28** 4

mares, golfos y bahías **70**

margarita **60** 5

Marina **48** 13, **48** 17

marinero **48** 14

marino **48** 18

mariposa **63** 3

mariposa nocturna **63** 21

mariquita **63** 14

mariscal de campo **93** 32

mariscos **11** D

marquesina **27** 2

Marte **74** 14

martillo **36** 13, **43** 12

Maryland **72** 20

máscara **23** 28

máscara del cácher **92** 3

Massachusetts **72** 21

mástil **59** 8

materia **47** 10

material **101** 4

matemáticas **79**

mazo **36** 11

(mazo de) paja **81** 13

mazorca de maíz **6** 12

mecánico **84** 2

mecanógrafa **83** 6

medias **22** 6, **22** 7

medias de invierno **19** 14

medicina **41**

medidas **79** E

medidor **55** 23

medidor de (la) gasolina **50** 9

medidor de tiempo **78** 13

medio **4** 26

medio fondo **22** 8

medio pollo **11** 17

medio trasero **93** 33

medios de comunicación y las artes **86** A

medusa **62** 12

mejilla **4** 35

mejillón(es) **11** 34

melocotón **9** 37

melón **9** 26, **9** 36

melón (verde) **9** 35

menear **31** 1

mensajero **85** 10, **86** 19

mentón **4** 3

menú **16** 7

meñique **4** 28

meple **61** 38

mercado de frutas y legumbres **45** 28

Mercurio **74** 11

mesa **29** 7

mesa de día de campo **88** 15

mesa de planchar **35** 13

mesa de reconocimiento **39** 6

mesa de trabajo **36** 22, **78** 24

mesera **16** 2

mesera (de bebidas) **16** 32

mesero **16** 5

meseta **88** 1

mesita **28** 29, **56** 22

mesita central **28** 26

mesita de noche **32** 27

mesita (portátil) **33** 9

meta **95** 21

meteoro **74** 5

metro **54** B

mezanine **99** 13

mezcladora de cemento **49** 13

Michigan **72** 22

mico **69** 14

microfilm **47** 13

microscopio **78** 30

mina de carbón **80** 6

mini-cámara **100** 2

mini-computadora **100** 31

Minnesota **72** 23

Misisipí **71** 58, **72** 24

Missouri **73** 25

mitón **19** 11

mocasín **21** 42

mochila **19** 4

mochila con armazón **89** 28

el, la modela **86** 5, **101** 7

módulo de comando **75** 9

módulo lunar **75** 7

mojado **25** 15

mojarra **65** 7

Mojave **71** 48

molde **30** 24

moler **31** 2

molinete **58** 23

molino de viento **80** 19

moluscos **11**

molusco(s) bivalvo(s) **11** 35

mondar **31** 5

moneda de cinco **13** 28

moneda de diez **13** 29

moneda de veinticinco **13** 30

monedas **13** 26

monitor **100** 32

mono de Asia **69** 15

monoriel **55** 29

Montana **73** 26

montaña **89** 19

Montañas Apalaches **71** 41

Montañas Cáucaso **71** 45

Montañas Rocallosas **71** 40

Montes Apalaches **71** 41

Montes Urales **71** 46

montículo **93** 11

moras **8** 12

morsa **68** 11

mortero **48** 28

mosca **63** 18

mosquitero **27** 19

mosquito **63** 13

mostaza **18** 1

mostrador **29** 29, **30** 27

mostrador de chequeo **15** 26, **47** 2

mostrador de fiambre y quesos **14** 1

motel **90** 3

moto pequeña **52** 29

motocicleta **52** 30, **53** 19

motor **51** F, **52** 32

motor exterior **59** 12

móvil **33** 2

mozo **56** 5

muchacha **2** 9

muchacho **2** 8

muchacho de los bates **93** 18

mudador **49** 12

mueble de pared **28** 19

muelle **58** 3

muestra en transparencia **78** 31

mujer **2** 1

muleta **39** 7

muñeca **4** 21, **33** 28

murciélago **66** 4

músculo **5** 62

música, baile/danza y teatro **99**

músico **99** 10

muslo **4** 18, **11** 19

nabo **7** 34

nadador **91** 28

nalgas **4** 15

naranja **8** 8

narciso **60** 8

nariz **4** 36, **57** 8

navajas para afeitar **23** 23

Naval **48** 13

naves espaciales **75** A

(con) neblina **25** 12

Nebraska **73** 27

nectarín **8** 17

Neptuno **74** 18

Nevada **73** 28

(con) nevado **25** 3

nevaja **94** 27

nevera **30** 19, **91** 41

nido **64** 31

nieta **2** 11

nieto **2** 12

(con) nieve **25** 3

Níger **71** 61

Nilo **71** 63

niña **2** 9

niño **2** 8

niños **2** 7

nochero **32** 27

norte **71** 71

Norteamérica **70** 1

nublado **25** 2

núcleo **80** 14

nudillo **4** 22

nueces **9**

nueva **24** 13

Nueva Hampshire **73** 29

Nueva Jersey **73** 30

Nueva York **73** 32

Nuevo México **73** 31

nuez (nueces) de nogal **9** 29

número de clasificación **47** 7

número del edificio **45** 24

nutria **68** 10

ñame **7** 24

Ob **71** 64

oboe **98** 15

obscuro **24** 10

océanos **70**

el, la oculista **84** 9

ocupaciones I: La calle principal en los
  Estados Unidos **84**

ocupaciones II **85**

ocupaciones III **86**

oeste **71** 74

oficial **86** 13

oficial de la corte **43** 19

(oficial de) policía **43** 6

oficina **83**

oficina de correo **44** 9

oficina de correos **46** B

Ohio **73** 35

oído **4** 34

ojal **101** 8

el ojo **5** D

ojo morado **40** 5

Oklahoma **73** 36

ola **91** 24

olla **30** 8, **30** 13

olmo **61** 36

operadora de conmutador **83** 1

operario **85** 12

el, la optico **84** 9

orangután **69** 18

órbita **74** 21

orden monetaria **46** 18

ordenar **17** 5

Oregon **73** 37

oreja **4** 34

orejeras **19** 10

órgano **98** 29

los órganos internos **5** F

orificio nasal **4** 37

orilla de la carretera **53** 22

orillero **33** 5

orquesta **99** 6

orquídea **60** 12

orza de deriva **59** 6

oso de peluche **33** 3

oso hormiguero **66** 5

(oso) Koala **66** 1

oso negro **69** 21

oso panda **69** 20

oso pardo **69** 23
oso polar **69** 22
osos **69**
ostión(es) **11** 33
ostra(s) **11** 33, **62** 2
Otoño **26**
otras actividades de costura **101** B
otras formas de transporte **55** E
otras plantas **61**
otros instrumentos **98**
óvalo **79** 18
oveja **10** 13, **67** 25
oveja pequeña **67** 24
ovejas **81** 10
overol **21** 30
paciente **39** 20
Pacífico del norte **70** 9
Pacífico del sur **70** 10
padre **3** 5
padres **2** 6
pagar **17** 7
paja **81** 13
pájaro azul **64** 8
pájaro carpintero **64** 17
pájaros **64**
pala **27** 31, **90** 17
pala de jardín **27** 27
pala de nieve **49** 5
palanca de cambios **50** 17
palanca de direccionales **50** 11
palanca de velocidades **50** 24, **52** 22
palco **99** 11
palear **26** 13
paleta **40** 12a, **94** 18
paleta (de agua) **59** 3
palitos **98** 19a
palitos de algodón **33** 10
palma **4** 29
palmera **61** 26
palo **94** 9
palo de cortina **34** 1
palo de hockey **92** 18
palo largo **94** 34, **95** 14
paloma **64** 1
palos de golf **95** 5
palta **9** 33
pan **14** 12

pan tostado **18** 34
panadería **44** 6
panadero **84** 8
pancakes **18** 5
páncreas **5** 71
pandereta **98** 17
panecillo **18** 7, **18** 19, **18** 27
panqueques **18** 5
pantaleta **22** 12
pantaleta (bikini) **22** 11
pantalla **100** 14
pantalla de gancho **23** 16
pantalla de lámpara **28** 27
pantalla de pinchar **23** 15
pantallas **23** 1
pantalón **20** 4
pantalón de mezclilla **19** 6
pantalón (de pana) **21** 27
pantalón de sudadera **20** 10
pantaloncillo **20** 14
pantalones impermeables para
    pescar **88** 10
pantimedia **22** 5
pantorrilla **4** 20
pants **20** 10
pantuflas **22** 18
pañal **33** 13
pañal desechable **33** 12
paño de platos **30** 18
pañuelos faciales **32** 13
papa al horno **18** 20
papalote **91** 22
papas fritas **18** 4, **18** 28
papas majadas **18** 17
papaya **8** 6
papa(s) **7** 23
papel absorbente **35** 23
papel de baño **34** 30
papel de gráficas **78** 11
papel filtro **78** 16
papel higiénico **34** 30
papitas **18** 4
paquete **12** 4, **13** 16, **46** 19
(paquete) correo express **46** 23
paquete de seis **13** 13
(paquetito de) azúcar **16** 13
paramédico **42** 7

el parabrisas **51** 45
paracaídas **48** 6
parada de autobús **44** 13
paraguas **20** 24
Paraná **71** 60
parasol **90** 21
pared **28** 3
párpado **5** 45
parque **87** 15
parques del vecindario **87**
parquímetro **45** 20
parrilla **27** 22, **88** 12
parte superior del brazo **4** 7
partidura **4** 31
pasa(s) **9** 24
pasaje **56** 4
pasajero **54** 6, **55** 25
pasamano **28** 11
pasar **96** 5
pascua **60** 15
pase de abordar **56** 18
paseo por agua **59**
pasillo **14** 10, **56** 23, **76** 12
paso a desnivel **53** 3
pasta de dientes **34** 16
pastelería **44** 6
pastelillo de fresa **18** 26
pastilla **13** 18
pastisal **81** 6
pasto **27** 15
pastor **69** 28
pastura **81** 6
pata **10** 14, **11** 20, **69** 29a
pata de foca **68** 12a
patas frontales **66** 3d
patas traseras **66** 3b
patear **96** 3
patilla **4** 33
patín **94** 26
patinaje en hielo **94**
patinar **97** 9
patines de hielo **19** 15
patín **101** 7
patio **27** 17
el patio interior **27** C
pato **11** 25, **64** 25
patrón **101** 7
pavo **11** 23, **64** 20

pavo real **64** 18

peaje **53** 27

peatón **44** 12

peces **65** A

peces y reptiles **65**

pecho **4** 12

pechicolorado **64** 9

pechuga **11** 21

pedal **39** 18, **52** 19

pedazo **13** 22

pega **76** 17

pegamento **37** 33, **76** 17

pegar **96** 1

peine **32** 6

peinilla **32** 6

pelar **31** 5

pelícano **64** 24

película **100** C

pelo **4** 30

pelota de playa **90** 11

pelota de softball **92** 10

peluquero **84** 3

Pennsylvania **73** 38

pensamiento **60** 2

pepinillo **18** 8

pepino(s) **7** 20

pepita **8** 8c

pequeña Liga de béisbol **92**

pequeño **24** 7

pequeño dedo del pie **5** 55

pequeño jugador de liga **92** 8

pera **8** 18

perfume **23** 27

perico **64** 16

periódico **21** 48

periquito **64** 15

periscopio **48** 8

perno **37** 38

perro caliente **18** 2

perro cobrador **69** 26

perro de aguas **69** 24

perros **69**

persianas **32** 12

persona de entrega **49** 10

persona que viaja pidiendo aventón **53** 9

personal **48** B

pesa **14** 17, **34** 32

pesa balanza **78** 4

pesas **78** 5

pesca **88**

pescado **11** 26

pescado entero **11** 27

pescador **58** 2

peseta **13** 30

pestañas **5** 46

pétalo **60** 18b

petirrojo **64** 9

petit pois **6** 17

petunia **60** 7

pez espada **65** 3

pez estrella **62** 7

pezón **33** 18

pezuña **67** 35b

piano **98** 1

picada **40** 3

picador **30** 26

picar **31** 11

pichón **64** 1

pico **64** 3a, **64** 24a, **89** 20

picolo **98** 12

el pie **5** E

pie de la cama **32** 24

pierna **10** 14, **11** 20, **4** 17

pieza **13** 22

pieza del patrón **101** 6

pijamas **22** 19

píldora **41** 7

piloto **56** 15

pimentero **29** 9

pimiento(s) **7** 22

pinches de ropa **35** 20

pincitas **78** 32

ping-pong **94**

pingüino **64** 27

pino **61** 34, **94** 5

Pintado **71** 49

pintar **26** 1

pintora **85** 7

pintura **28** 5, **37** 31

pinza **62** 13a

pinzas **35** 20, **36** 19, **78** 28, **78** 29

piña **8** 4

pipa **16** 26

piquete de insecto **40** 3

pirámide **79** 25

piso **32** 29

pista **57** 19, **94** 25, **94** 32

pista de carreras **95** D

pista para correr **87** 9

pistola **43** 7

pitillo **16** 10

pizarra **76** 5

pizarrón **76** 5

pizza **18** 30

placa **50** 28

plancha **35** 12

planchar **38** 11

planeador **57** 4

planeador de mar **91** 25

planeador pequeño de agua **91** 27

los planetas **74**

plantar **26** 4

plantas caseras **61** 39

plantas venenosas **61**

plantas y árboles **60**, **61**

plataforma **54** 11

plataforma de despegue **75** 15

plátanos **9** 20

platillo **29** 21, **90** 13

platillos **98** 18

platito **29** 21

platito de muestras **78** 3

platito para mantequilla y pan **29** 11

plato **29** 13

plato hondo **13** 23

plomera **85** 1

pluma **64** 7.a

pluma atómica **76** 22

plumero **35** 2

Plutón **74** 19

podar **26** 8

podio **99** 7

policía de tránsito **44** 10

pollería **11** B

pollito **64** 22

pollo **11** 24, **64** 23

pollo entero **11** 16

pollo frito **18** 29

pompa **13** 14, **52** 21

pompa de aire **53** 13

pompa de gasolina **53** 14

pompón **60** 13

poner la mesa **17** 8

ponero **53** 9

pony **67** 20

popa **58** 11

popote **16** 10, **78** 14

por encima de (el gato negro) **102** 2

porche **27** 6

porristas **93** 20

porta autos **49** 17

porta bustos **22** 13

porta carga **58** 4

porta compras **15** 19

porta ropa **56** 1

porta vaso **16** 27

portafolio **21** 37

portalón **58** 20

portaviones **48** 4

portero **85** 11, **92** 24

portilla **58** 21

poste de luz **45** 29

poste de servicio **80** 26

poste del gol **93** 35

pote **12** 9

potro **67** 22

pozo petrolero **80** 1

(pozo) tiro de elevador **80** 10

prendas **23** A

prendedor **23** 13, **23** 8

prender **17** 13

preposiciones de descripción **102**

preposiciones de movimiento **103**

presa **80** 18

presillas **101** 14

presión alta **40** 10

primates **69**

primavera **26**

primer cuarto **74** 23

primera base **93** 8

primo **3** 7

prisma **78** 1

proa **58** 5

procesador de palabras **83** 7

producción de energía **80** B

productos enlatados **14** 13

productos lácteos **14** 4

profundidad **79** 33

el programa espacial **75**

programador (de computadora) **86** 16

programas **99** 17

pronosticador del tiempo **86** 1

propina **55** 22

proveta **78** 9

proyector **100** 16

proyector de transparencias **100** 13

púa **66** 11a

publicaciones periódicas **47** 15

puerco espín **66** 11

el puerto **58**

puerta de carga **57** 13

puerta de salida **95** 20

puesto de periódicos y revistas **45** 30

puesto de refrescos **90** 2

pulidora **37** 26

pulir **38** 3

pulmón **5** 63

pulpo **62** 6

pulsera **23** 9

puntada **101** 19

puntadas **39** 21

punteado **24** 19

punto de partida **95** 13

puntos **39** 21

pupila **5** 48

puré de papas **18** 17

quemacoco **51** 44

quemador **30** 29, **78** 20

quemadura **40** 18

quemar **17** 14

quijada **4** 38

quilla **59** 6

rábano(s) **7** 29

radiador **51** 56

radio **50** 18, **79** 14

raíz **61** 35d

rama **61** 35a

ramita **61** 33a

rana **65** 17

rancho **81** C

ranura **46** 13

ranurador **37** 37

rápidos de río **89** 17

raqueta **94** 2, **94** 18, **94** 29

raqueta de lacrosse **92** 16

rasgar **77** 9

raspar **26** 15

rastrillar **26** 10

rastrillo **23** 20, **27** 30

rata **66** 7

ratón **66** 9

ratonera **35** 32

raya **4** 31

rayado **24** 17

rayo **52** 26

rayos x (equis) **39** 1

reactor nuclear **80** 13

rebanada **13** 21

rebanar **31** 10

reborde **45** 26

rebotar **97** 11

el, la recepcionista **86** 17

receptor **92** 2, **93** 16, **100** 21

recibidor **44** 2

recibo **15** 20, **55** 24

reclinador **28** 16

recogedor **35** 8

recoger **17** 6, **26** 7

recortar **26** 8

rectángulo **79** 19

red **92** 23, **95** 2

red de pesca **88** 9

red metálica **78** 6

refacción **51** 39

refinería **80** 12

reflector **52** 25, **99** 4

refajo **22** 10

refresco **16** 11

refrigerador **30** 19

regadera **27** 13, **34** 4

regadera de mano **27** 16

regar **26** 5

registro en el aeropuerto **56**

regla de carpintero **36** 1

regla **76** 23

reloj **76** 2

reloj de pulsera **23** 10

remitente **46** 8

remo **59** 3, **59** 22

remolacha **7** 33

remolcador **58** 13

renacuajo **65** 16

reparación y mantenimiento **85** A
reparar **38** 10
repisa **28** 7, **47** 26
repisa del gis **76** 9
repollo **6** 3
reportero **86** 11
repostería **14** 11
repuesta **51** 39
repuesto **35** 11
resbaladilla **87** 12
resfriado **40** 11
resfrío **40** 11
resfríos **40** 4
respaldo **50** 35
respirador **91** 34
restorán familiar **16** A
restorán familiar y bar **16**
restregar **38** 2
retroproyector **76** 27
revista **47** 16
revolvedora de cemento **49**
revolver **31** 1
revólver **43** 7
Rhode Island **73** 39
ribete **95** 16
riendas **94** 22
rifle **48** 21
rinoceronte **66** 16
riñón **5** 70
Río Grande **71** 57
ríos **71**
robalo **65** 7
roble **61** 33
roble venenoso **61** 43
rocas **88** 11
rociador **27** 13, **87** 14
rodilla **4** 19
rodillo **30** 25, **37** 29
roedores **66**
rollo **12** 11
rollo de película **100** 10
(rollo de) película **100** 17
rollo relleno de carne con verduras **18** 25
rolo **30** 25
rolodex **83** 14
rompecabezas **33** 31
romper **31** 7, **77** 9

rompeviento **19** 5
rondalla **37** 40
ropa de exteriores **19**
ropa del día **20, 21**
ropa interior y de dormir **22**
ropero **32** 9
rosa **60** 18
rosbí **10** 8
rosbif **10** 8
rosca **37** 42b
Rubalcali **71** 52
rubor **23** 32
rueda **52** 4
ruedas de entrenamiento **52** 1
ruedo **101** 11
sábana **32** 19
sacacopias **47** 18
sacacorcho **16** 17
sacapuntas **76** 20, **83** 30
saco de vestir **21** 33
saco "sport" **20** 2
sacudidor **35** 2
sacudir **38** 15
Sahara **71** 51
la sala **28**
sala de juicio **43** B
salamandra **65** 14
salero **29** 10
salir **77** 13
salón de clase **76**
salsa de tomate **16** 4
saltamonte **63** 6
salvavidas (objeto) **90** 9
el, la salvavidas (persona) **90** 6
sanocoho **10** 4, **18** 14
sandalia **20** 19
sandía **9** 26
sandwich **16** 16
sarpullido **40** 1
sartén **30** 5
sastre **84** 6
satélite climatológico **75** 3
satélite de comunicación **75** 2
Saturno **74** 16
sauce **61** 31
saxofón **98** 24
secador **30** 18, **34** 26

secadora **35** 24
secar **38** 5, **38** 9
sección **79** 15
sección de carga **75** 9
sección de referencia **47** 21
sección de revistas **47** 15
sección del saque **95** 1
seco **25** 14
secoya **61** 25
secretaria **83** 11
sedán (dos puertas) **51** D
segadora trilladora **81** 17
segunda base **93** 7
seguridad **56**
seguro **33** 11, **50** 1, **52** 13
seleccionador de rayos **56** 11
sello de correo **46** 9
semáforo **45** 21
semilla **8** 8c, **9** 37a
señal luminosa preventiva **51** 41
sencillo **13** 29
serrote **36** 8
serrucho **36** 8, **36** 18
servicios domésticos **85** B
servilleta **29** 14
servir **17** 3, **31** 4, **96** 2
seta(s) **7** 30
shampú **34** 8
shorts **20** 14
shorts de baño **91** 33
sierra **36** 3
sierra circular **36** 20
sierra eléctrica **27** 25
Sierra Madre **71** 42
silbato **90** 5
silla **29** 17
silla de mecanógrafa **83** 17
silla de montar **94** 20
silla de playa **90** 20
silla de ruedas **39** 2
silla del salvavidas **90** 8
silla del testigo **43** 18
(silla) mecedora **33** 16
silla para niño **16** 8
sillita **16** 8
silo **81** 4
sinfonola **16** 12

sintetizador **99** 21

sintonizador **100** 21

sirga **59** 11

el sistema postal de los Estados
    Unidos **46**

el sistema solar **74** B

sobaco **4** 10

sobre **83** 31, **102** 2

sobre (aéreo) **46** 16

sobre (la alfombra) **102** 5

sobre (la mesa) **102** 10

sobre (el puente) **103** 8

sobreabrigo **19** 20

sobrecama **32** 23

el, la sobrecargo **56** 20

sobrecito de azúcar **16** 13

sobretodo **19** 24

sobrina **3** 14

sobrino **3** 13

soga **89** 23

sofá **28** 25

softball **92**

sol **74** 7, **80** 3

solapa **20** 1

soldado **48** 16

soleadero **27** 24

soleado **25** 4

sólido **24** 20

sombra para ojos **23** 30

sombrero **19** 18

sombrero duro **21** 28

sombrilla **20** 24

sombrilla de playa **90** 21

sonaja **33** 21

soporte **39** 3, **52** 9

soporte del aro **78** 19

sorbeta **16** 10

sortija(s) **23** 2

sortija de boda **23** 4

sortija de compromiso **23** 3

sospechoso **43** 3

sostén **22** 13

sostén de ollas **30** 34

sostener **17** 12

spaniel **69** 24

suavizante **35** 27

subibaja **87** 18

submarino **48** 7

sucio **24** 5

sudadera **20** 8

Sudamérica **70** 2

suela **20** 6

suelto **24** 4

suéter abierto **21** 26

suéter cerrado **19** 7

suéter (cuello de tortuga) **19** 13

suéter (cuello V) **19** 23

sujeta papel **83** 28

sundae **18** 23

el supermercado **14**, **15**

sur **71** 72

surco **81** 18

suspensorio **22** 4

tabla **91** 25

tabla para cortar **30** 26

tablero **50** 19, **92** 19

tablero de anuncios **76** 7

tablero (de puntuación/puntaje) **93** 19

tablero para colgar herramientas **36** 15

tableta **41** 6

tablilla **47** 26, **50** 28

tablillo **14** 6

tablón de edictos **76** 7

tachuela **76** 25

taco **18** 24

tacón **20** 5

Takla Makan **71** 53

taladro **37** 43a, **39** 15

taladro de mano **36** 9

taladro eléctrico **37** 43

talco para bebé **33** 7

tallar **38** 2

taller de trabajo **36**, **37**

tallo **8** 2a, **60** 1a

talón **5** 50

tambor **98** 19

tambora **98** 21

tamborilero **99** 27

tamborina **98** 17

tanque **48** 10

tanque de gasolina **50** 34

tanque de oxígeno **91** 37

tapa **30** 9

tapabocina **50** 36

tapacubo **50** 36

tapete **32** 28, **50** 22

tapete de baño **34** 12

tapón **34** 10, **50** 36, **78** 10

taquilla **55** 19

taquilla de fichas **54** 13

tarifa **54** 5, **55** 21

tarjeta de biblioteca **47** 3

tarjeta informativa **47** 6

tarjeta postal **46** 17

tarjetero **47** 4

taxi **55** D, **55** 27

taxista **55** 26

taza **13** 19, **29** 20

tazón **13** 23, **78** 23

té **16** 15

teatro al aire libre **87** 2

techo **27** 4, **28** 2

teclado **98** 1a, **100** 33

técnica en reparación **84** 5

tee **95** 13

tejadillo de herramientas **27** 28

tejedora **101** 30

tejido **101** 22, **101** 30

tela **101** 4

telaraña **63** 15

teléfono **32** 26, **83** 15

teléfono público **44** 7

telescopio **74** 22

televisión **100** 5

televisor **28** 18, **100** 5

tema **47** 10

temperatura **25** 6

tenacillas **78** 32

tenazas **78** 28

tendedero **35** 19

tenedor **29** 12

tender (la cama) **38** 8

tenis **20** 11, **94**

Tennessee **73** 42

tentáculo **62** 12a

tercera base **93** 4

terminal **51** 55, **57** 16

termita **63** 11

termo **88** 14

termómetro **25** 5, **78** 22

ternero **67** 31

terrier **69** 25

testigo **43** 13

tetera **29** 19, **30** 28

tetilla **33** 18

Texas **73** 43

tía **3** 6

tiburón **65** 5

tienda de departamentos **44** 5

tierra **74** 8

Tierra **74** 13

tigre **68** 2

tijeras de césped **27** 29

tijeras de piquitos **101** 5

timbal **98** 21

timbre (de correo) **46** 10

timón **59** 5

tina **34** 11

tío **3** 3

tipos de correo **46** C

tirar **97** 10

título **47** 9

titabuzón **16** 17

tiza **76** 10

toalla calentadora **41** 3

toalla de baño **34** 24

toalla de manos **34** 23

toalla de playa **90** 15

toallero **34** 25

toallita **34** 22

toallitas para bebé **33** 8

tobillo **5** 49

toca cassettes **100** 25

toca discos compacto **100** 28

tocadiscos **100** 18

tocar **77** 2

tocineta **10** 11, **18** 33

tocino **10** 11, **18** 33

toldo **51** 47

tomar **17** 10

topo **66** 8

torcedura **40** 13

tornamesa **100** 18

tornillo **37** 42

tornillo de banco **36** 2, **37** 36

tornillo grande **37** 38

torniquete de entrada **54** 12

torno **54** 12

toro **67** 34

toronja **8** 7

torre blindada de armas **48** 12

torre de control **57** 20

torre enfriadora **80** 16

torres transmisoras **80** 23

tortuga **65** 12

tortuga gigante **65** 18

tostada **18** 34

tostador **30** 16

trabajo en fábrica **85** C

trabajos manuales **101**

tractor **81** 15

trailer **49** 15

traje de baño **90** 18

traje de buceo **91** 38

traje de tres piezas **21** 40

traje espacial **75** 6

trajecito **33** 19

trampa de arena **95** 11

transacciones bancarias **86** B

transatlántico **58** 27

transbordador **58** 17

el transbordador espacial **75** C

transbordador espacial **75** 14

transcripción **43** 15

transformador **80** 25

transmisión automática **50** A

transmisión manual **50** B

transparencias **100** 12

transportador **49** 17

el transporte público **54**, **55**

tranvía **55** 30

tranvía aéreo **55** 31

tranvía tirado por cable **55** 32

trapos **35** 4

tráquea **5** 60

trasero **23** 19, **93** 34

traspalar **26** 13

tratamientos y remedios **41**

trecho **95** 19

tren **55** C, **55** 14

tren de aterrizaje **57** 15

tren subterráneo **54** B

triángulo **79** 6

triángulo recto **79** 22

tribuna del testigo **43** 18

tribunal **43** 16

tribunal del jurado **43** 20

tribunas **93** 10

triciclo **52** 6

trigal **81** 16

trigo **60** 22

trinche **81** 14

tripié **100** 9

tripode **100** 9

tripulación **75** 12

trombón **98** 23

trompa **66** 17a

trompa (del avión) **57** 8

trompeta **98** 25

tronco **61** 35b

tronillo **78** 7

trompa **66** 17a

trucha **65** 2

tuba **98** 27

tubo **13** 15, **35** 18, **91** 29

tubo de hule **78** 18

tubo de vidrio **78** 14

tuerca **37** 39

tulipán **60** 1

turbina **57** 11

ukulele **98** 3

un cuarto **79** 31

un cuarto de pollo **11** 18

un medio **79** 30

(un par de) tijeras **101** 17

(un racimo de) uvas **8** 1

un tercio **79** 32

ungüento **41** 9

uniforme **21** 45, **92** 9

el Universo **74**

untar **17** 11

uña **4** 32, **83** 29, **98** 11a

uña del dedo del pie **5** 56

uñero **98** 11a

Urano **74** 17

usos y productos **80** C

Utah **73** 44

vaca **67** 32

vaca lechera **81** 11

vagón transportador **80** 8

vaina **6** 17a

vajilla **29** 1

válvula **52** 27

vaporera **30** 3
vaquera **81** 22
vaquero **81** 21
varilla del aceite **51** 58
varillas de uranio **80** 15
vaso **13** 20, **29** 6
vegetales **6**, **7**
vegetales mixtos **18** 16
vehículo de remolque para
   acampar **53** 16
vehículos y equipo **48** A
vejiga **5** 72
vela **29** 27, **59** 9
veleta **59** 15
vellón **13** 28
vellonera **16** 12
velocímetro **50** 10
vena **5** 68
venadito **67** 27
venado **67** 26
venda elástica **40** 13a
vendas (de gaza) **39** 24
vendedor **87** 3
vendedor(a) **86** 12
ventana **27** 7
ventanilla **46** 15, **58** 21
ventila **50** 21
ventilador **50** 21
ventilador de techo **28** 1
Venus **74** 12
Verano **26**

verbos relacionados con la cocina **31**
verbos relacionados con el deporte **96**, **97**
verbos relacionados con la escuela **77**
verbos relacionados con las estaciones
   del año **26**
verbos relacionados con el restorán **17**
verbos relacionados con el trabajo del
   hogar **38**
verdulera **84** 7
Verduras **6**, **7**
verduras mixtas **18** 16
Vermont **73** 45
vestido **20** 22
vía **54** 10
vía peatonal **44** 4
viajando en balsa **89**
viaje aéreo **56**
viaje por carretera **53**
viajero abonado **55** 17
viajero **56** 3
vibora **69** 9
víbora de cascabel **65** 10
video **100** A
videocassette (cinta) **100** 3
videograbadora **100** 4
vieja **24** 14
viento **80** 4
(con) viento **25** 13
vino **16** 19
viola **98** 8
violeta **60** 16

violín **98** 7
Virginia **73** 46
visera **50** 5
visor **91** 35
volante **50** 8
vólibol **92**, **92** 22
walkman **100** 30
Washington **73** 47
West Virginia **73** 48
Wisconsin **73** 49
Wyoming **73** 50
xilófono **98** 31
Yangtzé **71** 69
yema (del dedo) **5** 52
Yenisey **71** 65
yerba(s) **6** 9
yerbas y granos **60**
Yukón **71** 56
yuntas **23** 12
zafacón **34** 13, **44** 15
zanahoria(s) **7** 32
zancudo **63** 13
zapato **21** 49
zapatos de tacón (alto) **20** 25
zarzamoras **8** 12
zona de gol **93** 23
zoológico **87** 1
zorrillo **68** 8
zorro **68** 6
zumaque venenoso **61** 44